Alexander Maclaren

The Victor's Crowns

and other sermons

Alexander Maclaren

The Victor's Crowns
and other sermons

ISBN/EAN: 9783337271947

Printed in Europe, USA, Canada, Australia, Japan

Cover: Foto ©Lupo / pixelio.de

More available books at **www.hansebooks.com**

THE VICTOR'S CROWNS

And Other Sermons

BY

ALEXANDER MACLAREN, D.D.

LONDON
CHRISTIAN COMMONWEALTH PUBLISHING Co., Ld.
73, LUDGATE HILL, E.C.

OTHER WORKS BY

REV. ALEXANDER MACLAREN, D.D.

TRIUMPHANT CERTAINTIES.
CHRIST IN THE HEART.
A YEAR'S MINISTRY. (First Series).
A YEAR'S MINISTRY. (Second Series).
PICTURES AND EMBLEMS.

Crown 8vo. Cloth. Price 5s. each.

THE CHRISTIAN COMMONWEALTH PUBLISHING Co., LD.,
73, LUDGATE HILL, LONDON, E.C.

CONTENTS.

	PAGE
THE VICTOR'S CROWNS.—I.	1
THE VICTOR'S CROWNS.—II.	10
THE VICTOR'S CROWNS.—III.	21
THE VICTOR'S CROWNS.—IV.	31
THE VICTOR'S CROWNS.—V.	42
THE VICTOR'S CROWNS.—VI.	52
THE VICTOR'S CROWNS.—VII.	62
THE CHRIST OF THE SERMON ON THE MOUNT	73
FAITH IN 'HIS NAME.	83
"LOOKING UNTO JESUS".	93
PAUL AT CORINTH	104
"TO HIM THAT HATH SHALL BE GIVEN"	115
"ALL THINGS ARE YOURS"	126
THE EVIL EYE AND THE CHARM	136
PUTTING ON THE ARMOUR	146

CONTENTS.

	PAGE
DYING MEN AND THE UNDYING WORD	157
CITIZENSHIP IN HEAVEN	167
A FATHER'S DISCIPLINE	176
AHAB AND MICAIAH	186
THE ROYAL JUBILEE	196
"THE SPIRIT OF BURNING"	207
"SEEK YE."—"I WILL SEEK"	217
SOUND DOCTRINE OR HEALTHY TEACHING	226
TRUE GREATNESS	236
GREATNESS IN THE KINGDOM	246
"THE MATTER OF A DAY IN ITS DAY"	256
THE FOUNDER AND FINISHER OF THE TEMPLE	264
PETER'S DELIVERANCE FROM PRISON	273
A PAIR OF FRIENDS	282
A SOLDIER'S SHOES	290
A LIFE LOST AND FOUND	299
CHRIST'S MISSION THE REVELATION OF GOD'S LOVE	307

THE VICTOR'S CROWNS.—I.

"To him that overcometh will I give to eat of the tree of life, which is in the midst of the paradise of God."—REV. ii. 7.

THE seven-fold promises which conclude the seven letters to the Asiatic Churches, of which this is the first, are in substance one. We may, indeed, say that the inmost meaning of them all is the gift of Christ Himself. But the diamond flashes variously-coloured lights according to the angle at which it is held, and breaks into red and green and white. The one great thought may be looked at from different points of view, and sparkle into diversely splendid rays. The reality is single and simple, but so great that our best way of approximating to the apprehension of that which we shall never comprehend till we possess it is to blend various conceptions and metaphors drawn from different sources.

I have a strong conviction that the Christianity of this day suffers intellectually and practically, from its comparative neglect of the teaching of the New Testament as to the future life. We hear and think a great deal less about it than was once the case, and we are thereby deprived of a strong motive for action, and a sure comfort in sorrow. Some of us may, perhaps, be disposed to look with a little sense of lofty pity at the simple people who let the hope of heaven spur, or restrain, or console. But if there is a future life at all, and if the characteristic of it which most concerns us is that it is the reaping, in consequences, of the acts of the present, surely it cannot be such superior wisdom, as it sometimes pretends to be, to ignore it altogether; and perhaps the simplicity of the said people is more in accordance with the highest reason than is our attitude.

Be that as it may, believing, as I do, that the hope of immortality is meant to fill a very large place in the Christian life, and fearing, as I do, that it actually does fill a very small one with many of us, I have thought that it might do us all good to turn to this wealth of linked promises and to consider them in succession, so as to bring our hearts for a little while into contact with the motive for brave fighting which does occupy so large a space in the New Testament, however it may fail to do so in our lives.

I. I ask you to look first at the Gift.

Now, of course, I need scarcely remind you that this first promise, in the last book of Scripture, goes back to the beginning, to the old story in Genesis about Paradise and the Tree of Life. We may distinguish between the substance of the promise and the highly metaphorical form into which it is here cast. The substance of the promise is the communication of life; the form is a poetic and imaginative and pregnant allusion to the story on the earliest pages of Revelation.

Let me deal first with the substance. Now, it seems to me that if we are to pare down this word "life" to its merely physical sense of continuous existence, this is not a promise that a man's heart leaps up at the hearing of. To anybody that will honestly think, and try to realise, in the imperfect fashion in which alone it is possible for us to realise it, that notion of an absolutely interminable continuance of being, its awfulness is far more than its blessedness, and it overwhelms a man. It seems to me that the "crown of life," if life only means conscious existence, would be a crown of thorns indeed.

No, brethren, what our hearts crave, and what Christ's heart gives, is not the mere bare, bald, continuance of conscious being. It is something far deeper than that. That is the substratum, of course; but it is only the substratum, and not until we let in upon this word, which is one of the keywords of Scripture, the full flood of light that comes to it from John's gospel, and its use on the Master's lips there, do we begin to understand the meaning of this great promise. Just as we say of men who are sunk in gross animalism, or whose lives are devoted to trivial and transient aims, that theirs is not worth calling life, so we say that the only thing that deserves, and that in Scripture gets, the august name of "life," is a condition of existence in conscious union with, and possession of, God, who is manifested and communicated to mortals through Jesus Christ His Son. "In Him was life, and the life was manifested." Was that bare existence? And the life was not only manifested but communicated, and the essence of it is fellowship with God through Jesus Christ. The possession of "the spirit of life which was in Christ," and which in heaven will be perfectly communicated, will make men "free," as they never can be upon earth whilst implicated in the bodily life of this material world, "from the law of sin and death." The gift that Christ bestows to him that "overcometh" is not only conscious existence, but existence derived from, and, so to speak, embraided with the life of God Himself, and therefore blessed.

For such a life, in union with God in Christ, is the only condition in which all a man's capacities find their fitting objects, and all his activity finds its appropriate sphere, and in which, therefore, to live is to be blessed, because the heart is united with the source and fountain of all blessedness. Here is the deepest depth of that promise of future blessedness. It is not mainly because of any changes, glorious as these must necessarily be, which follow upon the dropping away of flesh, and the transportation into the light that is above, that heaven is a place of blessedness, but it is because the saints that are there are joined to God, and into their recipient hearts there pours for ever the fulness of the Divine life. That makes the glory and the blessedness.

But let us remember that all which can come hereafter of that full and perfect life is but the continuance, the development, the increase, of that which already is possessed. Here it falls in drops; there in floods. Here it is filtered; there poured. Here, the plant, taken from its native climate and soil, puts forth some pale blossoms, and grows but to a stunted height; there, set in their deep native soil, and shone upon by a more fervent sun, and watered by more abundant warm rains and dews, "they that" on earth "were planted in the house of the Lord shall," transplanted, "flourish in the courts of our God." The life of the Christian soul on earth, and of the Christian soul in heaven, is continuous, and though there is a break to our consciousness looking from this side—the break of death—the reality is that without interruption, and without a turn, the road runs on in the same direction. We begin to live the life of heaven here, and they who can say, "I was dead in trespasses and sins, but the life which I live in the flesh I live by the faith of the Son of God," have already the germs of the furthest development in the heavens in their hearts.

Notice, for a moment, the form that this great promise assumes here. That is a very pregnant and significant reference to the Tree of Life in the paradise of God. The old story tells how the cherub with the flaming sword was set to guard the way to it. And that paradise upon earth faded and disappeared. But it re-appears. "Then comes a statelier Eden back to man," for Jesus Christ is the Restorer of all lost blessings ; and the Divine purpose and ideal has not faded away amidst the clouds of the stormy day of earth's history, like the flush of morning from off the plains. Christ brings back the Eden, and quenches the flame of the fiery sword ; and instead of the repellent cherub, there stands Himself with the merciful invitation upon His lips : " Come ! Eat ; and life for ever."

"There never was one lost good ; what was shall live as before.

.   .   .   .   .   .

On the earth the broken arcs ; in heaven the perfect round."

Eden shall come back ; and the paradise into which the victors go is richer and fuller, by all their conflict and their wounds, than ever could have been the simpler paradise of which souls innocent, because untried, could have been capable. So much for the gift of life.

II. Notice, secondly, the Giver.

This is a majestic utterance; worthy of coming from the majestic Figure portrayed in the first chapter of this book. In it Jesus Christ claims to be the Arbiter of men's deserts and Giver of their rewards. That involves His judicial function, and therefore His Divine as well as human nature. I accept these words as truly His words. Of course, if you do not, my present remarks have no force for you; but if you do not, you ought to be very sure of your reasons for not doing so; and if you do, then I see not how any man who believes that Jesus Christ has said that He will give to all the multitude of faithful fighters, who have brought their shields out of the battle, and their swords undinted, the gift of life eternal, can be vindicated from the charge of taking too much upon him, except on the belief of His Divine nature.

But I observe, still further, that this great utterance of the Lord's, paralleled in all the other six promises, in all of which He is represented as the bestower of the reward, whatever it may be, involves another thing—viz., the eternal continuance of Christ's relation to men as the Revealer and Mediator of God. "I will give"—and that not only when the victor crosses the threshold and enters the Capitol of the heavens, but all through its secular ages, Christ is the Medium by which the Divine life passes into men. True, there is a sense in which He shall deliver up the kingdom to His Father, when the partial end of the present dispensation has come. But He is the Priest of mankind for ever; and for ever is His kingdom enduring. And through all the endless ages, which we have a right to hope we shall see, there will never come a point in which it will not remain as true as it is at this moment: "No man hath seen God at any time, nor can see Him; the only begotten Son, which is in the bosom of the Father, He hath declared Him." Christ is for ever the Giver of life, in the heavens as on earth.

Another thing is involved which I think also is often lost sight of. The Bible does not know anything about what people call "natural immortality." Life here is not given to the infant once for all, and then expended through the years, but it is continually being bestowed. My belief is that no worm that creeps, nor angel that soars, nor any of the beings between, is alive for one instant except for the continual communication from the fountain of life, of the life that they live. And still more certainly is it true about the future, that there all the blessedness and the existence, which is the substratum and condition of the blessedness, are only ours because, wavelet by wavelet, throbbing out as from a central fountain, there flows into the Redeemed a life communicated by Christ Himself. If I might so say—were that continual bestowment to cease, then heaven, like the vision of a fairy tale, would fade away; and there would be nothing left where the glory had shone. "I will give" through eternity.

III. Lastly, note the Recipients.

"To him that overcometh." Now, I need not say, in more than a sentence, that it seems to me that the fair interpretation of this promise, as of all the other references in Scripture to the future life, is that the reward is immediately consequent upon the cessation of the struggle. "To depart" is "to be with Christ," and to be with Christ, in regard of a spirit which has passed from the bodily environment, is to be conscious of His presence, and lapt in His robe, feeling the warmth and the pressure of His heart. So I believe that Scripture teaches us that at one moment there may be the clash of battle, and the whiz of the arrows round one's head, and next moment there may be the laurel-crowned quiet of the victor.

But that does not enter so much into our consideration now. We have, rather, here to think of just this one thing, that the gift is given to the victor because only the victor is capable of receiving it; that future life, interpreted as I have ventured to interpret it in this sermon, is no arbitrary bestowment that could be dealt all round miscellaneously to everybody, if the Giver chose so to give. Here on earth many gifts are bestowed upon men, and are neglected by them, and wasted like water spilled upon the ground; but this elixir of life is not poured out so. It is only poured into vessels that can take it in and hold it.

Our present struggle is meant to make us capable of the heavenly life. And that is—I was going to say the only, but at all events—incomparably the chiefest, of the thoughts which make life not only worth living, but great and solemn. Go into a mill, and in a quiet room, often detached from the main building, you will find the engine working, and seeming to do nothing but go up and down. But there is a shaft which goes through the wall and takes the power to the looms. We are working here, and we are making the cloth that we shall have to own, and say, "Yes, it *is* my manufacture!" when we get yonder. According to our life to-day will be our destiny in that great to-morrow. Life is given to the victor, because the victor only is capable of possessing it.

But the victor can only conquer in one way. "This," said John, when he was not an apocalyptic seer, but a Christian teacher to the Churches of Asia, "this is the victory that overcometh the world, even our faith." If we trust in Christ we shall get His power into our hearts, and if we get His power into our hearts, then " we shall be more than conquerors through Him that loved us." Christ gives life eternal, gives it here in germ and yonder in fulness. In its fulness only those who overcome are capable of receiving it. Those only who fight the good fight by His help overcome. Those only who trust in Him fight the good fight by His help. He gives to eat of the Tree of Life ; He gives it to faith, but faith must be militant. He gives it to the conqueror, but the conqueror must win by faith in Him who overcame the world for us, who will help us to overcome the world by Him.

Help us, O our God, we beseech Thee ; "teach our hands to war, and our fingers to fight." Give us grace to hold fast by the life which is in Jesus Christ; and, living by Him the lives which we live in the flesh, may we be made capable, by the discipline of earth's sorrows, of that rest and fuller "life which remaineth for the people of God."

THE VICTOR'S CROWNS.—II.

"He that overcometh shall not be hurt of the second death."—
Rev. ii. 11.

TWO of the seven Churches—viz., Smyrna, to which our text is addressed, and Philadelphia—offered nothing, to the pure eyes of Christ, that needed rebuke. The same two, and these only, were warned to expect persecution. The higher the tone of Christian life in the Church the more likely it is to attract dislike, and, if circumstances permit, hostility. Hence the whole gist of this letter is to encourage to steadfastness, even if the penalty is death.

That purpose determined at once the aspect of Christ which is presented in the beginning, and the aspect of future blessedness which is held forth at the close. The aspect of Christ is—"these things saith the First and the Last, which was dead and is alive;" a fitting thought to encourage the men who were to be called upon to die for Him. And, in like manner, the words of our text naturally knit themselves with the previous mention of death as the penalty of the Smyrneans' faithfulness.

Now, this promise is sharply distinguished from those to the other Churches by two peculiarities : one that it is merely negative, whilst all the rest are radiantly positive ;

the other that there is no mention of our Lord in it, whilst in all the others He stands forth with His emphatic and majestic "*I* will give"; "*I* will write upon him My new Name"; "*I* will make him a pillar in the temple of My God." The first peculiarity may partially account for the second, because the Giver is naturally more prominent in a promise of positive gifts, than in one of a merely negative exemption. But another reason is to be found for the omission of the mention of our Lord in this promise. If you will refer to the verse immediately preceding my text, you will find the missing positive promise with the missing reference to Jesus Christ: "I will give thee a crown of life." So that we are naturally led to link together both these statements when taking account of the hopes that were held forth to animate the Christians of Smyrna in the prospect of persecution even to the death; and we have to consider them both in conjunction now. I think I shall best do so by simply asking you to look at these two things: the Christian motive contained in the victor's immunity from a great evil, and the Christian motive contained in the victor's possession of a great good. "He shall not be hurt of the second death." "I will give thee a crown of life."

I. The Christian motive contained in the victor's immunity from a great evil.

Now, that solemn and thrilling expression "the second death" is peculiar to this book of the Apocalypse. The *name* is peculiar; the *thing* is common to all the New Testament writers. Here it comes with especial appropriateness, in contrast with the physical death which was about to be inflicted upon some members of the Smyrnean Church. But beyond that there lies in the phrase a very solemn and universally applicable meaning. I do not feel, dear brethren, that such a thing ought to be made matter of pulpit rhetoric. The bare vagueness of it seems to me to shake the heart a great deal more than any weakening expansion of it that we can give.

But yet, let me say one word. Then, behind that grim figure, the shadow feared of man that waits for all at some turn of their road, cloaked and shrouded, there rises a still grimmer and more awful form, " if form it can be called which form hath none." There *is* something, at the back of physical death, which can lay its grip upon the soul that is already separated from the body ; something running on the same lines somehow, and worthy to bear that name of terror and disintegration : "the second death." What can it be ? Not the cessation of conscious existence ; that is never the meaning of death. But let us apply the key which opens so many of the locks of the New Testament saying about the future, that the true and deepest meaning of *death* is separation from Him who is the fountain of life, and in a very deep sense is the only life of the universe. Separation from God ; *that* is death. What touches the surface of mere bodily life is but a faint shadow and parable, and the second death, like a second tier of mountains, rises behind and above it, sterner and colder than the lower hills of the foreground. What desolation, what unrest, what blank misgivings, what peeling off of capacities, faculties, opportunities, delights, may be involved in that solemn conception, we never can tell here—God grant that we may never know! Like some sea-creature, cast high and dry on the beach, and gasping out its pained being, the men that are separated from

God die whilst they live, and live a living death. The second is the comparative degree, of which the first is the positive.

Now, note again that immunity from this solemn fate is no small part of the victor's blessedness. At first sight we feel as if the mere negative promise of my text stands on a lower level than what I have called the radiantly positive ones in the other letters; but it is worthy to stand beside these. Gather them together, and think of how manifold and glorious the dim suggestions which they make of felicity and progress are, and then set by the side of them this one of our text as worthy to stand there. To eat of the Tree of Life; to have power over the nations; to rule them with a rod of iron; to blaze with the brightness of the morning star; to eat of the hidden manna; to bear the new name known only to those who receive it; to have that name confessed before the Father and His angels; to be a pillar in the Temple of the Lord; to go no more out; and to sit with Christ on His throne:—these are the positive promises, along with which this barely negative one is linked, and is worthy to be linked: "He shall not be hurt of the second death."

If this immunity from that fate is fit to stand in line with these glimpses of an inconceivable glory, how solemn must be the fate, and how real the danger of our falling into it! Brethren, in this day it has become unfashionable to speak of that future, especially of its sterner aspects. The dimness of the brightest revelations in the New Testament, the unwillingness to accept it as the source of certitude with regard to the future, the recoil from the stern severity of Divine retribution, the exaggerated and hideous guise in which that great truth was often presented in the past, the abounding worldliness of this day, many of its best tendencies and many of its worst ones concur in making some of us look with very little interest, and scarcely credence, at the solemn words of which the New Testament is full. But I, for my part, accept them; and I dare not but, in such proportion to the rest of Revelation as seems to me to be right, bring them before you. I beseech you, recognise the solemn teaching that lies in this thought, that this negative promise of immunity from the second death stands parallel with all these promises of felicity and blessedness.

Further, note that such immunity is regarded here as the direct outcome of the victor's conduct and character. I have already pointed out the peculiarities marking our text. The omission of any reference to our Lord in it is accounted for, as suggested, by that reference occurring in the immediately preceding context, but it may also be regarded as suggesting—when considered in contrast with the other promises, where He stands forward as the giver of heavenly blessedness— that that future condition is to be regarded not only as retribution, which implies the notion of a judge, and a punitive or rewarding energy on his part, but also as being the necessary result of the earthly life that is lived; a harvest of which we sow the seeds here.

Transient deeds consolidate into permanent character. Beds of sandstone rock, thousands of feet thick, are the sediment dropped from vanished seas, or borne down by long dried-up rivers. The actions which we often so unthinkingly perform, whatever may be the width and the permanency of their effects external to us, react upon ourselves, and tend to make our permanent bent or twist or character. The chalk cliffs at Dover are the skeletons of millions upon millions of tiny organisms, and our little lives are built up by the recurrence of transient deeds, which leave their permanent marks upon us. They make character, and character determines position yonder. As said the Apostle, with tender sparingness, and yet with profound truth, "he went to *his own place*," wherever that was. The surroundings that he was fitted for came about him, and the company that he was fit for associated themselves with him. So, in another part of this book, where the same solemn expression, "the second death," is employed, we read, "These shall have their *part* in ... the second death": the lot that belongs to them. Character and conduct determine position. However small the lives here, they settle the far greater ones hereafter, just as a tiny wheel in a machine may, by cogs and other mechanical devices, transmit its motion to another wheel at a distance, many times its diameter. You move this end of a lever through an arc of an inch, and the other end will move through an arc of yards. The little life here determines the sweep of the great one that is lived yonder. The victor wears his past conduct and character, if I may so say, as a fireproof garment, and if he entered the very furnace, heated seven times hotter than before, there would be no smell of fire upon him. "He that overcometh shall not be hurt of the second death."

II. Now note, secondly, the Christian motive contained in the victor's reception of a great good.

"I will give him a crown of life." I need not remind you, I suppose, that this metaphor of "the crown" is found in other instructively various places in the New Testament. Paul, for instance, speaks of his own personal hope of "the crown of righteousness." James speaks, as does the letter to the Smyrnean Church, of "the crown of life." Peter speaks "of the crown of glory." Paul, in another place, speaks of "the crown incorruptible." And all these express substantially the one idea. There may be a question as to whether the word employed here for the crown is to be taken in its strictly literal acceptation as meaning, not a kingly coronal, but a garland. But, seeing that, although that is the strict meaning of the word, it is employed, in a subsequent part of the letter, to designate what must evidently be kingly crowns—viz., in the fourth chapter— there seems to be greater probability in the supposition that we are warranted in including under the symbolism here both the aspects of the crown as royal, and also as laid upon the brows of the victors in the games or the conflict. I venture to take it in that meaning. Substantially, the promise is the same as that which we were considering in the previous letter, "I will give him to eat of the Tree of Life"; the promise of life in all the depth and fulness and sweep of that great encyclopædical word. But it is life considered from a special point of view that is set forth here.

It is a *kingly* life. Of course, that notion of regality and dominion, as the prerogative of the redeemed and glorified servants of Jesus Christ, is for ever cropping up in this book of the Revelation. And you remember how our Lord has set the example of its use when

He said, "Have thou authority over ten cities." What may lie in that great symbol it is not for us to say. The rule over ourselves, over circumstances, the deliverance from the tyranny of the external, the deliverance from the slavery of the body and its lusts and passions, these are all included. The man that can will rightly, and can do completely as he rightly wills, that man is a king. But there is more than that. There is the participation in wondrous, and for us inconceivable, ways, in the majesty and regality of the King of kings and Lord of lords. Therefore did the crowned Elders before the throne sing a new song to the Lamb, who made redeemed men out of every tribe and tongue, to be to God a kingdom, and priests who should reign upon the earth.

But, brethren, remember that this conception of a kingly life is to be interpreted, according to Christ's own teaching of that wherein royalty in His kingdom consists. For heaven, as for earth, the purpose of dominion is service, and the use of power is beneficence. "He that is chiefest of all, let him be servant of all," is the law for the regalities of heaven as well as for the lowliness of earth.

That life is a *triumphant* life. The crown was laid on the head of the victor in the games. Think of the victor as he went back, flushed and modest, to his village away up on the slopes of some of the mountain-chains of Greece. With what a tumult of acclaim he would be hailed! If we do our work, and fight our fight down here as we ought, we shall enter into the great city not unnoticed, not unwelcomed, but with the praise of the King and the pæans of His attendants.

"I will confess his name before My Father and the holy angels."

That life is a *festal* life. The garlands are twined on the heated brows of revellers, and the fumes of the wine and the closeness of the chamber soon make them wilt and droop. This Amaranthine crown fadeth never. And the feast expresses for us the felicities, the abiding satisfactions without satiety, the blessed companionship, the repose which belong to the Crowned. Royalty, triumph, festal goodness, all fused together, are incomplete, but they are not useless symbols. May we experience their fulfilment!

Brethren, the crown is promised not merely to the man that says, "I have faith in Jesus Christ," but to him who has worked out his faith into faithfulness, and by conduct and character has made himself capable of the felicities of the heavens. If that immortal crown were laid upon the head of another, it would be a crown of thorns; for the joys of that future require the fitness which comes from the apprenticeship to faith and faithfulness here on earth. We evangelical preachers are often taunted with preaching that future blessedness comes as the result of the simple act of belief. Yes: but only if, and when, the simple act of faith, which is more than belief, is wrought out in the loveliness of faithfulness. "We are made partakers of Christ, if we hold fast the beginning of our confidence firm unto the end."

Now, dear friends, I daresay that some of you may be disposed to brush aside these fears and hopes as very low motives, unworthy to be appealed to; but I cannot so regard them. I know that the appeal to fear is directed to the lower order of sentiments, but it is a legitimate motive. It is meant to stir us up to gird ourselves against the dangers which we wisely dread. And I, for my part, believe that we preachers are going aside from our Pattern, and are flinging away a very powerful weapon, in the initial stages of religious experience, if we are afraid to bring before men's hearts and answering consciences the solemn facts of the future which Jesus Christ Himself has revealed to us. We are no more to be blamed for it than the signalman for waving his red flag. And I fancy that there are some of my present hearers who would be nearer the love of God, if they took more to heart the fear of the Lord and of His judgment.

Hope is surely a perfectly legitimate motive to appeal to. We are not to be good because we thereby escape hell and secure heaven. We are to be good, because Jesus Christ wills us to be, and has won us to love Him, or has sought to win us to love Him, by His great sacrifice for us. But that being the basis, men can be brought to build upon it by the compulsion of fear and by the attraction of hope. And that being the deepest motive, there is a perfectly legitimate and noble sphere for the operation of these two other lower motives, the consideration of the personal evils that attend the opposite course, and of the personal good that follows from cleaving to Him. Am I to be told that Polycarp, Bishop of Smyrna, who went to his martyrdom, and was "faithful unto death," with the words on his lips: "Eighty and six years have I served Him, and He has done me nothing but good; how shall I deny my King and my Saviour?" was yielding to a low motive when to him the crown, that the Master promised to the Church of which he was afterwards bishop floated above the head that was soon to be shorn off, and on whose blood-stained brows it was then to fall? Would that we had more of such low motives! Would that we had more of such high lives as fear nothing because they "have respect to the recompense of the reward," and are ready for service or martyrdom, because they hear and believe the crowned Christ saying to them: "Be thou faithful unto death, and I will give thee a crown of life."

THE VICTOR'S CROWNS.—III.

"To him that overcometh will I give to eat of the hidden manna, and will give him a white stone, and in the stone a new name written, which no man knoweth saving he that receiveth it."—REV. ii. 17.

THE Church at Pergamos, to which this promise is addressed, had a sharper struggle than fell to the lot of the two Churches whose epistles precede this. It was set "where Satan's seat is." Pergamos was a special centre of heathen worship, and already the blood of a faithful martyr had been shed in it. The severer the struggle, the nobler the reward. Consequently the promise given to this militant Church surpasses, in some respects, those held out to the former two. They were substantially promised that life eternal, which indeed includes everything; but here some of the blessed contents of that life are expanded and emphasised.

There is a threefold promise given: "the hidden manna," "the white stone," a "new name" written. The first and the last of these are evidently the most important. They need little explanation; of the central one, the "white stone," a bewildering variety of interpretations—none of them, as it seems to me, satisfactory —have been suggested. Possibly there may be an allusion to the ancient custom of dropping the votes of the judges into an urn—a white pebble meaning innocence and acquittal; black meaning guilty—just as we, under somewhat similar circumstances, talk about "blackballing." But the objection to that interpretation lies in the fact that the "white stone" of our text is *given* to the person concerned, and not deposited elsewhere. There may be an allusion to a practice which antiquarians have hunted out, of conferring upon the victors in the games a little tile with a name inscribed upon it, which gave admission to the public festivals. But all the explanations are so doubtful that one hesitates to accept any of them. There remains one other alternative, which seems to me to be suggested by the very language of the text—viz., that the "white stone" is here named —with possibly some subsidiary thought of innocence and purity—merely as the vehicle for the name. And so I dismiss it from further consideration, and concentrate our thoughts on the remaining two promises.

I. We have the victor's food, the manna.

That seems, at first sight, a somewhat infelicitous symbol, because manna was wilderness food. But that characteristic is not to be taken into account. Manna, though it fell in the wilderness, came from heaven, and it is the heavenly food that is suggested by the symbol. When the warrior passes from the fight into the city, the food which came down from heaven will be given to him in fulness. It is a beautiful thought that, as soon as the man "spent with changing blows," and weary with conflict, enters the land of peace, there is a table spread for him; not, as before, in "the presence of his enemies," but in the presence of the companions of his repose. One moment hears the din of the battle-field, the next moment feels the refreshment of the heavenly manna.

But now there can be little need for dealing, by way of exposition, with this symbol. Let us rather try to lay it upon our hearts.

Now the first thing that it plainly suggests to us is the absolute satisfaction of all the hunger of the heart. It is possible, and for those that overcome it will one day be actual experience, that a man shall have everything that he wishes the moment that he wishes it. Here we have to suppress desires, sometimes because they are illegitimate and wrong, sometimes because circumstances sternly forbid their indulgence. There, to desire will be to have, and partly by the rectifying of the appetite, partly by the fulness of the supply, there will be no painful sense of vacuity, and no clamouring of the unsubdued heart for good that is beyond its reach. They—and you and I may be amongst them, and so we may say "*we*"—"shall hunger no more, neither thirst any more." Oh, brethren! to us who are driven into activity by desires, half of which go to water and are never fulfilled—to us who know what it is to try to tame down the hungering, yelping wishings and longings of our souls—to us who have so often spent our "money for that which is not bread, and our labour for that which satisfieth not" it ought to be a Gospel: "I will give him to eat of the hidden manna." Is it such to you? Do you believe it possible, and are you addressing yourselves to make the fulfilment of it actual in your case?

Then there is the other plain thing suggested here, that that satisfaction does not dull the edge of appetite or desire. Bodily hunger is fed, is replete, wants nothing more until the lapse of time and digestion have intervened. But it is not so with the loftiest satisfactions. There are some select, noble, blessed desires even here, concerning which we know that the more we have, the more we hunger with a hunger which has no pain in it, but is only the greatened capacity for greater enjoyment. You that know what happy love is know what that means—a satisfaction which never approaches satiety, a hunger which has in it no gnawing. And in the loftiest and most perfect of all realms, that co-existence of perfect fruition and perfect desire will be still more wondrously and blessedly manifest. At each moment the more we have, the wider will our hearts be expanded by possession, and the wider they are expanded the more will they be capable of receiving, and the more they are capable of receiving, the more deep and full and blessed and all-covering will be the inrush of the river of the water of life. Satisfaction without satiety, food which leaves him blessedly appetised for larger bestowments, belong to the victor.

Another thing to be noticed here is what we have already had occasion to point out in the previous promises: "I will give him." Do you remember our Lord's own wonderful words : " Blessed are those servants, whom the Lord when He cometh shall find watching : verily I say unto you, that He shall gird Himself, and shall come forth and serve them " ? The victor is seated at the board, and the Prince, as in some earthly banquet to a victorious army, Himself moves up and down amongst the tables, and supplies the wants of the guests. There was an old Jewish tradition, which perhaps may have influenced the form of this promise, to the effect that the Messiah, when He came, would bring again to the people the gift of the manna, and men should once more eat angels' food. Whether there is any allusion to that poetic fancy or no in the words of my text, the reality infinitely transcends it. Christ Himself bestows upon His servants the sustenance of their spirits in the realm above. But there is more than that. Christ is not only the Giver, but He is Himself the Food. I believe that the deepest meaning of this sevenfold cluster of jewels, the promises to these seven Churches, is in each case Christ. He is the Tree of Life; He is the Crown of Life, He *is*—as well as *gives*—" the hidden manna." You will remember how He Himself gives us this interpretation when, in answer to the Jewish taunt, " Our fathers did eat manna in the wilderness. What dost Thou work?" He said, " I am that Bread of God that came down from heaven."

So, then, once more, we come back to the all-important teaching that, whatever be the glories of the perfected flower and fruit in heaven, the germ and root of it is already here. The man that lives upon the Christ by faith, love, obedience, imitation, communion, aspiration, here on earth, has already the earnest of that feast. No doubt there will be aspects and sweetnesses and savours and sustenance in the heavenly form of our possession of, and living on, Him, which we here on earth know nothing about. But, no doubt also, the beginning and positive degree of all these sweetnesses and savours and sustenances yet to be revealed is found in the experience of the man who has listened to the cry of that loving voice, " Eat, and your souls shall live"; and has taken Jesus Christ Himself, the living person, to be not only the source but the nourishment of his spiritual life.

So, brethren, it is of no use to pretend to ourselves that we should like—as they put it in bald popular language—to "go to heaven," unless we are using and relishing that of heaven which is here to-day. If you do not like the earthly form of feeding upon Jesus Christ, which is trusting Him, giving your heart to Him, obeying Him, thinking about Him, treading in His footsteps, you would not like, you would like less, the heavenly form of that feeding upon Him. If you would rather have the strong-smelling garlic and the savoury leeks—to say nothing about the swine's trough and the husks—than "this light bread," the "angels' food," which your palates cannot stand and your stomachs cannot digest, you could not swallow it if it were put into your lips when you get beyond the grave; and you would not like it if you could. Christ forces this manna into no man's mouth; but Christ gives it to all who desire it and are fit for it. As is the man's appetite, so is the man's food; and so is the life that results therefrom.

II. Note the victor's new name.

I have often had occasion to point out to you that Scripture attaches, in accordance with Eastern habit, large importance to names, which are intended to be significant of character, or circumstances, or parental hopes or desires. So that, both in reference to God and man, names come to be the condensed expression of the character and the personality. When we read, "I will give him a stone, on which there is a new name written," we infer that the main suggestion made in that promise is of a change in the self, something new in the personality and the character. I need not dwell upon this, for we have no material by which to expand into detail the greatness of the promise. I would only remind you of how we are taught to believe that the dropping away of the corporeal, and removal from this present scene, carries with it, in the case of those who have here on earth begun to walk with Christ, and to become citizens of the spiritual realm, changes great, ineffable, and all tending in the one direction of making the servants more fully like their Lord. What new capacities may be evolved by the mere fact of losing the limitations of the bodily frame; what new points of contact with a new universe; what new analogues of what we here call our senses, and means of perception of the external world, may be the accompaniments of the disembarrassment from "the earthly house of this tabernacle," we dare not dream. We could not, if we were told, rightly understand. But, surely, if the tenant is taken from a clay hut and set in a Royal house, eternal, not made with hands, its windows must be wider and more transparent, and there must be an inrush of wondrously more brilliant light into the chambers.

But whatsoever be these changes, they are changes that repose upon that which has been in the past. And so the second thought that is suggested by this new name is that these changes are the direct results of the victor's course. Both in old times and in the peerage of England you will find names of conquerors, by land or by water, who carry in their designations and transmit to their descendants the memorial of their victories in their very titles. In like manner as a Scipio was called Africanus, as a Jervis became Lord St. Vincent, so the victor's "new name" is the concentration and memorial of the victor's conquest. And what we have wrought and fought here on earth we carry with us, as the basis of the changes from glory to glory which shall come in the heavens. "They rest from their labours; their works do follow them," and, gathering behind the laurelled victor, attend him as he ascends the hill of the Lord.

But once more we come to the thought that whatever there may be of change in the future, the main direction of the character remains, and the consolidated issues of the transient deeds of earth remain, and the victor's name is the summing up of the victor's life.

But, further, Christ gives the name. He changed the names of His disciples. Simon He called Cephas, James and John He called "Sons of Thunder." The act claimed authority, and designated a new relation to Him. Both these ideas are conveyed in the promise: "I will give him . . . a new name written." Only, brethren, remember that the transformation keeps true to the line of direction begun here, and the process of change has to be commenced on earth. They who win the new name of heaven are they of whom it would be truly said, while they bore the old name of earth, "If any man be in Christ he is a new creature." "Old things are passed away; behold, all things are become new."

III. Lastly, note the mystery of both the food and the name.

"I will give him the hidden manna . . . a new name . . . which no man knoweth saving he that receiveth it." Now, we all know that the manna was laid up in the

Ark, beneath the Shekinah, within the curtain of the holiest place. And, besides that, there was a Jewish tradition that the Ark and its contents, which disappeared after the fall of Jerusalem and the destruction of the first Temple, had been buried by the prophet Jeremiah, and lay hidden away somewhere on the sacred soil, until Messiah should return. There may be an allusion to that here, but it is not necessary to suppose it. The pot of manna lay in the Ark of the Covenant, of which we hear in another part of the symbolism in this book, within the veil in the holiest of all. And Christ gives the victor to partake of that sacred and secret food. The name which is given, "no man knoweth saving he that receiveth it." Both symbols point to the one thought, the impossibility of knowing until we possess and experience.

That impossibility besets all the noblest, highest, purest, Divinest emotions and possessions of earth. Poets have sung of love and sorrow from the beginning of time; but men must love to know what love means. Every woman has heard about the sweetness of maternity, but not till the happy mother holds her infant to her breast does she understand it. And so we may talk till Doomsday, and yet it would remain true that we must eat the manna, and look upon the white stone for ourselves, before we can adequately comprehend.

Since, then, experience alone admits to the knowledge, how vulgar, how futile, how absolutely destructive of the very purpose which they are intended to subserve, are all the attempts of men to forecast that ineffable glory. It is too great to be understood. The mountains that ring us round keep the secret well of the fair lands beyond. There are questions that bleeding hearts sometimes ask, questions which prurient curiosity more often ask, and which foolish people to-day are taking illegitimate means of solving, about that future life, which are all left—though some of them might conceivably have been answered—in silence. Enough for us to listen to the voice that says, " In My Father's house are many mansions "—room for you and me—" if it were not so I would have told you." For the silence is eloquent. The curtain is the picture. The impossibility of telling is the token of the greatness of the thing to be told. Hope needs but little yarn to weave her web with. I believe that the dimness is part of the power of that heavenly prospect. Let us be reticent before it. Let us remember that, though our knowledge is small and our eyes dim, Christ knows all, and we shall be with Him ; and so say, with no sense of pained ignorance, or unsatisfied curiosity, " It doth not yet appear what we shall be, but we know that when He shall appear we shall be like Him, for we shall see Him as He is." Cannot our hearts add, " It is enough for the servant that he be as his master " ?

An old commentator on this verse says, " Wouldst thou know what manner of new name thou shalt bear ? Overcome. It is vain for thee to ask beforehand. Hereafter thou shalt soon see it written on the white stone."

Help us, O Lord, to fight the good fight of faith, in the sure confidence that Thou wilt receive us, and refresh us, and renew us.

THE VICTOR'S CROWNS.—IV.

"He that overcometh, and keepeth My works unto the end, to him will I give power over the nations: and he shall rule them with a rod of iron; as the vessels of a potter shall they be broken to shivers: even as I. received of My Father. And I will give him the morning star."—REV. ii. 26-28.

THIS promise to the victors in Thyatira differs from the preceding ones in several remarkable respects. If you will observe, the summons to give ear to "what the Spirit saith to the churches" *precedes* the promises in the previous letters; here it follows that promise, and that order is observed in the three subsequent epistles. Now, the structure of all these letters is too careful and artistic to allow of the supposition that the change is arbitrary or accidental. There must be some significance in it, but I do not profess to be ready with the explanation, and I prefer acknowledging perplexity to pretending enlightenment.

Then there is another remarkable peculiarity of this letter—viz., the expansion which is given to the designation of the victor as "He that overcometh and *keepeth My works unto the end.*" Probably not unconnected with that expansion is the other peculiarity of the promise here, as compared with its precursors—viz., that they all regard simply the individual victor and promise to him " partaking of the tree of life "; a "crown of life"; immunity from "the second death"; "the hidden manna"; the "white stone"; and the "new name written"; which, like all the rest of the promises there, belonged to Himself alone; but here the field is widened, and we have others brought in on whom the victor is to exercise an influence. So, then, we enter upon a new phase of conceptions of that future life in these words, which not only dwell upon the sustenance, the repose, the glory that belong to the man himself, but look upon him as still an instrument in Christ's hands, and an organ for carrying out, by His activities, Christ's purposes in the worlds. So, then, I want you to look with me very simply at the ideas suggested by these words.

I. We have the victor's authority.

Now, the promise in my text is moulded by a remembrance of the great words of the second psalm. That psalm stands at the beginning of the Psalter as a kind of prelude; and, in conjunction with its companion psalm, the first, is a summing up of the two great factors in the religious life of the Hebrews—viz., the blessedness in the keeping of the law, and the brightness of the hope of the Messiah. The psalm in question deals with that Messianic hope under the symbols of an earthly conquering monarch, and sets forth His dominion as established throughout the whole earth. And our letter brings this marvellous thought, that the spirits of just men made perfect are, somehow or other, associated with Him in that campaign of conquest.

Now, there is much in these words which, of course, it is idle for us to attempt to expand or expound. We can only wait, as we gaze upon the dim brightness, for experience to unlock the mystery. But there is also much which, if we will reverently ponder it, may stimulate us to brave conflict and persistent diligence in keeping Christ's commandments. I, for my part, believe that Scripture is the only source of such knowledge as we have of the future life ; and I believe, too, that the knowledge, such as it is, which we derive from Scripture *is* knowledge, and can be absolutely trusted. And so, though I abjure all attempts at rhetorical setting forth of the details of this mysterious symbol, I would lay it upon our hearts. It is not the less powerful because it is largely inconceivable ; and the mystery, the darkness, the dimness, may be, and are part of the revelation and of the light. " *There* was the hiding of His power."

And so, notice that whatever may be the specific contents of such a promise as this, the general form of it is in full harmony with the words of our Lord whilst He was on earth. Twice over, according to the Gospel narratives—once in connection with Peter's foolish question, " What shall *we* have therefore ? " and once in a still more sacred connection, at the table on the eve of Calvary—our Lord gave His trembling disciples this great promise : " In the regeneration, when the Son of man shall sit on the throne of His glory, ye also shall sit on twelve thrones, judging the twelve tribes of Israel." Make all allowance that you like for the vesture of symbolism, the reality that lies beneath is that Jesus Christ, the Truth, has pledged Himself to this, that His servants shall be associated with Him in the activity of His royalty. And the same great thought, which we only spoil when we try to tear apart the petals which remain closed until the sun shall open them, underlies the twin parables of the pounds and the talents, in regard to each of which we have, "Thou hast been faithful over a few things; I will make thee ruler over many things;" and, linked along with the promise of authority, the assurance of union with the Master, "Enter thou into the joy of thy Lord." So this book of the Revelation is only following in the footsteps and expanding the hints of Christ's own teaching when it triumphs in the thought that we are made kings and priests to God; when it points onwards to a future wherein—we know not how, but we know, if we believe Him when He speaks, that it shall be so—they shall reign with Him for ever and ever.

My text adds further the image of a conquering campaign, of a sceptre of iron crushing down antagonism, of banded opposition broken into shivers, "as a potter's vessel" dashed upon a pavement of marble. And it says that in that final conflict and final conquest they that have passed into the rest of God, and have dwelt with Christ, shall be with Him, the armies of heaven following Him, clad in white raiment pure and glistening, and with Him subduing, ay! and converting into loyal love the antagonisms of earth. I abjure all attempts at millenarian prophecy, but I point to this, that all the New Testament teaching converges upon this one point, that the Christ who came to die shall come again to reign, and that He shall reign, and His servants with Him. That is enough; and that is all. For all the rest is conjecture and fancy, and sometimes folly; and details minimise, and do not magnify, the great, undetailed, magnificent fact.

But all the other promises deal not with something in the remoter future, but with something that begins to take effect the moment the dust, and confusion, and garments rolled in blood, of the battle-field are swept away. At one instant the victors are fighting, at the next they are partaking of the Tree of Life, and on their locks lies the crown, and their happy lips are feeding upon "the hidden manna." And so, I think, that though, no doubt, the main stress of the promise of authority here points onwards, as our Lord Himself has taught us, to the time of "the regeneration, when the Son of man shall sit on the throne of His glory," the incidence of the promise is not to be exclusively confined thereto. There must be something in the present for the blessed dead, as well as for them in the future. And this is, that they are united with Jesus Christ in His present activities, and through Him, and in Him, and with Him, are even now serving Him. The servant, when he dies, and has been fitted for it, enters at once on his government of the ten cities.

Thus this promise of my text, in its deepest meaning, corresponds with the deepest needs of a man's nature. For we can never be at rest unless we are at work; and a heaven of doing nothing is a heaven of *ennui* and weariness. Whatever sneers may have been cast at the Christian conception of the future, which find vindication, one is sorry to say, in many popular representations and sickly bits of hymns, the New Testament notion of what that future life is to be is noble with all energy, and fruitful with all activity, and strenuous with all service. This promise of my text comes in to supplement the three preceding. They were addressed to the legitimate, wearied longings for rest and fulness of satisfaction for oneself. This is addressed to the deeper and nobler longing for larger service. And the words of my text, whatever dim glory they may partially reveal, as accruing to the victor in the future, do declare that, when he passes beyond the grave, there will be waiting for him nobler work to do than any that he ever has done here.

But let us not forget that all this access of power and enlargement of opportunity are a consequence of Christ's royalty and Christ's conquering rule. That is to say, whatever we have in the future we have because we are knit to Him, and all our service there, as all our blessedness here, flows from our union with that Lord. So when He says, as in the words that I have already quoted, that His servants shall sit on thrones, He presents Himself as on the central throne. The authority of the steward over the ten cities is but a consequence of the servant's entrance into the joy of the Lord. Whatever there lies in the heavens, the germ of it all is this, that we are as Christ, so closely identified with Him that we are like Him, and share in all His possessions. He says to each of us, "All Mine is thine." He has taken part of our flesh and blood that we may share in His Spirit. The bride is endowed with the wealth of the bridegroom, and the crowns that are placed on the heads of the redeemed are the crown which Christ Himself has received as the reward of His Cross—"even as I have received of My Father."

II. Note the victor's starry splendour.

The second symbol of my text is difficult of interpretation, like the first: "I will give him the morning star." Now, no doubt, throughout Scripture a star is a symbol of royal dominion; and many would propose so to interpret it in the present case. But it seems to me that whilst that explanation—which makes the second part of our promise simply identical with the former, though under a different garb—does justice to one part of the symbol, it entirely omits the other. For the emphasis is here laid on "morning" rather than on "star." It is "the morning star," not any star that blazes in the heavens, that is set forth here as a symbolical representation of the victor's condition. Then another false scent, as it were, on which interpretations have gone, seems to me to be that, taking into account the fact that in the last chapter of the Revelation our Lord is Himself described as "the bright and morning star," they bring this promise down simply to mean "I will give him Myself." Now, though it is quite true that, in the deepest of all views, Jesus Christ Himself is the gift as well as the giver of all these seven-fold promises, yet the propriety of representation seems to me to forbid that He should here say, "I will give them Myself!"

So I think we must fall back upon what any touch of poetic imagination would at once suggest to be the meaning of the promise, that it is the dawning splendour of that planet of hope and morning, the harbinger of day, which we are to lay hold of. Hebrew prophets, long before, had spoken of Lucifer, "light-bringer," "the son of the morning." Many a poet sang of it before Milton with his

> "Hesperus, that led the starry host,
> Rode brightest."

So that I think we are just to lay hold of the thought

that the starry splendour, the beauty and the lustre that will be poured upon the victor is that which is expressed by this symbol here.' What that lustre will consist in it becomes us not to say. That future keeps its secret well, but that it shall be the perfecting of human nature up to the most exquisite and consummate height of which it is capable, and the enlargement of it beyond all that human experience here can conceive, we may peaceably anticipate and quietly trust.

Only, note, the advance here on the previous promises is as conspicuous as in the former part of this great promise. There the Christian man's influence and authority were set forth under the emblem of regal dominion. Here they are set forth under the emblem of lustrous splendour. It is the spectators that see the glory of the beam that comes from the star. And this promise, like the former, implies that in that future there will be a sphere in which perfected spirits may ray out their light, and where they may gladden and draw some eyes by their beams. I have no word to say as to the sky in which the rays of that star may shine, but I do feel that the very essence of this great representation is that Christian souls, in the future, as in the present, will stand forth as the visible embodiments of the glory and lustre of the unseen God.

Further, remember that this image, like the former, traces up the lustre, as that traced the royalty, to communion with Christ, and to impartation from Him. "*I* will *give* him the morning star." We shall shine as the "brightness of the firmament, and as the stars for ever," as Daniel said—not by inherent but by reflected light. We are not suns, but planets, that move round the Sun of Righteousness, and flash with His beauty.

III. Lastly, mark the condition of the authority and of the lustre.

Here I would say a word about the remarkable expansion of the designation of the victor, to which I have already referred: "He that overcometh, and keepeth My works unto the end." We do not know why that expansion was put in, in reference to Thyatira only, but if you will glance over the letter you will see that there is more than usual about works—works to be repented of, or works which make the material of a final retribution and judgment.

Whatever may be the explanation of the expanded designation here, the lesson that it reads to us is a very significant and a very important one. Bring the metaphor of a victor down to the plain, hard, prose fact of doing Christ's work right away to the end of life. Strip off the rhetoric of the fight, and it comes down to this—dogged, persistent obedience to Christ's commandments. "He that keepeth My works" does not appeal to the imagination as "He that overcometh" does. But it is the explanation of the victory, and one that we all need to lay to heart.

"My works": that means the works that He enjoins. No doubt; but look at a verse before my text: "I will give unto every one of you according to *your* works." That is, the works that you *do*, and Christ's works are not only those which He enjoins, but those of which He Himself set the pattern. He will "give according to works"; He will give authority; give the morning star. That is to say, the life which has been moulded according to Christ's pattern, and shaped in obedience to Christ's commandments is the life which is capable of being granted participation in His dominion, and invested with reflected lustre. If here we do His work we shall be able to do it more fully yonder. "The works that I do shall he do also." That is the law for life—ay, and it is the promise for heaven. "And greater works than these shall he do, because I go to My Father." When we have come to partial conformity with Him here we may hope—and only then have we the right to hope—for entire assimilation to Him hereafter. If here, from this dim spot which men call earth, and amid the confusion and dust and distances of this present life, we look to Him, and with unveiled faces behold Him, and here, in degree and part, are being changed from glory to glory, there He will turn His face upon us, and, beholding it, in righteousness, "we shall be satisfied when we awake with His likeness."

Brethren, it is for us to choose whether we shall share in Christ's dominion or be crushed by his iron sceptre. It is for us to choose whether, moulding our lives after His will and pattern, we shall hereafter be made like Him in completeness. It is for us to choose whether, seeing Him here, we shall, when the brightness of His coming draws near, be flooded with gladness, or whether we shall call upon the rocks and the hills to cover us from the face of Him that sitteth on the Throne. Time is the mother of Eternity. To-day moulds to-morrow, and when all the to-days and to-morrows have become yesterdays, they will have determined our destiny, because they will have settled our characters. Let us keep Christ's commandments, and we shall be invested with dignity and illuminated with glory, and entrusted with work, far beyond anything that we can conceive here, though, in their furthest reach and most dazzling brightness, these are but the continuation and the perfecting of the feeble beginnings of earthly conflict and service.

THE VICTOR'S CROWNS.—V.

"He that overcometh, the same shall be clothed in white raiment; and I will not blot out his name out of the book of life, but I will confess his name before My Father, and before His angels."—REV. iii. 5.

THE brightest examples of earnest Christianity are generally found amidst widespread indifference. If a man does not yield to the prevailing tone, it is likely to quicken him into strong opposition. So it was in this Church of Sardis. It was dead. That was the summing-up of its condition. It had a name to live, and the name only made the real deadness more complete. But there were exceptions: souls ablaze with Divine love, who in the midst of corruption had kept their robes clean, and whom Christ's own voice declared to be worthy to walk with Him in white.

That great eulogium, which immediately precedes our text, is referred to in the first of its triple promises; as is even more distinctly seen if we read our text as the *Revised Version* does: "He that overcometh, the same shall thus be clothed in white raiment"; the "thus" pointing back to the preceding words, and widening the promise to the faithful few in Sardis so as to extend to all victors in all Churches throughout all time.

Now, the remaining two clauses of our text also seem to be coloured by the preceding parts of this letter. We read in it, "Thou hast a *name* that thou livest";

and again, " Thou hast a few *names* even in Sardis which have not defiled their garments." Our text catches up the word, and moulds its promises accordingly. One is more negative, the other more positive ; both link on to a whole series of Scriptural representations.

Now, all these declarations of the blessedness of the victors are, of course, intensely symbolical, and we can but partially translate them. I simply seek now to take them as they stand, and to try to grasp at least some part of the dim but certain hopes which they partly reveal and partly hide. There are, then, three things here.

I. The victor's robes.

"He that overcometh, the same shall (thus) be clothed in white raiment." White, of course, is the festal colour. But it is more than that: it is the heavenly colour. In this book we read of white thrones, white horses, hairs "white as snow," white stones. But we are to notice that the word here employed does not merely mean a dead whiteness, which is the absence of colour, but a lustrous and glistering white, like that of snow smitten by sunshine, or like that which dazzled the eyes of the three on the Mount of Transfiguration, when they saw the robes of the glorified Christ "whitened as no fuller on earth could white them." So that we are to associate with this metaphor, not only the thoughts of purity, festal joy, victory, but likewise the thought of lustrous glory.

Then the question arises, can we translate that metaphor of the robe into anything that will come closer to the fact ? Now, I may remind you that this figure runs through the whole of Scripture. We find, for instance, in one of the old prophets, a vision in which the taking away of Israel's sin is represented by the High Priest, the embodiment of the nation, standing in filthy garments, which were stripped off him and fair ones put on him. We find our Lord giving forth a parable of a man who came to the feast, not having on a wedding garment. We find the Apostle Paul speaking frequently, in a similar metaphor, of putting off an ancient nature and putting on a new one. We find in this book, not only the references in my text and the context, but the great saying concerning those that have "washed their robes and made them white in the blood of the Lamb," and the final benediction pronounced upon those who washed their robes, that they may "have a right to enter through the gate into the city."

Putting all these things together—and the catalogue might be extended—we have to observe that the signification of this symbol is not that of something wholly external to or apart from the man, but that it is rather that part of his nature, so to speak, which is visible to beholders, and we may translate it very simply—the robe is character. So the promise of my text, brought down so far as we can bring it to its primary element, is of a purity and lustrous glory of personal character, which shall be visible to any eye that may look upon the wearer. What more there may be found in it when we are "clothed upon with our house which is from heaven," if so be that "being clothed we shall not be found naked," I do not presume to say. I do not speculate, I simply translate the plain words of Scripture into the truth which they represent.

But now I would have you notice that this, like all the promises of the New Testament in regard to a future life, lays main stress on what a man is. Not where we are ; not what we have ; not what we do or know, make heaven, but *what we are.* The promises are clothed for us, as they must needs be, in sensuous images, which sensuous men have interpreted in far too low a sense ; or sometimes have not been even at the trouble of interpreting. But in reality there are but two facts that we *know* about that future, and they are smelted together, as cause and effect, in the great saying of the most spiritual of the Apostles : " We shall be like Him "—that is what we shall be—" for we shall see Him as He is." So, then, purity of character, when all the stains on the garments, spotted by the flesh, shall have melted away ; purity of character, when temptations shall have no more food in us and so conflict shall not be needful ; purity like Christ's own, and derived from the vision of Him, according to the great law that beholding is transformation, and the light we see is the light which we reflect—this is the heart of this great promise.

But notice that the main thing about it is that this lustrous purity of a perfected character is declared to be the direct outcome of the character, that was made by effort and struggle carried on in faith here upon earth. In this clause the familiar " I will give " does not appear ; and the thought of the condition upon earth working itself out into the glory of lustrous purity in the heavens is made even more emphatic by the adoption of the reading to which I have referred : " Shall *thus* be clothed," which points us backwards to what preceded, where our Lord's own voice declares that the men who have not defiled their garments upon earth are they who "shall walk with Him in white." The great law of continuity and of increase, so that the dispositions cultivated here rise to sovereign power hereafter, and that what was tendency, and struggle, and imperfect realisation upon earth becomes fact and complete possession in the heavens, is declared in the words before us.

What solemn importance that thought gives to the smallest of our victories or defeats here on earth! They are threads in the web out of which our garment is to be cut. After all, yonder as here, we are dressed in homespun, and we make our clothing and shape it for our wear. That truth is perfectly consistent with the other truth on which it reposes—that the Christian man owes to Christ the reception of the new garment of purity and holiness. The evangelical doctrine, "not by works of righteousness which we have done," and its complement in the words of my text, are perfectly harmonious. We cannot weave the web except Christ gives us yarn, nor can we work out our own salvation except Christ bestows upon us the salvation which we work out. The two things go together. Let us remember that, whilst in one aspect the souls that were all clad in filthy garments are arrayed as a bridegroom decketh his bride with a fair vesture, in another aspect we ourselves, by our own efforts, by our own struggles, by our own victories, have to weave and fashion and cut and sew the dress which we shall wear for ever.

II. Notice here the victor's place in the Book of Life.

"I will not blot out his name out of the Book of Life." I have pointed out that in the former clause the characteristic "I will give" is omitted, in order that emphatic expression might be secured for the thought that in one aspect the reward of the future is automatic or self-working. But that thought is by no means a complete statement of the truth with regard to this matter; and so, in both of the subsequent clauses, we have our Lord representing Himself (for it is never to be forgotten that these promises are Christ's own words from heaven) as clothed with His judicial functions, and as determining the fates of men. "I will not blot out his name out of the Book of Life." That is a solemn and tremendous claim, that Christ's finger can write, and Christ's finger can erase, a name from that register.

Now, I have said that all these clauses link themselves on to a whole series of Scriptural representatives. I showed that briefly in regard to the former; I would do so in regard to the present one.

You will remember, perhaps, in the early history of Israel, that Moses, with lofty self-devotion, prayed God to blot his name out of His book, if only by that sacrifice Israel's sin might be forgiven. You may recall too, possibly, how one of the prophets speaks of "those that are written amongst the living in Jerusalem," and how Daniel, in his eschatological vision, refers to those whose names were or were not written in the book. I need not remind you of how our Lord commanded His disciples to rejoice not in that the spirits were subject to them, but rather to rejoice because their names were written in heaven. Nor need I do more than simply refer to the Apostle's tender and pathetic excuse for not remembering the names of some of His fellow-workers, that it mattered very little, because their names were written in the Book of Life. Throughout this Apocalypse, too, we find subsequent allusions of the same nature, just as in the Epistle to the Hebrews we read of the "Church of the first-born whose names are written in heaven." Now, all these, thus put together, suggest two ideas: one which I do not deal with here—viz., that of a burgess-roll—and the other that of a register of those who truly live. And that is the thought that is suggested here. The promise of my text links on to the picture in the letter, of the condition of the Church at Sardis, which was dead, and says that the victor will truly and securely and for ever possess life, with all the clustered blessednesses which, like a nebula unresolved, gather themselves, dim yet radiant, round that great word.

But what I especially note here is, not so much this reiteration of the fundamental and all-embracing promise which has met us in preceding letters, the promise of a secure, eternal life, as that plain and solemn implication that a name *may* be struck out of that book. Theological exigencies compelled our fathers to deny that, but surely the words of our text are too plain to be neglected or misunderstood. It is possible that a name, like the name of a dishonest attorney, shall be struck off the rolls. Do not let any desire for theological symmetry blind you, brother, to that fact. Take it into account in your daily lives. It is possible for a man to "cast away his confidence." It is possible for him to make shipwreck of the faith. Some of you will remember that pathetic story of Cromwell's deathbed, when he asked one of his ghostly counsellors whether it was true that "once in the covenant, always in the covenant?" He got the answer, "Yes"; and then he said, "I know I once was," and so died. Brethren, it is the victors whose names are kept upon the roll. These people at Sardis had a name to live, and they thought that their names were in the Book of Life. And when it was opened, lo! a blot. Some of us have seen upon the granite of Egyptian temples the cartouches of a defeated dynasty chiselled out by their successors. The granite on which this list is written is not so hard but that a man, by his own sin, falling away from the Master, may chisel out his name. A student goes up for his examination. He thinks he has succeeded. The pass-lists come out, and his name is not there. Take care that you are not building upon past faith, but remember that it is the *victor's* name that is not blotted out of the Book of Life.

III. Lastly, the victor's recognition by the Commanding Officer.

"I will confess his name before My Father, and before His angels." There, too, we have a kind of mosaic, made up of previous Scripture declarations. Our Lord, twice in the Gospels—and on neither occasion in the Gospel according to St. John—has similar sayings; once about confessing the name of him who confesses His name "before the Father"; once about confessing it "before the holy angels." Here these are smelted together into the one great recognition by Jesus Christ of the victor as being His.

Now, I need not remind you of how emphatically, to this clause also, the remark which I have made with regard to the former one applies, and how tremendous and inexplicable, except on one hypothesis, is this same assumption by Christ of judicial functions which determine the fate and the standing of men.

But I would rather point to the thought that this promise carries with it not only Christ's judicial recognition of the victor, but also the thought of loving relationship, of close friendship, of continual regard. He "confesses the name"—that means that He takes to His heart, and loves, and cares for the person.

Is it not the highest honour that can be given to any soldier, to have honourable mention in the General's despatches? It matters very little what becomes of our names upon earth, though there they be dark, and swift oblivion devours them almost as soon as we are dead, except in so far as they may live for a little while in the memory of two or three that loved us. That is the fate of most of us. And surely "the hollow wraith of dying fame" may "fade wholly," and we "exult," if Jesus Christ confess our name. It matters little who forgets us if He remember us. It matters even less what the judgments pronounced in our obituaries may be, if He says, "That man is Mine, and I own him." Ah! brethren, what a reversal of the world's judgments there will be one day; and how names that have been blown through a thousand trumpets, and had hosannas sung to them, and been welcomed with a tumult of acclaim through generations, will sink into oblivion and never be heard of any more, and the unseen and obscure men who lived by, and for, and with Jesus Christ, will come to the front! Praise from Him is praise indeed.

Now, brethren, the upshot of it all is that life here derives its meaning and its consecration from life hereafter. The question for us is, do we habitually realise that we are weaving the garment we must wear, be it a poisoned robe that shall eat into our flesh like fire, or be it a fair vesture, clean and white? Do we brace ourselves for the obscure struggles of our little lives, feeling that they are not small because they carry eternal consequences? Are we content to be unknown because well known by Him, and to live so that He shall acknowledge us in the day when to be acknowledged by Him means glory and blessedness beyond all hopes and all symbols; and to be disowned by Him means ruin and despair? You know the conditions of victory. Lay them to heart, and its issues, and the tragical results of defeat; and then cleave, with mind and heart and will, to Him who can make you more than conquerors, who will change your frayed and dinted armour for the fine linen, clean and white, and will point to you, before His Father and the universe, and say, " This man was one of My faithful soldiers." That will be honour indeed. Do you see to it that you make it yours.

THE VICTOR'S CROWNS.—VI.

"Him that overcometh will I make a pillar in the temple of My God, and he shall go no more out: and I will write upon him the name of My God, and the name of the city of My God, which is New Jerusalem, which cometh down out of heaven from My God: and I will write upon him My new name."—REV. iii. 12.

THE eyes which were as a flame of fire saw nothing to blame in the Philadelphian Church, and the lips out of which came the two-edged sword that cuts through all hypocrisy to the discerning of the thoughts and intents of the heart, spoke only eulogium—" Thou hast kept My word, and hast not denied My name." But however mature and advanced may be Christian experience, it is never lifted above the possibility of temptation; so, with praise, there came warning of an approaching hour which would try the mettle of this unblamed Church. Christ's reward for faithfulness is not immunity from, but strength in, trial and conflict. As long as we are in the world there will be forces warring against us; and we shall have to fight our worse selves and the tendencies which tempt us to prefer the visible to the unseen, and the present to the future. So the Church which had no rebuke received the solemn injunction: " Hold fast that thou hast; let no man take thy crown." There is always need of struggle, even for the most mature, if we would keep what we have. The treasure will be filched from slack hands; the crown will be stricken from a slumbering head. So it is not inappropriate that the promise to this Church should be couched in the usual terms, "to him that *overcometh*," and the conclusion to be drawn is the solemn and simple one that the Christian life is always a conflict, even to the end.

The promise contained in my text presents practically but a twofold aspect of that future blessedness; the one expressed in the clause, "I will make him a pillar"; the other expressed in the clauses referring to the writing upon him of certain names. I need not do more than again call attention to the fact that here, as always, Jesus Christ represents Himself as not only allocating the position and determining the condition, but as shaping, and moulding, and enriching the characters of the redeemed, and ask you to ponder the question, What in Him does that assumption involve?

Passing on, then, to the consideration of these two promises more closely, let us deal with them singly. There is, first, the steadfast pillar; there is, second, the three-fold inscription.

I. The steadfast pillar.

Now, I take it that the two clauses which refer to this matter are closely connected. "I will make him a pillar in the temple of My God, and he shall go no more out." In the second clause the figure is dropped, and the point of the metaphor is brought out more clearly. The stately column in the temples, with which these Philadelphian Christians, dwelling in the midst of the glories of Greek architecture, were familiar, might be, and often has been, employed as a symbol of many things. Here it cannot mean the office of sustaining a building, or pre-eminence above others, as it naturally lends itself sometimes to mean. For instance, the Apostle Paul speaks of the three chief Apostles in Jerusalem, and says that they "seemed to be pillars"; by which pre-eminence and the office of maintaining the Church are implied. But that obviously cannot be the special application of the figure here, inasmuch as we cannot conceive of even redeemed men sustaining that temple in the heavens; and also, inasmuch as the promise here is perfectly universal, and is given to all that overcome —that is to say, to all the redeemed. We must, therefore, look in some other direction. Now, the second of the two clauses which are thus linked together seems to me to point in the direction in which we are to look. "He shall go no more out." A pillar is a natural emblem of stability and permanence, as poets in many tongues and in many lands have felt it to be. I remember one of our own quaint English writers who speaks of men who "are bottomed on the basis of a firm faith, mounting up with the clear shaft of a shining life, and having their persevering tops garlanded about, according to God's promise, "I will give thee a crown of life." That idea of stability, of permanence, of fixedness, is the one that is prominent in the metaphor here.

But whilst the general notion is that of stability and permanence, do not let us forget that it is permanence and stability in a certain direction, for the pillar is " in the temple of My God." Now, I would recall to you the fact that in other parts of Scripture we find the present relation of Christian men to God set forth under a similar metaphor: "Ye are the temple of the living God"; or again, "In whom ye are builded for a habitation of God through the Spirit"; or again, in that great word which is the foundation of all such symbols, "We will come and make our abode with Him." So that the individual believer and the community of all such are, even here and now, the dwelling place of God. And whilst there are ideas of dignity and grace attaching to the metaphor of the pillar, the underlying meaning of it is substantially that the individual souls of redeemed men shall be themselves parts of, and collectively shall constitute, the temple of God in the heavens.

This book of the Apocalypse has several points of view in regard to that great symbol. It speaks, for instance, of there being "no temple therein," by which is meant the cessation of all material and external worships such as belong to earth. It speaks also of God and the Lamb as themselves being "the Temple thereof." And here we have the converse idea that not only may we think of the redeemed community as dwelling in God and Christ, but of God and Christ as dwelling in the redeemed community. The promise, then, is of a thrilling consciousness that God is in us, a deeper realisation of His presence, a fuller communication of His grace, a closer touch of Him, far beyond anything that we can conceive of on earth, and yet being the continuation and the completion of the earthly experiences of those in whom God dwells by their faith, their love, and their obedience. We have nothing to say about the new capacities for consciousness of God which may come to redeemed souls when the veils of flesh and sense, and the absorption in the present drop away. We have nothing to say, because we know nothing, about the new manifestations and more intimate touches which may correspond to these new capacities. There are vibrations of sound too rapid or too slow for our ears as at present organised to catch. But whether these be too shrill or too deep to be heard, if the ear were more sensitive there would be sound where there is silence, and music in the waste places. So with new organs, with new capacities, there will be a new and a deeper sense of the presence of God; and utterances of His lips too profound to be caught by us now, or too clear and high to be apprehended by our limited sense, will then thunder into melody and with clear notes sound His praises. There are rays of light in the spectrum, at both ends of it, as yet not perceptible to human eyes; but then "we shall, in Thy light, see light" flaming higher and deeper than we can do now. We dwell in God here if we dwell in Christ, and we dwell in Christ if He dwell in us, by faith and love. But in the heavens the indwelling shall be more perfect, and transcend all that we know now.

The special point in regard to which that perfection is expressed here is to be kept prominent. "He shall go no more out." Permanence, and stability, and uninterruptedness in the communion and consciousness of an indwelling God, is a main element in the glory and blessedness of that future life. Stability in any fashion comes as a blessed hope to us, who know the curse of constant change, and are tossing on the unquiet waters of life. It is blessed to think of a region where the seal of permanence will be set on all delights, and our blessednesses will be like the bush in the desert, burning and yet not consumed. But the highest form of that blessedness is the thought of stable, uninterrupted, permanent communion with God and consciousness of His dwelling in us. The contrast forces itself upon us between that equable and unvarying communion and the ups and downs of the most uniform Christian life here—to-day thrilling in every nerve with the sense of God, to-morrow dead and careless. Sometimes the bay is filled with flashing waters that leap in the sunshine; sometimes, when the tide is out, there is only a long stretch of grey and oozy mud. It shall not be always so. Like lands on the Equator, where the difference between midsummer and midwinter is scarcely perceptible, either in length of day or in degree of temperature, that future will be a calm continuance, a uniformity which is not monotony, and a stability which does not exclude progress.

I cannot but bring into contrast with that great promise "he shall go no more out" an incident in the Gospels. Christ and the Twelve were in the upper room, and He poured out His heart to them, and their hearts burned within them. But "they went out to the Mount of Olives"—He to Gethsemane and to Calvary; Judas to betray and Peter to deny; all to toil and suffer, and sometimes to waver in their faith. "He shall go no more out." Eternal glory and unbroken communion is the blessed promise to the victor who is made by Christ "a pillar in the temple of My God."

II. Now, secondly, notice the threefold inscription.

We have done with the metaphor of the pillar

altogether. We are not to think of anything so incongruous as a pillar stamped with writing, a monstrosity in Grecian architecture. But it is the man himself on whom Christ is to write the threefold name. The writing of a name implies ownership and visibility.

So the first of the triple inscriptions declares that the victor shall be conspicuously God's. "I will write upon him the name of My God." There may possibly be an allusion to the golden plate which flamed in the front of the High Priest's mitre, and on which was written the unspoken name of Jehovah. But whether that be so or no, the underlying ideas are these two which I have already referred to—complete ownership, and that manifested in the very front of the character.

How do we possess one another? How do we belong to God? How does God belong to us? There is but one way by which a spirit can possess a spirit—by love, which leads to self-surrender and to practical obedience. And if—as a man writes his name in his books, as a farmer brands on his sheep and oxen the marks that express his ownership—on the redeemed there is written the name of God, that means, whatever else it may mean, perfect love, perfect self-surrender, perfect obedience, that the whole nature shall be owned, and know itself owned, and be glad to be owned, by God. That is the perfecting of the Christian relationship which is begun here on earth. And if we here yield ourselves to God and depart from that foolish and always frustrated attempt to be our own masters and owners, so escaping the misery and burden of self-hood, and entering into the liberty of the children of God, we shall reach that blessed state in which there will be no murmuring and incipient rebellions, no disturbance of our inward submission, no breach in our active obedience, no holding back of anything that we have or are ; but we shall be wholly God's—that is, wholly possessors of ourselves, and blessed thereby. " He that loveth his life shall lose it ; and he that loseth his life, the same shall find it." And that Name will be stamped on us, that every eye that looks, whoever they may be, shall know " whose we are and whom we serve."

The second inscription declares that the victor conspicuously belongs to the City. Our time will not allow of my entering at all upon the many questions that gather round that representation of " the New Jerusalem which cometh down out of heaven." I must content myself with simply pointing to the possible allusion here to the promise in the preceding letter to Sardis. There we were told that the victor's name should not " be blotted out of the Book of Life " ; and that Book of Life suggested the idea of the burgess-roll of the city, as well as the register of those that truly live. Here the same thought is suggested by a converse metaphor. The name of the victor is written on the rolls of the city, and the name of the city is stamped on the forehead of the victor. That is to say, the affinity which, even here and now, has knit men who believe in Jesus Christ to an invisible order, where is their true mother-city and metropolis, will then be uncontradicted by any inconsistencies, unobscured by the necessary absorption in daily duties and transient aims and interests, which often veils to others, and renders less conscious to ourselves, our true belonging to the city beyond the sea. The name of the city shall be stamped upon the victor.

That, again, is the perfecting and the continuation of the central heart of the Christian life here, the consciousness that we are come to the city of the living God, the heavenly Jerusalem, and belong to another order of things than the visible and material around us.

The last of the triple inscriptions declares that the victor shall be conspicuously Christ's. "I will write upon him My new name." All the three inscriptions link themselves, not with earlier, but with later parts of this most artistically constructed book of the Revelation; and in a subsequent portion of it we read of a new name of Christ's, which no man knoweth save Himself. What is that new name? It is an expression for the sum of the new revelations of what He is, which will flood the souls of the redeemed when they pass from earth. That new name will not obliterate the old one—God forbid! It will not do away with the ancient, earth-begun relation of dependence and faith and obedience. "Jesus Christ is the same . . . for ever"; and His name in the heavens, as upon earth, is Jesus the Saviour. But there are abysses in Him which no man moving amidst the incipiencies and imperfections of this infantile life of earth can understand. Not until we possess can we know the depths of wisdom and knowledge, and of all other blessed treasures which are stored in Him. Here we touch but the fringe of His great glory; yonder we shall penetrate to its central flame.

That new name no man fully knows, even when he has entered on its possession and carries it on his forehead; for the infinite Christ, who is the manifestation of the infinite God, can never be comprehended, much less exhausted, even by the united perceptions of a redeemed universe; but for ever and ever more and more will well out from Him. His name shall last as long as the sun, and blaze when the sun himself is dead.

"I will write upon him My new name" was said to a Church of which the eulogium was, "Thou hast not denied My name." If we are to pierce to the heart of the glory there, we must begin on its edges here. If the name is to be on our foreheads then, we must shrine it in our hearts now, by faith and love, and bear in our body the marks of the Lord Jesus—the brand of ownership impressed on the slave's palm. In the strength of that name we can overcome; and if we overcome His name will hereafter blaze on our foreheads—the token that we are completely His for ever, and the pledge that we shall be growingly made like unto Him.

THE VICTOR'S CROWNS.—VII.

"To him that overcometh will I grant to sit with Me in My throne, even as I also overcame, and am set down with My Father in His throne."—REV. iii. 21.

THE Church at Laodicea touched the lowest point of Christian character. It had no heresies, but that was not because it clung to the truth, but because it had not life enough to breed even them. It had no conspicuous vices, like some of the other communities. But it had what was more fatal than many vices—a low temperature of religious life and feeling, and a high notion of itself. Put these two things together —they generally go together—and you get the most fatal condition for a Church. It is the condition of a large part of the so-called "Christian world" to-day, as that very name unconsciously confesses; for "world" is the substantive, and "Christian" only the adjective, and there is a great deal more "world" than "Christian" in many so-called "Churches."

Such a Church needed, and received, the sharpest rebuke. A severe disease requires drastic treatment. But the same necessity which drew forth the sharp rebuke drew forth also the loftiest of the promises. If the condition of Laodicea was so bad, the struggle to overcome became proportionately greater, and, consequently, the reward the larger. The least worthy may rise to the highest position. It was not to the victors over persecution at Smyrna, or over heresies at Thyatira, nor even to the blameless Church of Philadelphia, but it was to the faithful in Laodicea, who had kept the fire of their own devotion well alight amidst the tepid Christianity round them, that this climax of all the seven promises is given.

In all the others Jesus Christ stands as the bestower of the gift. Here He stands, not only as the bestower, but as Himself participating in that which He bestows. The words beggar all exposition, and I have shrunk from taking them as my text. We seem to see in them, as if looking into some sun with dazzled eyes, radiant forms moving amidst the brightness, and in the midst of them one like unto the Son of man. But if my words only dilute and weaken this great promise, they may still help to keep it before your own minds for a few moments. So I ask you to look with me at the two great things that are bracketed together in our text; only I venture to reverse the order of consideration, and think of—

I. The Commander-in-Chief's conquest and royal repose.

"I also overcame, and am set down with My Father in His throne." It seems to me that, wonderful as are all the words of my text, perhaps the most wonderful of them all are those by which the two halves of the promise are held together—"Even as I also." The Captain of the host takes His place in the ranks, and, if I may so say, shoulders His musket like the poorest private. Christ sets Himself before us as pattern of the struggle, and as pledge of the victory and reward. Now let me say a word about each of the two halves of this great thought of our Lord's identification of Himself with us in our fight, and identification of us with Him in His victory.

As to the former, I would desire to emphasise, with all the strength that I can, the point of view from which Jesus Christ Himself, in these final words from the heavens, directed to all the Churches, looks back upon His earthly career, and bids us think of it as a true conflict. You remember how, in the sanctities of the upper room, and ere yet the supreme moment of the crucifixion had come, our Lord said, when within a day of the Cross and an hour of Gethsemane, "I have overcome the world." This is an echo of that never-to-be-forgotten utterance, that the aged Apostle had heard when leaning on his Master's bosom in the seclusion and silence of that sacred upper chamber. Only here our Lord, looking back upon the victory, gathers it all up into one as a past thing, and says, "I overcame," in those old days long ago.

Brethren, the orthodox Christian is tempted to think of Jesus Christ in such a fashion as to reduce His conflict on earth to a mere sham fight. Let no supposed theological necessities induce you to weaken down in your thoughts of Him what He Himself has told us— that He, too, struggled, and that He, too, overcame. That temptation in the wilderness, where the necessities of the flesh and the desires of the spirit were utilised by the Tempter as weapons with which His unmoved obedience and submission were assailed, was repeated over and over again all through His earthly life. We believe—at least I believe—that Jesus Christ was in nature sinless, and that temptation found nothing in Him on which it could lay hold, no fuel or combustible material to which it could set light. But notwithstanding, inasmuch as He became partaker of flesh and blood, and entered into the limitations of humanity, His sinlessness did not involve His incapacity for being tempted, nor did it involve that His righteousness was not assailed, nor His submission often tried. We believe—or, at least I believe—that He "did no sin, neither was guile found in His mouth." But I also reverently listen to Him unveiling, so far as may need to be unveiled, the depths of His own nature and experience, and I rejoice to think that He fought the good fight, and Himself was a soldier in the army of which He is the General. He is the Captain, the Leader, of the long procession of heroes of the faith; and He is the "perfecter" of it, inasmuch as His own faith was complete and unbroken.

But I may remind you, too, that from this great word of condescending self-revelation and identification, we may well learn what a victorious life really is. "I overcame;" but from the world's point of view, He was utterly beaten. He did not gather in many who would listen to Him or care for His words. He was misunderstood, rejected; lived a life of poverty; died, when a young man, a violent death; was hunted by all the Church dignitaries of His generation as a blasphemer; spit upon by soldiers, and execrated after His death. And that is victory, is it? Well, then, we shall have to revise our estimates of what is a conquering career. If He, the pauper-martyr, if He, the misunderstood enthusiast, if He conquered, then some of our notions of a victorious life are very far astray.

Nor need I say a word, I suppose, about the completeness, as well as the reality, of that victory of His. From heaven He claims in this great word just what He claimed on earth, over and over again, when He fronted His enemies with " Which of you convinceth Me of sin ? " and when He declared in the sanctities of His confidence with His friends, " I do always the things that please Him." The rest of us partially overcome, and partially are defeated. He alone bears His shield out of the conflict undinted and unstained. To do the will of God, to dwell in continual communion with the Father, never to be hindered by anything that the world can present or my sins can suggest, whether of delightsome or dreadful, from doing the will of the Father in heaven from the heart—that is victory, and all else is defeat. And that is what the Captain of our salvation, and only He, did.

Turn for a moment now to the other side of our Lord's gracious identification of Himself with us. " Even as I also am set down with My Father in His throne." That points back, as the Greek original shows even more distinctly, to the historical fact of the Ascension. It recalls the great words by which, with full consciousness of what He was doing, Jesus Christ sealed His own death-warrant in the presence of the Sanhedrim when He said : " Henceforth ye shall see the Son of man sitting on the right hand of power." It carries us still farther back to the psalm which our Lord Himself quoted, and thereby stopped the mouths of Scribes and Pharisees : " The Lord said unto My Lord, sit Thou at My right hand till I make Thine enemies Thy footstool." He laid His hand upon that great promise, and claimed that it was to be fulfilled in His case. And here, stooping from amidst the blaze of the central royalty of the Universe, He confirms all that He had said before, and declares that He shares the Throne of God.

Now, of course, the words are intensely figurative, and have to be translated as best we can, even though it may seem to weaken and dilute them, into less concrete and sensible forms than the figurative representation. But I think we shall not be mistaken if we assert that, whatever lies in this great statement far beyond our conception in the present, there lie in it three things—repose, royalty, communion of the most intimate kind with the Father.

There is repose. You remember how the first martyr saw the opened heavens and the ascended Christ, in that very hall, probably, in which Christ had said, " Henceforth ye shall see the Son of man sitting at the right hand of power." But Stephen, as he declared, with rapt face smitten by the light into the likeness of an angel's, saw Him standing at the right hand. We have to combine these two images, incongruous as they are in prose, literally, before we reach the conception of the essential characteristic of that royal rest of Christ's. For it is a repose that is full of activity. " My Father worketh hitherto," said He on earth, " and I work." And that is true with regard to His unseen and heavenly life. The verses which are appended to the close of Mark's gospel draw a picture for us—" They went everywhere preaching the Word": He sat at "the right hand of God." The two halves do not fuse together. The Commander is in repose; the soldiers are bearing the brunt of the fight. Yes! But then there comes the word which links the two halves together. "They went everywhere preaching, the Lord also working with them."

Christ's repose indicates, not merely the cessation from, but much rather the completion of, His work on earth, which culminated on the Cross; which work on earth is the basis of the still mightier work which He is doing in the heavens. So the Apostle Paul sets up a great ladder, so to speak, which our faith climbs by successive stages, when He says, "He that died—yea, rather that is risen again—who is even at the right hand of God—who also maketh intercession for us." His repose is full of beneficent activity for all that love Him.

Again, there is set forth royalty, participation in Divine dominion. The highly metaphorical language of our text, and of parallel verses elsewhere, presents this truth in two forms. Sometimes we read of "sitting at the right hand of God"; sometimes, as here, we read of "sitting on the throne." The "right hand of God" is everywhere. It is not a local designation. "The right hand of the Lord" is the instrument of His omnipotence, and to speak of Christ as sitting on the right hand of God is simply to cast into symbolical words the great thought that He wields the forces of Divinity. When we read of Him as enthroned on the Throne of God, we have, in like manner, to translate the figure into this overwhelming and yet most certain truth, that the Man Christ Jesus is exalted to supreme, universal dominion, and that all the forces of omnipotent Divinity rest in the hands that still bear, for faith, the prints of the nails.

But again that session of Christ with the Father suggests the thought, about which it becomes us not to speak, of a communion with the Father—deep, intimate, unbroken, beyond all that we can conceive or speak. We listen to Him when He says, " Glorify Thou Me with the glory which I had with Thee before the world was." We bow before the thought that what He asked in that prayer was the lifting of one of ourselves, the humanity of Jesus, into this inseparable unity with the very glory of God. And then we catch the wondrous words : " Even as I also."

II. That brings me to the second of the thoughts here, which may be more briefly disposed of after the preceding exposition, and that is, the private soldier's share in the Captain's victory and rest. "I will grant to sit with Me in My throne, even as I also."

Now, with regard to the former of these, our share in Christ's triumph and conquest, I only wish to say one thing, and it is this—I thankfully recognise that to many who do not share with me in what I believe to be the teaching of Scripture—viz., the belief that Christ was more than example, their partial belief, as I think it, in Him as the realised ideal, the living Pattern of how men ought to live, has given strength for far nobler and purer life than could otherwise have been reached. But, brethren, it seems to me that we want a great deal more than a pattern, a great deal closer and more intimate union with the Conqueror, than the mere setting forth of the possibility of a perfect life as realised in Him, ere we can share in His victory. What does it matter to me, after all, except for stimulus and for rebuke, that Jesus Christ should have lived the life? Nothing ; but when we can link the words in the upper room, " I have overcome," and the words from heaven, " Even as I also overcame," with the same Apostle's words in his epistle, " This is the victory that overcometh the world ; even our faith," then we share in the Captain's victory in an altogether different manner from that which *they* do who can see in Him only a pattern that stimulates and inspires. For if we put our trust in that Saviour, then the very life which was in Christ Jesus, and which conquered the world in Him, will pass into us ; and the law of the spirit of life in Christ will make us more than conquerors through Him that loved us.

And then the victory being secured, because Christ lives in us and makes us victorious, our participation in His throne is secure likewise.

There shall be repose, the cessation of effort, the end of toil. There shall be no more aching heads, strained muscles, exhausted brains, weary hearts, dragging feet. There will be no more need for resistance. The helmet will be antiquated, the laurel crown will take its place. The heavy armour, that rusted the garment over which it was braced, will be laid aside, and the trailing robes, that will contract no stain from the golden pavements, will be the attire of the redeemed. We have all had work enough, and weariness enough, and battles enough, and beatings enough, to make us thankful for the thought that we shall *sit* on the throne.

But if it is a rest like His, and if it is to be the rest of royalty, there will be plenty of work in it; work of the kind that fits us and is blessed. I know not what new elevation, or what sort of dominion will be granted to those who, instead of the faithfulness of the steward, are called upon to exercise the activity of the Lord over ten cities. I know not, and I care not; it is enough to know that we shall sit on His throne.

But do not let us forget the last of the thoughts: "They shall sit *with Me*." Ah! There you touch the centre—"To depart and to be with Christ, which is far better;" "Absent from the body; present with the Lord." We know not how. The lips are locked that might, perhaps, have spoken; only this we know, that, not as a drop of water is absorbed into the ocean and loses its individuality, shall we be united to Christ. There will always be the two, or there would be no blessedness in the two being one; but as close as is compatible with the sense of being myself, and of His being Himself, will be our fellowship with Him. "He that is joined to the Lord is one spirit."

Brethren, this generation would be a great deal the better for thinking more often of the promises and threatenings of Scripture with regard to the future. I believe that no small portion of the lukewarmness of the modern Laodicean is owing to the comparative neglect into which, in these days, the Christian teachings on that subject have fallen. I have tried in these sermons on these seven promises to bring them at least before your thoughts and hearts. And I beseech you that you would, more than you have done, "have respect unto the recompense of reward," and let that future blessedness enter as a subsidiary motive into your Christian life.

We may gather all these promises together, and even then we have to say, "the half hath not been told us." "It doth not yet appear what we shall be." Symbols and negations, and these alone, teach us the little that we know about that future; and when we try to expand and concatenate these, I suppose that our conceptions correspond to the reality about as closely as would the dreams of a chrysalis as to what it would be when it was a butterfly. But certainty and clearness are not necessarily united. "It doth not yet appear what we shall be, but we *know* that when He shall appear we shall be like Him." Take "even as I also" for the key that unlocks all the mysteries of that glorious future. "It is enough for the servant that he be as his Master."

THE CHRIST OF THE SERMON ON THE MOUNT.

"He taught them as one having authority, and not as the scribes."—MATT. vii. 29.

"I DO not care about doctrines; give me the Sermon on the Mount." So say some, many of whom, no doubt, admire the said Sermon a good deal more than they obey it. But they are right in so far as the so-called Sermon is not a summary of Christian doctrine, but of Christian morals. It is not a gospel, or a creed; it is the law of the kingdom given by the King Himself, but the truths on which it reposes, and still more the power by which it can be obeyed, are to be looked for elsewhere.

Still, though that is true, this collection of our Lord's ethical teachings does go farther into the region of Christian doctrine than some of its admirers seem to see. And I have taken this text, not so much for the purpose of speaking about it specially, as because it sums up the impression that was made upon our Lord's hearers, and may serve as a starting point for our considering what is implied in regard to some very important matters, by the teaching of this Sermon on the Mount.

I wish to look at what Jesus Christ says about Himself in it, and to ask to what conclusion that points. We shall not do justice to this non-doctrinal summary of Christian morals, unless we recognise that the conclusion to which it leads is no less solemn and lofty than that to which the plainest words of our Lord's self-revelation conduct us. If any man will accept the Jesus of the Sermon on the Mount at His own valuation, he will have to go farther than perhaps he thinks towards accepting the Christ of John's Gospel, of the Epistles, and of the Apocalypse. So I gather together the scattered intimations that drop from our Lord's lips in this discourse concerning Himself, and note the impression that it made on His hearers. I begin with that feature which is brought out in the words that I have taken for a kind of text.

I. Note, first, the unique air of *authority* that breathes through the whole of this discourse.

A great many attempts have been made, and that very conspicuously in recent days, to trace the influence of Jewish tradition on our Lord's teachings; and I am by no means concerned to deny that such influence may to a certain extent be traced, or to assert that His human development was altogether independent of the circumstances in which He grew up. But these attempts have generally been made in the interests of a purely natural explanation of our Lord and His work, and in order to make out that He was, like every man, a creature of his times. Now, it may be worth our while to notice that, as my text and other places of Scripture tell us, the broad, outstanding impression which His teaching made upon His contemporaries, who, perhaps, knew as much about Rabbinical teaching as modern scholars do, was precisely the opposite one—viz., its utter unlikeness to the kind of thing that they were accustomed to hear from those learned lips. Originality was a sin in the schools of the scribes. Their whole ingenuity—and it was great—was directed to deducing consequence after consequence, ever more fine-spun and fantastic, from the admitted principles of early teachers. But here was a man that quotes nobody, that never argued, that did not base what He said upon anything previously said by any one, but who stood before them making this impression—that He was a teacher, clean out of the rut in which Rabbi This trod wearisomely after the footsteps of Rabbi That, that He saw things with His own eyes, and drew water out of His own well. "He taught them as one having authority, and not as the scribes," and if anybody wants to understand the difference between Jesus Christ and the teachers of the day in which He lived, let him, if he can, get hold of a page of the Talmud, and then read the Sermon on the Mount, and he will find out that the unlikeness is a great deal more conspicuous than the similarity.

We need only to turn to this great discourse in order to get proof of this. For what is the first thing that would strike a reader, if he were to come to it with fresh eyes? I suppose it would be, not so much the wisdom, or the reasonableness, or the elevation of the individual precepts contained in it, as the strange air of having the right to command which breathes through it. This man speaks to the listeners as if He were their master, and our master, and everybody's master; with a royal tone, condescending to no vindication of His right to command, but, with clear-cut, sharp definiteness, laying His orders upon every human heart.

We cannot say that, in thus speaking, He is hiding His own personality behind the truths that He is uttering. That may be the explanation of much of the apparent dogmatism of moral teachers. It does not usually matter who says the thing; what is said, and not who says it, is the important matter for us. But in this case, Jesus Christ thrusts His own personality into the front; and the only vindication that He gives through all the sermon of the autocratic imperativeness of His tone, is not by referring to the elevation or the self-evident reasonableness of His commandments, but "I say unto you." What right has He to plant Himself opposite humanity, and to speak as if He had the authority to bid them, as His servants, "Go," and they would go; "Come," and they would come; "Do this," and they would do it? The right is based on what is articulately uttered elsewhere, but is implied in the very discourse itself.

I do not need to ask you to set by the side of that characteristic the tone which becomes all other moralists and guides. If Jesus Christ is only what they are, one of a class, the peculiarity which distinguishes His teaching from theirs puts Him beneath, and not above, them. For no one of the rest has

> "made the important stumble
> Of saying that he, the sage and humble,
> Is likewise One with the Creator."

That is what He did. It was not arrogance for Him to push His personality into the front, as the all-sufficient sanction of His commands. It matters not what is the shape of the lampstand if the light is blazing. But here the lampstand is the light; and we do not understand Jesus Christ unless we have found the reason for His authoritativeness in His Divinity.

II. Let me ask you to consider our Lord's attitude, in this Sermon, to earlier Revelation.

That is all summed up in one word of the Sermon. "I came not to destroy" [the law and the prophets], "but to fulfil." Now, I have no time to dwell upon the significance, though it is important, of that introductory word "I came." I must leave that for other occasions. But I ask you to notice what is meant by that great word "to fulfil," and how much Jesus Christ asserts about Himself and His relation to that past Revelation, which He and His hearers equally regarded as being sent from God, by that declaration, "I came . . . to fulfil."

To fulfil? That refers primarily, as I take it, to the fact that He has discharged to the full, in His individual life, all the obligations which that ancient set of commandments laid upon men, that He had done all that Moses and the prophets had required, as God's organs, that men should do. And this assertion, though it be entirely incidental, carries with it great weight in reference to His consciousness of sinlessness, and is in conformity with all His utterances. From the very beginning of His career never a word drops from His lips to express that He has any experience of that which is common to us all, the sense of imperfection, or the sting of remorse. He begins His course with "It becometh us to fulfil all righteousness." In the midst of it He could ask, "Which of you convinceth Me of sin?" and assert, "I do always the things that please Him." At the last He could say, "It is finished!" and look back upon a life of uninterrupted and complete conformity to the will of the Father in Heaven. Thus He fulfilled the law. What right had He to say that? Was He right or wrong in saying it? If He was right, how came it that there has been a man in the world uninfected by the universal disease, and one heart in which there was no drop of the poison that has trickled into all others? The Sermon on the Mount craves for an answer to that question.

He came to fulfil the prophets. He asserted that He, standing there in the midst, the Son of the carpenter in a little village, was the goal towards which the whole solemn march of progressive Revelation through the centuries had been tending, and that in Him all the purposes and premonitions of that earlier Revelation centred and were fulfilled. That is a strange claim for a *man* to make. The Sermon on the Mount makes that. And we have to answer the questions, why? and what then?

But, further, the fulfilment of which our Lord spoke was not merely His own personal realisation of the ideal set forth in the ancient law, or His being the theme and the goal of ancient prophecy and prophetic rites and ceremonial, but it was a fulfilment of a kind, of which He went on to give a series of illustrations. That fulfilment was that He laid His hand on the law of Sinai, which He and His hearers believed to have come straight from God, and assumed the right of modifying it, of expanding it, of putting it in some measure on one side, of shifting its incidence and enlarging its scope. What business had He to do that? Nor is that all, but He uses a daring antithesis: "It has been said to them of old time." Said when? In the giving of the law. Said by whom? By Moses, as the mouthpiece of God. "It has been said to them of old time"—and now, side by side with that, "*I* say unto you." So He makes the authority of His own utterances co-ordinate with those of that ancient law, and asserts that He, too, has the power thus to modify, to republish, and to enlarge, the very law of God Himself.

Put these three things together. What must a man have thought of himself, who asserted that he was the realised ideal of humanity as God had willed it to be; who asserted that he was the pivot on which the world's history turned, the centre to which all the rays of the earlier Revelation converged, and who dared to put his "I say unto you" side by side with Moses' "Jehovah hath said"? What must he have thought of himself? Answer the question. That is the Christ of the Sermon on the Mount.

III. Note our Lord's attitude to the followers who He anticipated would gather around Him.

There are three things which He says upon that subject, each of which may require just a word; and all of which, put together, bring out a wonderful outline of what He requires from and will give to His disciples.

He demands from us absolute obedience and implicit trust. "He that heareth these sayings of Mine and doeth them; I will show you what he is like. He is like a wise man that built his house upon a rock." That is to say, this Jesus, shut up in that little strip of country, surrounded by circumstances altogether different from ours, with no knowledge, so far as we are told, of the deep things that philosophers have taught and argued about, long before the dawn of European civilisation, industrial progress, and physical science, fronted the world, in all its ages, in far distant lands, and down the stream of time to the very end, and to all idiosyncrasies of character, to all in every condition, dared to say, "If you will build your life on My commandments, you will build upon a rock. Do as *I* bid you, and your being will be stable and eternal." What right had He to say that?

Again, He expects of His followers a devotion so entire that they will be glad to suffer even to the death for His sake. "Blessed are ye when men shall persecute you and speak all manner of evil against you falsely for My sake. Rejoice, and be exceeding glad, for great is your reward in heaven." What reason is there for a man's yielding himself up thus to that Lord? He demands it, and He tells us that we shall be wise if thus we fling away our lives for His dear love. And men have done it by the hundred and the thousand; and the noble army of martyrs has proved the truth of that gracious promise, when they had admitted the rightfulness of that solemn demand. Why should the Christ of the Sermon on the Mount expect men to go to the death gladly for His sake? Because the Christ of the Sermon on the Mount is "the Lamb of God" whose sacrifice "taketh away the sin of the world." I know no other ground on which He has the title to build that demand, or to cherish that anticipation.

One word more. He promises that His followers shall receive an illumination and a perfecting which will make them the light and the salt of the world. They are to be these, because they are His disciples. That is to say, He knows Himself to be able to touch the deadest into life, to kindle the darkest into flame, to turn the most putrid, not only into a thing sweet and sound itself, but capable of diffusing sweetness and soundness through the corrupt mass. The man that makes these claims, that expects this sacrifice, that holds out these promises, is the Christ of the Sermon on the Mount.

IV. Lastly, and only a word. Note our Lord's revelation of Himself as in future the Judge of Mankind.

Remember the solemn words, "Many will say to Me in that day, Lord, Lord, have we not prophesied in Thy name? . . . . And I will profess unto them, I never knew you; depart from Me all ye that work iniquity." That is in accordance with all the rest of our Lord's teaching upon that subject. Whatever drapery there may be about the New Testament representations of the general judgment, however much there may be of parable in the picture of the bar and the gathered universe, and the sheep on the one hand and the goats on the other, the two facts of a judgment of every man beyond the grave, and of Christ as the administrator of that judgment, stand out clear, and in my belief undeniable. He that sat on the mountain, and opened His lips and spake this Sermon, is to sit on the throne of His glory; and from His lips is to come my sentence and yours, and that of all men. That is the Christ of the Sermon on the Mount. You do not like doctrines; you like it. Do you accept its teaching that He is the

Judge of all the earth? Do you believe that He is able infallibly to appreciate the character, and absolutely and irreversibly to determine the fate, of every man? Do you believe that His sentence will be just and conclusive? Do you believe that not to be known by Him is ruin, and to depart from Him eternal death? These statements are in the Sermon on the Mount. You say that you accept *it;* do you accept *them*?

Brethren, gather all these things together and let me again put the question to you—where do all these characteristics lead us except to the conclusion, " God, who at sundry times and in divers manners spake unto the fathers by the prophets, hath in these last days spoken unto us by His Son, whom He appointed Heir of all things "? This Christ has the right to speak with authority, and to deal freely with ancient sacred words, because He is Himself the Eternal Word, the climax of all Revelation. He has the right to demand absolute trust and obedience, even up to the suffering of death, because He has tasted death for every man. He has the right to promise light and healing, because He Himself is the Fountain thereof, and, being the Light of the World, can kindle a kindred flame in us. He has the right to judge mankind, because He is the Son of man and Son of God. He made these claims for Himself in this Sermon on the Mount ; and the Voice from another mount, that of the Transfiguration, countersigned them all when it proclaimed, " This is My beloved Son ; hear ye Him."

FAITH IN HIS NAME.

"The faith of our Lord Jesus Christ, the Lord of glory."—JAMES ii. 1.

THE rarity of the mention of Jesus in this Epistle must strike every attentive reader; but the character of the references that *are* made is equally noticeable, and puts beyond doubt that, whatever is the explanation of their fewness, lower thoughts of Jesus, or less devotion to Him than belonged to the other New Testament writers, are not the explanation. James mentions Christ unmistakeably only three times. The first occasion is in his introductory salutation, where, like the other New Testament writers, he describes himself as "the slave of God and of the Lord Jesus Christ"; thus linking the two names in closest union, and proffering unlimited obedience to his Master. The second case is that of my text, in which our Lord is set forth by this solemn designation, and is declared to be the object of faith. The last is in an exhortation to patience in view of the coming of the Lord to be our Judge.

So James, like Peter and Paul and John, looked to Jesus, who was probably the brother of James by birth, as being the Lord, whom it was no blasphemy nor idolatry to name in the same breath as God, and to whom the same absolute obedience was to be rendered; who was to be the object of men's unlimited trust, and who was to come again to be our Judge.

Here we have, in this remarkable utterance, four distinct designations of that Saviour, a constellation of glories gathered together; and I wish now in a few remarks, to isolate, and gaze at the several stars —"the faith of our Lord—Jesus—Christ—the Lord of glory."

I. Christian faith is faith in Jesus.

We often forget that that name was common, wholly undistinguished, and borne by very many of our Lord's contemporaries. It had been borne by the great soldier whom we know as Joshua; and we know that it was the name of one at least of the disciples of our Master. Its disuse after Him, both by Jew and Christian, is easily intelligible. But though He bore it with special reference to His work of saving His people from their sins, He shared it, as He shared manhood, with many another of the sons of Abraham. Of course, Jesus is the name that is usually employed in the Gospels. But when we turn to the Epistles, we find that it is comparatively rare for it to stand alone, and that in almost all the instances of its employment by itself, it brings with it the special note of pointing attention to the manhood of our Lord Jesus. Let me just gather together one or two instances which may help to elucidate this matter.

Who does not feel, for example, that when we read "let us run with patience the race that is set before us, looking unto Jesus, the author and finisher of faith," the fact of our brother Man having trodden the same path, and being the pattern for our patience and perseverance, is tenderly laid upon our hearts? Again, when we read of sympathy as being felt to us by the great High Priest who can be "touched with a feeling of our infirmities, even Jesus," I think we cannot but recognise that His humanity is pressed upon our thoughts, as securing to us that we have not only the pity of a God, but the compassion of a Man, who knows by experience the bitterness of our sorrows.

In like manner we read sometimes that "*Jesus* died for us," sometimes that "*Christ* died for us"; and, though the two forms of the statement present the same fact, they present it, so to speak, from a different angle of vision, and suggest to us different thoughts. When Paul, for example, says to us, "If we believe that *Jesus* died and rose again," we cannot but feel that he is pressing on us the thought of the true manhood of that Saviour who, in His death, as in His resurrection, is the Forerunner of them that believe upon Him, and whose death will be the more peaceful, and their rising the more certain, because He, who, "forasmuch as the children were partakers of flesh and blood likewise took part of the same," has thereby destroyed death, and delivered them from its bondage. Nor, with less emphasis, and strengthening triumphant force, do we read that this same *Jesus*, the Man who bore our nature in its fulness and is kindred to us in flesh and spirit, has risen from the dead, hath ascended up on high, and is the Forerunner, who for us, by virtue of His humanity, has entered in thither. Surely the most insensitive ear must catch the music, and the deep significance of the word which says, "We see not yet all things put under him (*i.e.*, man), but we see *Jesus* crowned with glory and honour.

So, then, Christian faith first lays hold of that manhood, realises the suffering and death as those of a true humanity, recognises that He bore in His nature "all the ills that flesh is heir to," and that His human life is a brother's pattern for ours; that, He having died, death hath no more terrors for, or dominion over, us, and that whither the Man Jesus has gone, we sinful men need never fear to enter, nor doubt that we shall enter, too.

If our faith lays hold on Jesus the Man, we shall be delivered from the misery of wasting our earthly affections on creatures that may be false, that may change, that must be feeble, and will surely die. If our faith lays hold on the Man Jesus, all the treasures of the human love, trust and obedience, that are so often squandered, and return as pain on our deceived and wounded hearts, will find their sure, sweet, stable object in Him. Human love is sometimes false and fickle, always feeble and frail; human wisdom has its limits, and human perfection its flaws; but the Man Jesus is the perfect, the all-sufficient and unchangeable object for all the love, the trust, and the obedience that the human heart can pour out before Him.

II. Christian faith is faith in Jesus Christ.

The earliest Christian confession, the simplest and sufficient creed, was, Jesus is the Christ. What do we mean by that? We mean, first and plainly, that He is the realisation of the dim figure which arose, majestic and enigmatical, through the mists of a partial revelation. We mean that He is, as the word signifies etymologically, "anointed" with the Divine Spirit, for the discharge of all the offices which, in old days, were filled by men who were fitted and designated for them by outward unction—prophet, priest, and King. We mean that He is the substance of which ancient ritual was the shadow. We mean that He is the goal to which all that former partial unveiling of the mind and will of God steadfastly pointed. This, and nothing less, is the meaning of the declaration that Jesus is the Christ; and that belief is the distinguishing mark of the faith which this Hebrew of the Hebrews, writing to Hebrews, declares to be the Christian faith.

Now, I know, and I am thankful to know, that there are many men who earnestly and reverently admire and obey Jesus, but think that they have nothing to do with these old Hebrew ideas of a Christ. It is not for me to decide which individual is His follower, and which is not; but this I say, that the primitive Christian confession was precisely that Jesus was the Christ, and that I, for my part, know no reason why the terms of the confession should be altered. Ah! these old Jewish ideas are not, as one great man has called them, "Hebrew old clothes"; and I venture to assert that they are not to be discarded without wofully marring the completeness of Christian faith.

The faith in Jesus must pass into faith in Christ; for it is the office described in that name, which gives all its virtue to the Manhood. Glance back for a moment to those instances which I have already quoted of the use of the name suggesting simple humanity, and note how all of them require to be associated with this other thought of the function of Christ, and His special designation by the anointing of God, in order that their full value may be made manifest.

For instance, "Jesus died." Yes, that is a fact of history. The Man was crucified. What is that to me more than any other martyrdom and its story, unless it derives its significance from the clear understanding of *who* it was that died upon the Cross? So, we can understand the significant selection of terms, when the same Apostle, whose utterances I have been already quoting in the former part of this sermon, varies the name, and says, "This is the gospel which I declared unto you, how that *Christ* died for our sins according to the Scriptures."

Again, suppose we think of the example of *Jesus* as the perfect realised ideal of human life. That may become, and I think often does become, as impotent and as paralysing as any other specimen without flaw, that can be conceived of or presented to man. But if we listen to the teaching that says to us, "*Christ* died for us, leaving us an example that we should follow His steps," then the ideal is not like a cold statue that looks down repellent even in its beauty, but is a living person who reaches a hand down to us to lift us to His own level, and will put His spirit within us, that, as the Master is, so may also the servants be.

Again, if we confine ourselves to the belief that the Man named *Jesus* has risen again, and has been exalted to glory, then, as a matter of fact, the faith in His Resurrection and Ascension will not long co-exist with the rejection of anything beyond simple humanity in His Person. If, however, that faith could last, then He might be conceived of as filling a solitary throne, and there might be no victory over death for the rest of us in His triumph. But when we can ring out as the Apostle did, "Now is *Christ* risen from the dead," then we can also say, "and is become the first fruits of them that slept."

So, brethren, lift your faith in Jesus, and let it be sublimed into faith in Christ. "Whom say ye that I am?" The answer is—may we all from our hearts and from our minds make it!—"Thou art the Christ, the Son of the living God."

III. Christian faith is faith in Jesus Christ the Lord.

Now, I take it that that name is here used neither in its lowest sense, as a mere designation of politeness, as we employ "sir," nor in its highest sense in which, referred to Jesus Christ, it is not unfrequently used in the New Testament as being equivalent to the "Jehovah" of the Old; but that it is employed in a middle sense as expressive of dignity and sovereignty.

Jesus is Lord. Our brother, a Man, is King of the universe. The new thing in Christ's return to "the glory which He had with the Father before the world was" is that He took the Manhood with Him into indissoluble union with the Divinity, and that a man is Lord. So you and I can cherish that wonderful hope: "I will give to him that overcometh to sit with Me on My throne." Nor need we ever fear but that all things concerning ourselves and our dear ones, and the Church and the world, will be ordered aright; for the hand that sways the universe is the hand that was many a time laid in blessing upon the sick and the maimed, and that gathered little children to His bosom.

Christ is Lord. That is to say, supreme dominion is based on suffering. Because the vesture that He wears is dipped in blood, therefore there is written upon it, "King of kings, and Lord of lords." The Cross has become the Throne. There is the basis of all true rule, and there is the assurance that His dominion is an everlasting dominion. So our faith is to rise from earth, and, like the dying martyr, to see the Son of man at the right hand of the majesty of the heavens.

IV. Lastly, Christian faith is faith in Jesus Christ, "the Lord of glory."

Now, the last words of my text have given great trouble to commentators. A great many explanations, with which I need not trouble you, have been suggested with regard to them. One old explanation has been comparatively neglected; and yet it seems to me to be the true one. "The Lord" is a supplement which ekes out *a* meaning, but, as I think, obscures *the* meaning. Suppose we strike it out and read straight on. What do we get? "The faith of our Lord Jesus Christ, the Glory."

And is that not intelligible? Remember to whom James was writing—Jews. Did not every Jew know what the Shekinah was, the light that used to shine between the Cherubim, as the manifest symbol of the Divine presence, but which had long been absent from the Temple? And when James falls back upon that familiar Hebrew expression, and recalls the vanished lustre that lay upon the mercy-seat, surely he would be understood by his Hebrew readers, and should be understood by us, as saying no more and no other than another of the New Testament writers has said with reference to the same symbolical manifestation—namely, "The Word became flesh and tabernacled among us; and we beheld

His glory, the glory as of the only Begotten of the Father, full of grace and truth." James's sentence runs on precisely the same lines as other sentences of the New Testament. For instance, the Apostle Paul, in one place, speaks of " Our Lord Jesus Christ, our hope." And this statement is constructed in exactly the same fashion, with the last name put in apposition to the others, " The Lord Jesus Christ, the Glory."

Now, what does that mean? This, that the true presence of God, the true lustrous emanation from, and manifestation of, the abysmal brightness, is in Jesus Christ, " the effulgence of His glory and the express image of His person." For the central blaze of God's glory is God's love, and that rises to its highest degree in the name and mission of Jesus Christ our Saviour. Men conceive of the glory of the Divine nature as lying in the attributes which separate it most widely from our impotent, limited, changeable, and fleeting being. God conceives of His highest glory as being in that love, of which the love of earth is a kindred spark ; and whatever else there may be of majestic and magnificent in Him, the heart of the Divinity is a heart of love.

Brethren, if we would see God, our faith must grasp the Man, the Christ, the Lord, and, as climax of all names —the Incarnate God, the Eternal Word, who has come among us to reveal to us men the glory of the Lord.

So, brethren, let us make sure that the fleshy tables of our hearts are not like the mouldering stones that antiquarians dig up on some historical site, bearing half-obliterated inscriptions and fragmentary names of mighty kings of long ago, but bearing the many-syllabled Name written firm, clear, legible, complete upon them, as on some granite block fresh from the stone-cutter's chisel. Let us, whilst we cling with human love to the Man that was born in Bethlehem, discern the Christ that was prophesied from of old, to whom all altars point, of whom all prophets spoke, who was the theme and the end of all the earlier Revelation. Let us crown Him Lord of All in our own hearts, and let us, beholding in Him the glory of the Father, lie in His Light until we are changed into the same image. Be sure that your faith is a full-orbed faith; grasp all the many sides of the Name that is above every name. And let us, like the Apostles of old, rejoice if we are counted worthy to suffer shame for the Name. Let us go forth into life for the sake of the Name, and, whatsoever we do in word or deed, let us do all in the name of the Lord Jesus Christ, the Glory.

"LOOKING UNTO JESUS."

Looking unto Jesus."—HEB. xii. 2.

IN the preceding chapter the writer has been calling over the muster-roll of the heroes of faith. In this one he proceeds to draw the practical lessons from their lives. "Wherefore, seeing we also are compassed about with a great cloud of witnesses, let us run the race set before us." We are in the arena, appointed to run, to wrestle, or to fight. They, like the spectators in the amphitheatre, fill the crowded benches, rising tier upon tier above the sand, like a luminous cloud. They are witnesses as well as spectators, for they testify to the power of God by which they have overcome, and in their calm repose they witness to the end of a faithful life.

But they are not all that look upon us, or on whom we are to look. One figure parts itself from the clouds; and though it is that of a man who fought, still He stands distinct, and His brightness dims all else. It is as it was on the Mount of Transfiguration, where, for a brief space, the Lawgiver and the Chief of the Prophets stood by the side of the Christ; and then the three Apostles "lifted up their eyes, and saw no man any more save Jesus only." The cloud melts; the sun shines out. " We are compassed with witnesses " ; but we are " looking unto Jesus."

I. So we have here the one object of Christian contemplation.

We have to carry with us the metaphor which underlies the whole representation. There, on the benches of the amphitheatre, sit not only the multitudinous ranks of the spectator-witnesses, but yonder in the midst, parted off from them by the purple curtains, and surrounded by lictors with their flashing axes, is throned the Emperor. It is to Him that gladiator and athlete and runner are to look. And what if the Emperor was Himself once a fighter, and was down there where they now are, before He sat yonder on the throne? Nero lost caste, if I may so say, and was disgraced even in the eyes of his flattering courtiers, because he once condescended to dress himself in the vesture, and to fill the part, of a gladiator in the arena. But our King has been down in the strife, and, as the writer immediately goes on to say, " He is the author and the finisher of faith."

So, then, the main aspect in which it concerns a Christian fighter to look steadfastly to Jesus is as being Himself the perfect Example of the conflict and the race. Christianity as a revelation is all condensed and concentrated in Jesus, so that it is no exaggeration to say Christianity is Christ. And Christianity as a life may almost all be gathered up, with regard at all events to the inner side of it, in this one expression of my text— gazing upon Christ.

It is not in vain, nor with any rhetorical exaggeration, that the words appropriate to bodily vision are transferred unhesitatingly, in the New Testament, to the vision which belongs to the gladsome eye of faith. For it is possible that we may have a sight as real, as direct, as immediate as, and more reliable than, the sight that is given to us by sense when, with believing hearts and thoughts, we realise for ourselves the past of that Christ who fought, the present of that Christ who reigns.

But this great idea, which is wrought out in the subsequent part of our verse, is not a familiar one to very many Christian hearts. The "author of faith," says the writer. It is the same word which is translated in the Acts of the Apostles "the *Prince* of life," and in another part of this letter, " the *Captain* of salvation." It literally means one who makes a beginning, or who leads on a series or succession of events or of men. And when we read of the "author of faith," (for the word "our" in the Authorised Version is a very unfortunate supplement), we are not to take the writer as intending to say that Christ gives to men the faith by which they grasp Him—for that is neither a Scriptural doctrine nor would it be relevant to the present context—but to regard him as meaning that Jesus Christ is, as it were, the Captain of the great army that has been deployed before us in the preceding chapter. He came first in order of time, yet, like other commanders-in-chief, He rides in the centre of the march ; and He *is* the first that ever lived a life of perfect and unbroken faith. So He is the Leader of the army, and in the true sense of the name, which is usurped by a very unworthy earthly monarch, is the " Commander of the Faithful."

This is the only place in Scripture, so far as I know,

in which faith is directly predicated of the Man Jesus, and as being the very secret of His human life. But there is a closely parallel passage in the earlier part of this letter, where the writer adduces it as one of the signs of our Lord's true brotherhood that He takes upon His own lips the ancient Psalmist's words, " I will put my trust in Him."

So faith, which we regard mainly and usually as finding its Object in Christ, finds also its Example and its Pattern in Him. For what is faith? Is it dependence upon God? If so, was there ever a life which more absolutely hung on the Father than did the life of the Man Christ Jesus, who said, when He would lay bare the deepest secret of His personality, "I live by the Father"? Is faith communion with God? Was there ever a life which kept up so unbroken a conscious fellowship with Him, as that of the Man who could say, "The Father hath not left Me alone, for I do always the things that please Him"? Is faith "the substance of things hoped for, the evidence of things not seen," a vivid realisation of the future? Is there anything more manifestly stamped on the human life of Christ, as recorded for us, than the continual presence to Him of the Invisible, so that it might truly be said of Him that, even whilst He walked here amongst us, He " was the Son of man which is in Heaven"? Is faith a realisation of the future reward? Then this very context tells us that the secret of Christ's patient suffering was that, " for the joy set before Him, He endured the cross." Thus, from whatever side we contemplate that great Christian idea of faith, Jesus Christ is the Example of it; and we are to look to Him as its perfect Pattern.

But there is another thought suggested also by the context. We are not only to realise and make our own by contemplation the past of the Jesus who fought, but the present of the Jesus who reigns. Sight, in its lowest sense, of course, cannot travel thither, and in the mere physical signification of the word, He is to us, by an altogether unique and unparalleled experience, the Christ " whom, having not seen, we love." There is nothing in the whole world the least like that strange fact that love, which in general needs the air of corporeal vision, at some stage or other, should, perfectly independently of that, gush out in such exuberant streams towards a Man that has been dead for nineteen centuries, and whom none of His lovers have ever beheld. The gathering mists of oblivion wrap all other great names around. Contrast the poor, pale, phantom regards which we have for any other of the great names of the past, with the warm, solid, living grasp which Christian hands lay on the unseen hand of the Lord, and you will understand something of the uniqueness of the Christian relation to the Christ. But whilst thus the lower kind of sight fails, the higher kind survives, and all the more because of the defect and dropping away of the other. So that it is no piece of rhetorical rhodomontade when this writer says, " We see not yet all things put under Him "—that is, with the bodily eye—" but," as he triumphantly goes on to say, " we see Jesus crowned with glory and honour." And that coronation of the Christ is the pledge that we, too, if we look to Him, shall one day sit amongst the witnesses lapped in rest and adorned with glory.

Let me press upon you, brethren, that this, the

suffering and exalted Christ, is to be the object of our *habitual* contemplation. Nothing great reveals itself to a hasty glance. No great book can be read by snatches. No great picture can be understood or felt by the man, who runs through a gallery and looks at a hundred in half an hour. The secrets of no fair landscape will impart themselves to the hasty tripper, who casts a lack-lustre gaze for a minute over it. This modern life of ours, with its hurry and its bustle, about which so many people are so proud, is fatal, unless we exercise continual watchfulness over ourselves, to all deep and noble things. The most of us spend our lives as some amateur photographers do their days, in taking snapshots ; and, of course, the mystery, and the beauty, and the secret, and the power escape us. Sit down and let the loveliness soak into you, if you want to understand the fairest scenes of Nature. Sit down in front of Jesus Christ, and take your time, and as you look you will learn that which no hasty glance, no couple of minutes in the morning before you go to work, no still more abbreviated and drowsy moments at night before you go to sleep, will ever reveal to you. You must " summer and winter " with Him

"ere that to you
He will seem worthy of your love."

II. And now, secondly, note the resolute shutting-off of other objects needed to secure this vision.

Many of you, no doubt, know that the word rendered " looking " is a compound expression which would be fully represented by " looking off," looking away from other things, in order to look on to Jesus Christ. Now, that is no more than every object of pursuit, either in the intellectual or in the practical world, demands for its successful prosecution. Science will give no favours to vagrant suitors. If we are to hold anything we must relinquish much that we have ; to concentrate ourselves and to give up the attempt to "intermeddle with all knowledge" if we would know any one thing thoroughly. So that Christianity is doing no more than your shop, your business, your profession, or than your studies, your pursuits, your recreations even, demand, when it demands the exclusion of much in order that you may truly hold it. Astronomers put what they call diaphragms into their telescopes, which narrow the field of vision. What for ? In order to secure a sharper definition. And we have to do the same thing, to shut off a great deal, to do as a man does that is looking at the white gleam, for instance, away yonder questionable on the horizon, which may be the foam of a billow or a gull's wing, or the ship that he is expecting. He puts his hand to his brows, in order to shut out everything else, and fixes his gaze. That is what we have to do. Look off if you would look on. Look away from the intrusive and vulgar brilliancy of "the things that are seen and temporal." You will never see the stars in a street blazing with electric lamps; and you will never see Christ as you ought to see Him, if your thoughts and desires and aims are all squandered upon this fleeting present. A worldly Christian—and, alas ! that is the right name of thousands of them, and of many of us— a worldly Christian will see but a dim Christ. Such, and nothing more, is the Christ that a great many of you have seen. The little things near shut out the great things remote. I know that I am speaking to many a one who has so turned his or her current of life to the things of this present world, as that there is no force left to drive the wheels of a higher life. I beseech you, do not be like John Bunyan's man with the muck-rake, who was so busy in piling together the manure and the rotten straw that he never lifted his eye to the crown that was dangling above, but never would alight on, his heedless and earth-turned head. Look away from the present if you would see Christ.

Look away from the cloud of witnesses—from the men living and dead whose examples may, in some measure, stimulate, but who have no power to reproduce in us their own likenesses.

Look away from the living. They can do much for us. Thank God for human love, and earthly companionship, and family ties, and friendship and all its sweetness. But each human soul needs more than any human soul can give. Never mind men's judgments. The racer has to neglect the crowd, whether they roar applause or yell disapprobation, as he speeds past them. They cannot help us; Christ can. Look away from them, and look to Him.

Look away from difficulties. No race will be run, if we begin by counting up the roughnesses and the obstacles. There is nothing more weakening than that habit of anticipating difficulties in our course. "He that observeth the wind shall not sow; and he that regardeth the clouds shall not reap." The difference between the successful and the unsuccessful man consists largely in this, that the one looks out from the harbour, and is so frightened with the crests of the white sea-horses outside that he will not put forth into them, or loses his head if he does; and that the other looks at them, and gathers himself up to front them. Difficulties? they are things to be overcome. The climber that looks down will *go* down, in many cases. The only safety is to look up, away from the arena, and up to the Emperor.

Look away from yourselves. You will never make yourselves strong by groaning over your weaknesses. You may get some hints as to what you should avoid and so forth, by self-examination, and I am not dehorting from that. But I say there are few more widely operative causes of imperfect and unprogressive Christian lives than that habit of always looking at ourselves, and recounting to ourselves our own failures. That is not the way to get strength. "Look off unto Jesus."

III. And now there is only one last thought to which I point, that is—the strength for duty which comes from the look.

The construction of my text shows that "looking unto Jesus" is the principal means which the writer suggests for "running with patience the race that is set before us." That look will bring to us the strength that comes from the contemplation of a perfect Example. When we try to grasp the unseen hand in the darkness; when we try tremblingly to bow our wills, and to say, "Though He slay me, yet will I trust Him"; when we try to nerve ourselves for duty and for sacrifice; when we try to shut out the gaudy brightnesses of to-day, and to make solid the vision of the future, and to "endure the cross," "despising the shame," it is a priceless source of inspiration and of power to us to think that Jesus Christ in all these things went before us, and did the very same.

Lives of great men all remind us—and of good men still more—how we may make our lives great and good ; but they have little power to help us. Jesus Christ can help us, and His example is more than example.

That look will bring to us the strength of a continual presence with us. Our yearning hearts often ask, Are our dead near us ? We get no answer. But Jesus Christ is near us, and as surely as the man who lifts his face to the sun has his face irradiated and his eyes illuminated by its brightness, so surely will Jesus Christ lift up the light of His countenance on every eye that looks to Him and make it glad.

"The sun, whose beams most glorious are,
Disdaineth no beholder,"

and every eye has the bright ray coming straight to itself through all the distant fields of space.

That look will give strength for the race by making us certain of the prize. " The Forerunner hath for us entered." So, brethren, look off to Jesus. The stars do give light, but the sun drowns their twinkle. He is the Example ; therefore looking to Him will give us instruction and strength. He is the goal ; therefore looking to Him will be no hindrance, nor will it entangle our feet. He is the Judge ; therefore looking to Him will stimulate. He is the Reward ; therefore looking to Him will wing our feet with hopes which are certainties. If from the dust of earth we look up to Him from afar, He will make our feet like hinds' feet ; and when the race is run, He will carry us thither whither our looks and our hearts have travelled before. And then the far-off gaze from this dim spot will be changed for the closer vision, which shall transform the beholder into the image of that which is beheld, and the great promise will be fulfilled : " As for me, I shall behold Thy face in righteousness. I shall be satisfied when I awake in Thy likeness."

Help us, O Lord, we beseech Thee, to look unto Christ in all our conflict and struggle. Turn away our eyes from seeing vanity; and may we, looking unto Him from the ends of the earth, be saved.

PAUL AT CORINTH.

"And when Silas and Timotheus were come from Macedonia, Paul was pressed in the spirit, and testified."—ACTS xviii. 5.

THE Revised Version, in concurrence with most recent authorities, reads, instead of "pressed in the spirit," "constrained by the word." One of these alterations depends on a diversity of reading, the other on a difference of translation. The one introduces a significant difference of meaning; the other is rather a change of expression. The word rendered here "pressed," and by the Revised Version "constrained," is employed in its literal use in "Master, the multitude throng Thee and *press* Thee," and in its metaphorical application in "The love of Christ constraineth us." There is not much difference between "constrained" and "pressed," but there is a large difference between "in the spirit" and "by the word." "Pressed in the spirit" simply describes a state of feeling or mind; "constrained by the word" declares the force which brought about that condition of pressure and constraint." What, then, does "constrained by the word" refer to? It indicates that Paul's message had a grip of him, and held him hard, and forced him to deliver it.

One more preliminary remark is that our text evidently brings this state of mind of the Apostle, and the coming of his two friends Silas and Timothy, into relation as cause and effect. He had been alone in Corinth. His work had not been encouraging of late. He had been comparatively silent there, and had spent most of his time in tent-making. But when his two friends came a cloud was lifted off his spirit, and he sprang back again, as it were, to his old form and to his old work.

Now, if we take that point of view with regard to the passage before us, I think we shall find that it yields valuable lessons, some of which I wish to try to enforce now.

I. Let me ask you to look with me at the downcast Apostle.

"Downcast," you say; "is not that an unworthy word to use about a minister of Jesus Christ inspired as Paul?" By no means. We shall very much mistake both the nature of inspiration and the character of this inspired Apostle, if we do not recognise that he was a man of many moods and tremulously susceptible to external influences. Such music would never have come from him, if his soul had not been like an Æolian harp hung in a tree, that vibrated in response to every breeze. And so we need not hesitate to speak of the Apostle's mood, as revealed to us in the section before us, as being downcast.

Now, notice that in the verses preceding my text his conduct is extremely abnormal, and unlike his usual procedure. He goes into Corinth, and he does next to nothing in evangelistic work. He repairs to the synagogue once a week, and talks to the Jews there. But that is all. The notice of his reasoning in the synagogue is quite subordinate to the notice that he was occupied in finding a lodging with another pauper Jew and stranger in the great city, and that these two poor men went into a kind of partnership, and tried to earn a living by hard work. Such procedure makes a singular contrast to Paul's usual methods in a strange city.

Now, the reason for that slackening of impulse, and comparative cessation of activity, is not far to seek. The first Epistle to Thessalonica was written immediately after these two brethren rejoined Paul. And how does the Apostle describe in that letter his feelings before they came? He speaks of "all our distress and affliction." He tells that he was tortured by anxiety as to how the new converts in Thessalonica were getting on, and could not forbear to try to find out whether they were still standing steadfast. Again, in the first Epistle to the Corinthians you will find that there, looking back to this period, he describes his feelings in similar fashion and says, "I was with you in weakness and in fear, and in much trembling." And if you look on a verse or two in our chapter, you will find that there came a vision to our Apostle, which presupposes that some touch of fear, and some temptation to silence, were busy in his heart. For God shapes His communications according to our need, and would not have said, "Do not be afraid, and hold not thy peace, but speak," unless there had been a danger both of his being frightened and of his being dumb.

And what thus brought a cloud over his sky? A little exercise of historical imagination will very sufficiently answer that. A few weeks before, in obedience, as he believed, to a direct Divine command, Paul had made a plunge, and ventured upon an altogether new phase of work. He had crossed into Europe, and from the moment that he landed at the harbour of Philippi, up to the time when he took refuge in some quiet little room in Corinth, he had had nothing but trouble and danger and disappointment. The prison at Philippi, the riots that hounded him out of Thessalonica, the stealthy, hurried escape from Berœa, the almost entire failure of his first attempt to preach the Gospel to Greeks in Athens, his loneliness, and the strangeness of his surroundings in the luxurious, wicked, wealthy Greek city of Corinth—all these things weighed on him, and there is no wonder that his spirit went down, and he felt that now he must lie fallow for a time and rest, and pull himself together again.

So here, we have, in this great champion of the faith, in this strong runner of the Christian race, in this chief of men, an example of the fluctuation of mood, the variation in the way in which we look at our duties and our obligations and our difficulties, the slackening of the impulse which dominates our lives, that is too familiar to us all. It brings Paul nearer to feel that he, too, knew these ups and downs. The force that drove this meteor through the darkness varied, as the force that impels us varies to our consciousness. It is the prerogative of God to be immutable; men have their moods and their fluctuations. Kindled lights flicker; the sun burns steadily. An Elijah to-day beards Ahab and Jezebel and all their priests, and to-morrow hides his head in his hands, and says, " Take me away, I am not better than my fathers." There will be ups and downs in the Christian vigour of our lives, as well as in all other regions, as long as men dwell in this material body and are surrounded by their present circumstances.

Brethren, it is no small part of Christian wisdom and providence to recognise this fact, both in order that it may prevent us from becoming unduly doubtful of ourselves when the ebb tide sets in on our souls, and also in order that we may lay to heart this other truth, that because these moods and changes of aspect and of vigour *will* come to us, therefore the law of life must be effort, and the duty of every Christian man be to minimise, in so far as possible, the fluctuations which, in some degree, are inevitable. No human hand has ever drawn an absolutely straight line. That is the ideal of the mathematician, but all ours are crooked. But we may indefinitely diminish the magnitude of the curves. No two atoms are so close together as that there is no film between them. No human life has ever been an absolutely continuous, unbroken series of equally holy and devoted thoughts and acts, but we may diminish the intervals between kindred states, and may make our lives so far uniform as that to a bystander they shall look like the bright circle, which a brand whirled round in the air makes the impression of, on the eye that beholds. We shall have times of brightness and of less brilliancy, of vigour and of consequent reaction and exhaustion. But Christianity has, for one of its objects, to help us to master our moods, and to bring us nearer and nearer, by continual growth, to the steadfast, unmovable attitude of those whose faith is ever the same.

Do not forget the plain lesson that comes from the incident before us—viz., that the wisest thing a man can do, when he feels that the wheels of his religious being are driving heavily, is to set himself doggedly to the plain, homely work of daily life. Paul did not sit and bemoan himself because he felt this slackening of impulse, but he went away to Aquila, and said, "Let us set to work and make camel's-hair cloth and tents." Be thankful for your homely, prosaic, secular daily work. You do not know how many sickly fancies it saves you from, and how many breaches in the continuity of your Christian feeling it may bridge over. It takes you away from thinking about yourselves, and you cannot think about anything less profitably sometimes. So stick to your work ; and if ever you feel, as Paul did, "cast down," be sure that the workshop, the office, the desk, the kitchen will prevent you from being "destroyed," if you give yourselves to the plain duties which no moods alter, but which can alter a great many moods.

II. And now, note the constraining word.

I have already said that the return of the two, who had been sent to see how things were going with the recent converts in the infant Churches, brought the Apostle good tidings, and so lifted off a great load of anxiety from his heart. No wonder. He had left raw recruits under fire, with no captain, and he might well doubt whether they would keep their ranks. But they did. So the pressure was lifted off, and the pressure being lifted off, spontaneously the old impulse gripped him once more ; like a spring which leaps back to its ancient curve when some alien force is taken from it. It must have been a very deep and a very habitual impulse, which thus instantly reasserted itself the moment that the pressure of anxiety was taken out of the way.

The word constrained him. What to do? To declare it. Paul's example brings up two thoughts—that that impulse may vary at times, according to the pressure of circumstances, and may even be held in abeyance for a while; and that if a man is honestly and really a Christian, as soon as the incumbent pressure is taken away, he will feel, "Necessity is laid upon me, yea! woe is me if I preach not the Gospel." For, though Paul's sphere of work was different from ours, his obligation to work and his impulse to work were such as are, or should be, common to all Christians. The impulse to utter the word that we believe and live by seems to me to be, in its very nature, inseparable from earnest Christian faith. All emotion demands expression; and if a man has never felt that he must let his Christian faith have vent, it is a very bad sign. As certainly as fermentation or effervescence demands outgush, so certainly does emotion demand expression. We all know that. The same impulse that makes a mother bend over her babe with unmeaning words and tokens that seem to unsympathetic onlookers foolish, ought to influence all Christians to speak the name they love. All conviction demands expression. There may be truths which have so little bearing upon human life that he who perceives them feels little obligation to say anything about them. But these are the exceptions; and the more weighty, and the more closely affecting human interests, anything that we have learned to believe as truth is, the more do we feel in our hearts that, in making us its believers, it has made us its apostles. Christ's saying, "What ye hear in the ear that preach ye on the housetops," expresses a universal truth which is realised in many regions, and ought to be most emphatically realised in the Christian. For surely of all the truths that men can catch a glimpse of, or grapple to their hearts, or store in their understandings, there are none which bring with them such tremendous consequences, and therefore are of so solemn import to proclaim to all the children of men, as the truth that we profess we have received, of personal salvation through Jesus Christ.

If there never had been a single commandment to that effect, I know not how the Christian Church or the Christian individual could have abstained from declaring the great and sweet Name to which it and he owe so much. I do not care to present this matter as a commandment, nor to speak now of obligation or responsibility. The *impulse* is what I would fix your attention upon. It is inseparable from the Christian life. It may vary in force, as we see in the incident before us. It will vary in grip, according as other circumstances and duties insist upon being attended to. The form in which it is yielded to will vary indefinitely in individuals. But if they are Christian people it is always there.

Well, then, what about the masses of so-called Christians that know nothing of any such constraining force? And what about the many that know enough of it to make them feel that they are wrong in not yielding to it, but not enough to make their conduct be influenced by it? Brethren, I venture to believe that the measure in which this impulse to speak the word, and use direct efforts for somebody's conversion, is felt by Christians, is a very fair test of the depth of their own religion. If a vessel is half empty it will not run over. If it is full to the brim, the sparkling treasure will fall on all sides. A weak plant may never push its green leaves above the ground, but a strong one will come into the light. A spark may be smothered in a heap of brushwood, but a steady flame will burn its way out. If this word has not a grip of you, impelling you to its utterance, I would have you not to be too sure that you have a grip of it.

III. Lastly, we have here the witness to the word.

He was constrained by the word, *testifying.*" Now, I do not know whether it is imposing too much meaning upon a non-significant difference of expression, if I ask you to note the difference between that phrase and the one which describes his previous activity; " He *reasoned* in the synagogue every Sabbath, and tried to persuade " the Jews and the Greeks. But when the old impulse came back in new force, *reasoning* was far too cold a method, and he took to *testifying.* Whether that be so or no, mark that the witness of one's own personal conviction and experience is the strongest weapon that a Christian can use. I do not despise the place of reasoning, but arguments do not often change opinions; they never change hearts. Logic and controversial discoursing may prepare the way of the Lord, but it is in the wilderness. But when a man calls aloud, " Come and hear all ye, and I will declare what God hath done for my soul " ; or when he tells his brother, " We have found the Messias " ; or when he sticks to " One thing I know, that, whereas I was blind, now I see " it is difficult for anybody to resist, and impossible for anybody to answer, that way of testifying.

It is a way that we can all adopt if we will. Christian men and women can all say that. I do not forget that there are indirect ways of spreading the Gospel. Some of you think that you do enough when you give your money and your interest in order to help these. You can buy a substitute in the militia, but you cannot buy a substitute in Christ's service. You have each some congregation to which you can speak, if it is no bigger than Paul's—namely, two people, Aquila and Priscilla. What talks they would have in their lodging, as they plaited the wisps of black hair into rough cloth, and stitched the strips into tents! Aquila was not a Christian when Paul picked him up, but he became one very soon; and it was the preaching in the workshop, amidst the dust, that made him one. If we want to speak about Christ we shall find plenty of people to speak to. "Ye are my witnesses, saith the Lord."

Now, dear friends, I have only one word more. I have no doubt there are some of my hearers who have been saying, "This sermon does not apply to me at all." Does it not? If it does not, what does that mean? It means that you have not the first requisite for spreading the word—viz., personal faith in the word. It means that you have put away, or at least neglected to take in, the word and the Saviour of whom it speaks, into your own lives. But it does *not* mean that you have got rid of the word thereby. It will not in that case lay the grip of which I have been speaking upon you, but it will not let you go. It will lay on you a far more solemn and awful clutch, and, like a gaoler with his hand on the culprit's shoulder, will "constrain" you into the presence of the Judge.

You can make it a savour of life unto life, or of death unto death. And if you do not grasp *it*, it grasps and holds *you*. "The word that I speak unto him, the same shall judge him at the last day."

"TO HIM THAT HATH SHALL BE GIVEN."

"Whosoever hath, to him shall be given, and he shall have abundance; but whosoever hath not, from him shall be taken away even that he hath."—MATT. xiii. 12.

THERE are several instances in the Gospels of our Lord's repetition of sayings which seem to have been, if we may use the expression, favourites with Him; as, for instance, "There are first which shall be last, and there are last which shall be first"; or, again, "The servant is not greater than his master, nor the disciple than his lord." My text is one of these. It is here said as part of the explanation why He chose to speak in parables, in order that the truth, revealed to the diligent and attentive, might be hidden from the careless.

Again, we find it in two other Gospels, in a somewhat similar connection, though with a different application, where Jesus enunciates it as the basis of His warning, "Take heed how"—or, in another version, "what"—"ye hear." Again, He employs it in this Gospel in the parable of the talents, as explaining the principle on which the retribution to the slothful servant was meted out. And we find it yet once more in the parable of the pounds in Luke's Gospel, which, though entirely different in conception and purpose from that of the talents, is identical in the portion connected with the slothful servant.

So, there are two very distinct directions in which this saying looks, as it was used by our Lord—one in reference to the attitude of men towards the Revelation of God, and one in reference to the solemn subject of future retribution. I wish, now, mainly to try and illustrate the great law which is set forth here, and to follow out the various spheres of its operation, and estimate the force of its influence. For I think that large and very needful lessons for us all may be drawn therefrom. The principle of my text shapes all life. It is a paradox, but it is a deep truth. It sounds harsh and unjust, but it contains the very essence of righteous retribution. The paradox is meant to spur attention, curiosity, and inquiry. The key to it lies here—to use is to have. There is a possession which is no possession. That I have rights of property in a thing, as contradistinguished to your rights, does not make it, in any deep and real sense, mine. What I use I have; and all else is, as one of the other Evangelists has it, but "seeming" to have.

So much, then, by way of explanation of our text. Now, let me just ask you to come with me into two or three of the regions where we shall find illustrations of its working.

I. Take the application of this principle to common life.

The lowest of these are material possessions. It is a complaint that is made against the present social arrangements and distribution of wealth, that money makes money; that wealth has a tendency to clot; the rich man to get richer, and the poor man to get poorer. Just as in a basin of water when the plug is out, and circular motion is set up, the little bits of foreign matter that may be there all tend to get together, so it is in regard to these external possessions. "To him that hath shall be given"; and people grumble about that and say, "It never rains but it pours, and the man that needs more money least gets it most easily." Of course. Treasure used grows; treasure hoarded rusts and dwindles. The millionaire will double his fortune by a successful speculation. The man with half-a-dozen large shops drives the poor little tradesman out of the field. So it is all round; "To him that hath shall be given; but from him that hath not shall be taken even that he hath."

Next, go a step higher. Look at how this law works in regard of powers of body. That is a threadbare old illustration. The blacksmith's arm we have all heard about; the sailor's eye, the pianist's wrist, the juggler's fingers, the surgeon's deft hand—all these come by use. "To him that hath shall be given." And the same man who has cultivated one set of organs to an almost miraculous fineness or delicacy or strength will, by the operation of the other half of the same principle, have all but atrophied another set. So with the blacksmith's arm, which has grown muscular at the expense of his legs; part of the physical being has monopolised what might have been distributed throughout the whole. Use is strength; use makes growth. We have what we employ. And even in regard of our bodily frame the organs that we do not use we carry about with us rather as a weight attached to us than as a possession.

Again, come a little higher. This great principle largely goes to determine our position in the world and our work. The man that can do a thing gets it to do. In the long run the tools come to the hand that can use them. So here is one medical man's consulting-room crammed full of patients, and his neighbour next door has scarcely one. The whole world runs to read A, B, or C's books. The briefless barrister complains that there is no middle course between having nothing to do and being overwhelmed with briefs. "To him that hath shall be given"—the man can do a thing, and he gets it to do—"and from him that hath not shall be taken away even that which he hath." That law largely settles every man's place in the world.

Let us come still higher. The same law has much—not all, but much—to do in making men's characters. For it operates in its most intense fashion, and with results most blessed or most disastrous, in the inner life. The great example that I would adduce is conscience. Use it; obey it; listen for its voice; never thwart it, and it grows and grows and grows, and becomes more and more sensitive, more and more educated, more and more sovereign in its decisions. Neglect it; still more, go in its teeth, and it dwindles and dwindles and dwindles; and I suppose it is possible—though one would fain hope that it is a very exceptional case—for a man, by long-continued indifference to the voice within that says "Thou shalt" or "Thou shalt not," to come at last to never hearing it at all, or to its never speaking at all.

It is "seared as with a hot iron," says one of the Apostles; and in seared flesh there is no feeling any more. Are any of you, dear friends, bringing about such a state? Are you doing what you know you ought not to do? Then you will be less and less troubled as the days go on; and, by neglecting the voice, you will come at last to be like the profligate woman in the book of Proverbs, who, after her sin, "wipes her mouth and says, I have done no harm." Do you think *that* is a desirable state—to put out the eyes of your soul, to stifle the nearest approach to God's voice that you will ever hear? Do you not think that it would be wiser to get the blessed half of this law on your side, instead of the dreadful one? Listen to that voice. Never, as you value yourselves, neglect it. Cultivate the habit of waiting for its monitions, its counsels, prohibitory or commendatory, and then you will have done much to secure that your spirit shall be enriched by the operations of this wide-spread law.

Take another illustration. People who, by circumstances, are placed in some position of dependence and subordination, where they have seldom to exercise the initiative of choice, but just to do what they are bid, by degrees all but lose the power of making up their minds about anything. And so a slave set free is proverbially a helpless creature, like a bit of driftwood, and children who have been too long kept in a position of pupilage and subordination, when they are sent into the world are apt to turn out very feeble creatures, for want of a good, strong backbone of will in them. So, many a woman that has been accustomed to leave everything in her husband's hands, when the clods fall on his coffin finds herself utterly helpless and bewildered, just because in the long, happy years she never found it necessary to exercise her own judgment or her own will about practical matters.

So do not get into the habit of letting circumstances

settle what you are going to do, or you will lose the power of dominating them, before very long. And if a man for years leaves himself, as it were, to be guided by the stream of circumstances, like long green weeds in a river, he will lose the power of determining his own fate, and the Will will die clean out of him. Cultivate it, and it will grow.

Again, this same principle largely settles our knowledge, our convictions, the operations and the furniture of our understandings. If a man holds any truth slackly, or, in the case of truths that are meant to influence life and conduct, does not let it influence these, then that is a kind of having truth that is sure to end in losing it. If you want to lose your convictions grasp them loosely—do not act upon them, do not take them for guides of your life—and they will soon relieve you of their unwelcome presence. If you wish mind and knowledge to grow, grip with a grip of iron what you do know, and let it dominate you, as it ought. He that truly *has* his learning will learn more, and pile by slow degrees stone upon stone, until the building is complete.

So, dear friends, here, in these illustrations, which might have been indefinitely enlarged, we see the working of a principle which has much to do in making men what they are. What you use you increase; what you leave unused you lose. There are grey heads in this chapel to-night who, when they were young men, had dreams and aspirations that they bitterly smile at now. There are men here who began life with possibilities that have never blossomed or fruited, but have died on the stem. Why? Because they were so much occupied with the vulpine craft of making their position and their "pile," that generous emotions and noble sympathies and lofty aspirations, intellectual or otherwise, were all neglected, and so they are dead; and the men are the poorer incalculably, because of what has thus been shed away from them. You make your characters by the parts of yourselves that you choose to cultivate and employ. Do you think that God gave us all of an intellectual and emotional and moral kind that is in us in order that it might be all used up in Portland Street? A very much scantier outfit would have done for all that is wanted there. But there are abortive and dormant organs in your spiritual nature, as there are in the corporeal, which tell you what you were meant for, and which it is your sin to leave undeveloped. Brethren, the law of my text shapes us in the two ways, that whatever we cultivate, be it noble or be it bestial, will grow, and whatever we repress or neglect will die. Choose which of the two halves of yourselves you will foster, and on which you will frown.

So much, then, for the first general application of these words. Now, let me turn for a moment to another.

II. I would note, secondly, the application of this two-fold law in regard to God's revelation of Himself.

That is the bearing of it in the immediate context from which our text is taken. Our Lord explains that teaching by parable—a transparent veil over a truth—was adopted in order that the veiled truth might be a test as well as a revelation. And although I do not believe that the Christian revelation has been made in any degree less plain and obvious than it could have been made, I cannot but recognise the fact that the necessities of the case demand that, when God speaks to us, He should speak in such a fashion as that it is possible to say, " Tush ! It is not God that is speaking ; it is only Eli ! " and so to turn about the young Samuel's mistake the other way. I do not believe that God has diminished the evidence of His Revelation in order to try us ; but I do maintain that the Revelation which He has made does come to us, and must come to us, in such a form as that, not by mathematical demonstration but by moral affinity, we shall be led to recognise and to bow to it. He that will be ignorant, let him be ignorant, and he that will come asking for truth, it will flood his eyeballs with a blessed illumination. The veil will but make more attractive to some eyes the outlines of the fair form beneath it, whilst others are offended at it and say, " Unless we see the truth undraped, we will not believe that it is truth at all."

So, brethren, let me remind you—what is really but a repetition in reference to another subject—of what I have already said, that in regard to God's speech to men, and especially in regard to what I, for my part, believe to be the complete and ultimate and perfect speech of God to men, in Jesus Christ our Saviour, the principle of my text holds good.

" To him that hath shall be given." If you will make that truth your own by loyal faith and honest obedience, if you will grapple it to your heart, then you will learn more and more. Whatever tiny corner of the great whole you have grasped, hold on by that and draw it into yourselves, and you will by degrees get the entire, glorious, golden web to wrap round you. " If any man wills to do His will he shall know." That is Christ's promise; and it will be fulfilled to us all. "To him that hath shall be given."

If, on the other hand, you have Christian truth and Christ, who is the Truth, in the fashion in which so many of us have it and Him, as a form, as a mere intellectual possession, so that we can, when we go to church, repeat the creed without feeling that we are telling a lie, but when we go to market do not carry the Commandments with us—if that is our Christianity, then it will dribble away into nothing. We shall not be much the poorer for the loss of such a sham possession, but it will go, and the evidence of it will go. It drops out of the hands that are not clasped to hold it. It is just that a thing so neglected shall some day be a thing withdrawn. So, in regard to Revelation and a man's perception and reception of it, my text holds good in both its halves.

III. Lastly, look at the application of these words in the future.

That is our Lord's own application of them, twice out of the five times in which the saying appears in the three Gospels: in the parable of the talents and in the parallel portion of the parable of the pounds. I do not venture into the regions of speculation about that future, but there come clearly enough out from the words before us two aspects of it. The man with the ten talents got more; the man that had hid the talent or the pound in the ground was deprived of that which he had not used.

Now, with regard to the former there is no difficulty in translating the representations of the parables, sustained as they are by distinct statements of other portions of Scripture. They come to this, that, for the life beyond, indefinite progress in all that is noble and blessed and godlike in heart and character, in intellect and power, are certain; that faith, hope, love here cultivated but putting forth few blossoms and small fruitage, there, in that higher house where these be planted, will flourish in the courts of the Lord, and will bear fruit abundantly; that here the few things faithfully administered will be succeeded yonder by the many things royally ruled over; that here one small coin, as it were, is put into our palm—namely, the present blessedness and peace and strength and purity of a Christian life; and that yonder we possess the inheritance of which what we have here is but the earnest. It used to be the custom when a servant was hired for the next term-day to give him one of the smallest coins of the realm as what was called "arles" —wages in advance, to seal the bargain. Similarly in buying an estate a bit of turf was passed over to the purchaser. We get the earnest here of the broad acres of the inheritance above. "To him that hath shall be given."

And the other side of the same principle works in some terrible ways that we cannot speak about. "From him that hath not shall be taken away even that which he hath." I have spoken of the terrible analogy to this solemn prospect which is presented us by the imperfect experiences of earth. And when we see in others, or discover in ourselves, how it is possible for unused faculties to die entirely out, I think we shall feel that there is a solemn background of very awful truth, in the representation of what befell the unfaithful servant. Hopes unnourished are gone ; opportunities unimproved—gone ; capacities undeveloped—gone ; fold after fold, as it were, peeled off the soul, until there is nothing left but the naked self, pauperised and empty-handed for evermore. "Take it from him ;" he never was the better for it ; he never used it ; he shall have it no longer.

Brethren, cultivate the highest part of yourselves, and see to it that, by faith and obedience, you truly have the Saviour whom you have by the hearing of the ear and by outward profession. And then death will come to you, as a nurse might to a child that came in from the fields with its hands full of worthless weeds and grasses, and empty them in order to fill them with the flowers that never fade. You can choose whether death—and life, too, for that matter—shall be the porter that will open to you the door of the treasure-house of God, or the robber that will strip you of misused opportunities and unused talents.

"ALL THINGS ARE YOURS."

" They fought from heaven; the stars in their courses fought against Sisera."—JUDGES v. 20.

"Thou shalt be in league with the stones of the field: and the beasts of the field shall be at peace with thee."—JOB v. 23.

THESE two poetical fragments present the same truth on opposite sides. The first of them comes from Deborah's triumphant chant. The singer identifies God with the cause of Israel, and declares that heaven itself fought against those who fought against God's people. There may be an allusion to the tempest which Jewish tradition tells us burst over the ranks of the enemy, or there may be some trace of ancient astrological notions, or the words may simply be an elevated way of saying that Heaven fought for Israel. The silent stars, as they swept on their paths through the sky, advanced like an avenging host, embattled against the foes of Israel and of God. All things fight against the man that fights against God.

The other text gives the other side of the same truth. One of Job's friends is rubbing salt into his wounds by insisting on the commonplace, which needs a great many explanations and limitations before it can be accepted as true, that sin is the cause of sorrow, and that righteousness brings happiness; and in the course of trying to establish this heartless thesis to a heavy heart he breaks into a strain of the loftiest poetry in describing the blessedness of the righteous. All things, animate and inanimate, are upon his side. The ground, which Genesis tells us is cursed for his sake, becomes his ally, and the very creatures whom man's sin set at enmity against him are at peace with him. All things are the friends and servants of him who is the friend and servant of God.

I. So, putting these two texts together, we have first the great conviction to which religion clings, that God being on our side all things are for us, and not against us.

Now, that is the standing faith of the Old Testament, which no doubt was more easily held in those days, because, if we accept its teaching, we shall recognise that Israel lived under a system in so far supernatural as that moral goodness and material prosperity were a great deal more closely and indissolubly connected than they are to-day. So, many a psalm and many a prophet break out into apostrophes, warranted by the whole history of Israel, and declaring how blessed are the men who, apart from all other defences and sources of prosperity, have God for their help and Him for their hope.

But we are not to dismiss this conviction as belonging only to a system where the supernatural comes in, as it does in the Old Testament history, and as antiquated under a dispensation such as that in which we live. For the New Testament is not a whit behind the Old in insisting upon this truth. "All things work together for good to them that love God." "All things are yours, and ye are Christ's and Christ is God's." "Who is he that will harm you if ye be followers of that which is good?" The New Testament is committed to the same conviction as that to which the faith of Old Testament saints clung as the sheet anchor of their lives.

That conviction cannot be struck out of the creed of any man, who believes in the God to whom the Old and the New Testament alike bear witness. For it rests upon this plain principle, that all this great universe is not a chaos, but a cosmos, that all these forces and creatures are not a rabble, but an ordered host.

What is the meaning of that great Name by which, from of old, God in His relations to the whole universe has been described—the Lord of Hosts? Who are the "hosts" of which He is "the Lord," and to whom, as the centurion said, He says to this one, "Go!" and he goeth; and to another, "Come!" and he cometh; and to another, "Do this!" and he doeth it? Who are "the hosts"? Not only these beings who are dimly revealed to us as rational and intelligent, who "excel in strength," because they "hearken to the voice of His word," but also in the ranks of that great army are embattled all the forces of the universe, and all things living or dead. "All are Thy servants;" "they continue this day"—angels, stars, creatures of earth—"according to Thy ordinances."

And if it be true that the All is an ordered whole, and all are obedient to the touch and to the will of that Divine Commander, then all His servants must be on the same side, and cannot turn their arms against each other. As an old hymn says about another subject—

"All the servants of our King
In heaven and earth are one."

And none of them can injure, wound, or slay a fellow-servant. If all are travelling in the same direction there can be no collision. If all are enlisted under the same standard they can never turn their weapons against each other. If God sways all things, then all things that God sways must be on the side of the men that are on the side of God. "Thou shalt make a league with the stones of the field: and the beasts of the field shall be at peace with thee."

II. Note the difficulties arising from experience, in the way of holding fast by this conviction of faith.

The grim facts of the world, seen from their lowest level, seem to shatter it to atoms. Talk about "the stars in their courses fighting" for or against anybody! In one aspect it is superstition, in another aspect it is a dream and an illusion. The prose truth is that they shine down, silent, pitiless, cold, indifferent, on battle-fields or on peaceful homes; and the moonlight is as pure when it falls upon broken hearts as when it falls upon glad ones. Nature is utterly indifferent to the moral or the religious character of its victims. It goes on its way unswerving and pitiless; and whether the man that stands in its path is good or bad, it matters not. If he gets into a typhoon he will be wrecked; if he tumbles over Niagara he will be drowned. And what has become of all the talk about an embattled universe on the side of goodness, in the face of the plain facts of life—of nature's indifference, nature's cruelty, which has led some men to believe in two sovereign powers, one beneficent and one malicious, and has led others to say, "God is a superfluous hypothesis, and to believe in Him brings more enigmas than it solves," and which has led others to say, "Why, why, if there *is* a God, does it look as if either He was not all-powerful, or was not all-merciful?" Nature has but ambiguous evidence to give in support of this conviction.

Then, if we turn to what we call Providence and its mysteries, the very book of Job, from which my second text is taken, is one of the earliest attempts to grapple with the difficulty and to untie the knot; and I suppose everybody will admit that, whatever may be the solution which is suggested by that enigmatical book, the solution is by no means a complete one, though it is as complete as the state of religious knowledge at the time at which the book was written made possible to be attained. The seventy-third psalm shows that even in that old time when, as I have said, supernatural sanctions were introduced into the ordinary dealings of life, the difficulties that cropped up were great enough to bring a devout heart to a stand, and to make the Psalmist say, "My feet were almost gone; my steps had well-nigh slipped." Providence, with all its depths and mysteries, often to our aching hearts seems in our own lives to contradict that truth, and when we look out over the sadness of humanity, still more does it seem impossible for us to hold fast by the faith "that all which we behold is full of blessings."

I doubt not that there are many in this audience whose lives, shadowed, darkened, hemmed in, perplexed, or made solitary for ever, seem to them to be mysteries hard to reconcile with this cheerful faith upon which I am trying to insist. Brethren, cling to it in the darkness. Be sure of this, that amongst all our mercies there are none more truly merciful than these forms which come to us shrouded in dark garments, and in questionable shapes. Let nothing rob us of the confidence that "all things work together for good."

III. I come, lastly, to consider the higher form in which this conviction is true for ever.

I have said that the facts of life seem often to us, and are felt often by some of us, to shatter it to atoms; to riddle it through and through with shot. But, if we bring the Pattern-life to bear upon the illumination of all life, and if we learn the lessons of the Cradle and the Cross, and rise to the view of human life which emerges from the example of Jesus Christ, then we get back the old conviction, transfigured indeed, but firmer than ever. We have to alter the point of view. Everything depends on the point of view, always. We have to alter one or two definitions. Definitions come first in geometry and in everything else. Get them right, and you will get your theorems and problems right.

So, looking at life in the light of Christ, we have to give new contents to the two words "good" and "evil," and a new meaning to the two words "for" and "against." And when we do that, then the difficulties straighten themselves out, and there are not any more knots, but all is plain; and the old faith of the Old Testament, which reposed very largely upon abnormal and extraordinary conditions of life, comes back in a still nobler form, as possible to be held by us amidst the common-place of our daily existence.

For everything is my friend, is for me and not against me, that helps me nearer to God. To live for Him, to live with Him, to be conscious ever of communion with

Himself, to feel the touch of His hand on my hand, and the pressure of His breast against mine, at all moments of my life, is my true and the highest good. And if it is true that the river of the water of life which flows from the Throne of God is the only draught that can ever satisfy the immortal thirst of a soul, then whatever drives me away from the cisterns, and to the fountain, is on my side. Better to dwell in a dry and thirsty land, where no water is, if it makes me long for the water that rises at the gate of the true Bethlehem—the house of bread—than to dwell in a land flowing with milk and honey, and well watered in every part. If the cup that I would fain lift to my lips has poison in it, or if its sweetness is making me lose my relish for the pure and tasteless water that flows from the Throne of God, there can be no truer friend than that calamity, as men call it, which strikes the cup from my hands, and shivers the glass before I have raised it to my lips. Everything is my friend that helps me towards God.

Everything is my friend that leads me to submission and obedience. The joy of life, and the perfection of human nature, is an absolutely submitted will, identified with the Divine, both in regard to doing and to enduring. And whatever tends to make my will flexible, so that it corresponds to all the sinuosities, so to speak, of the Divine will, and fits into all its bends and turns, is a blessing to me. The raw hides, stiff with dirt and blood, are put into a bath of bitter infusion of oak-bark. What for? For the same end as when they are taken out they are scraped with sharp steels, —that they may become flexible. When that is done the useless hide is worth something.

> "Our wills are ours, we know not how;
> Our wills are ours, to make them Thine."

And whatever helps me to that is my friend.

Everything is a friend to the man that loves God, in a far sweeter and deeper sense than it can ever be to any other. Like a sudden burst of sunshine upon a gloomy landscape, the light of union with God and friendship with Him flooding my daily life flashes it all up into brightness. The dark ribbon of the river that went creeping through the black copses, when the sun glints upon it, gleams up into links of silver, and the trees by its bank blaze out into green and gold. Brethren, "who follows pleasure follows pain"; who follows God finds pleasure following Him. There can be no surer way to set the world against me than to try to make it for me, and to make it my all. They tell us that if you want to count those stars that, "like a swarm of fire-flies tangled in a silver braid," make up the Pleiades, the surest way to see the greatest number of them is to look a little on one side of them. Look away from the joys and friendships of creatural things right up to God, and you will see these sparkling and dancing in the skies, as you never see them when you gaze at them alone. Make them second and they are good and on your side. Make them first, and they will turn to be your enemies and fight against you.

This conviction will be established still more irrefragably and wonderfully in that future. Nothing lasts but goodness. "He that doeth the will of God abideth for ever." To oppose it is like stretching a piece of pack-thread across the rails before the express comes; or putting up some thin wooden partition on the beach on one of the Western Hebrides, exposed to the whole roll of the Atlantic, which will be battered into ruin by the first winter's storm. So is the end of all those who set themselves against God.

But there comes a future in which, as dim hints tell us, these texts of ours shall receive a fulfilment beyond that realised by the present condition of things.

"Then comes the statelier Eden back to man," and in a renewed and redeemed earth "they shall not hurt nor destroy in all My holy mountain"; and the ancient story will be repeated in higher form. The servants shall be like the Lord who, when He had conquered temptation, was with the wild beasts that forgot their enmity, and angels ministered unto Him. That scene in the desert may serve as a prophecy of the future when, under conditions of which we know nothing, all God's servants shall, even more markedly and manifestly than here, help each other; and every man that loves God will find a friend in every creature.

If we take Him for our Commander, and enlist ourselves in that embattled host, then all weathers will be good; stormy winds, fulfilling His word, will blow us to our port; the wilderness will rejoice and blossom as the rose; and the whole universe will be radiant with the light of His presence, and ringing with the music of His voice.

But if we elect to join the other army—for there is another army, and men have wills that enable them to lift themselves up against God, the Ruler of all things—then the old story, from which my first text is taken, will fulfil itself again in regard to us—"the stars in their courses will fight against" us; and Sisera, lying stiff and stark, with Jael's tent-peg through his temples, and the swollen corpses being swirled down to the stormy sea by "that ancient river, the river Kishon," will be a grim parable of the end of the men that set themselves against God, and so have the universe against them. "Choose ye this day whom ye will serve."

THE EVIL EYE AND THE CHARM.

"Who hath bewitched you, that ye should not obey the truth, before whose eyes Jesus Christ hath been evidently set forth, crucified among you?"—GAL. iii. 1.

THE Revised Version gives a shorter, and probably correct, form of this vehement question. It omits the two clauses "that ye should not obey the truth" and "among you." The omission increases the sharpness of the thrust of the interrogation, whilst it loses nothing of the meaning.

Now, a very striking metaphor runs through the whole of this question, which may easily be lost sight of by ordinary readers. You know the old superstition as to the Evil Eye, almost universal at the date of this letter and even now in the East, and lingering still amongst ourselves. Certain persons were supposed to have the power, by a look, to work mischief, and by fixing the gaze of their victims, to suck the very life out of them. So Paul asks who the malign sorcerer is that has thus fascinated the fickle Galatians, and is draining their Christian life out of their eyes.

Very appropriately, therefore, if there is this reference, which the word translated "bewitched" carries with it, he goes on to speak about Jesus Christ as having been displayed before their eyes. They had seen Him.

How did they come to be able to turn away to look at anything else?

But there is another observation to be made by way of introduction, and that is as to the full force of the expression "evidently set forth." The word employed, as commentators tell us, is that which is used for the display of official proclamations, or public notices, in some conspicuous place, as the Forum or the market, that the citizens might read. So, keeping up the metaphor, the word might be rendered, as has been suggested by some eminent scholars, "placarded"—"Before whose eyes Jesus Christ has been placarded." The expression has acquired somewhat ignoble associations from modern advertising, but that is no reason why we should lose sight of its force. So, then, Paul says, "In my preaching, Christ was conspicuously set forth. It is like some inexplicable enchantment that, having seen Him, you should turn away to gaze on others." It is insanity which evokes wonder, as well as sin which deserves rebuke; and the fiery question of my text conveys both.

I. Keeping to the metaphor, I note first the placard which Paul had displayed.

"Jesus Christ crucified has been conspicuously set forth before you," he says to these Galatians. Now, he is referring, of course, to his own work of preaching the Gospel to them at the beginning. And the vivid metaphor suggests very strikingly two things. We see in it the Apostle's notion of what He had to do. His had been a very humble office, simply to hang up a proclamation. The one virtue of a proclamation is that it should be brief and plain. It must be authoritative, it must be urgent, it must be "writ large," it must be easily intelligible. And he that makes it public has nothing to do except to fasten it up, and make sure that it is legible. If I might venture into modern phraseology, what Paul means is that he was neither more nor less than a bill-sticker, that he went out with the placards and fastened them up.

Ah! if we ministers universally acted up to the implications of this metaphor, do you not think the pulpit would be more frequently a centre of power than it is to-day? And if, instead of presenting our own ingenuities and speculations, we were to realise the fact that we have to hide ourselves behind the broad sheet that we fasten up, there would be a new breath over many a moribund Church, and we should hear less of the often warrantable sarcasms about the inefficiency of the modern pulpit.

But I turn from Paul's conception of the office to his statement of his theme. "*Jesus* was displayed amongst you." If I might vary the metaphor a little, the placard that Paul fastened up was like those that modern advertising ingenuity displays upon all our walls. It was a picture-placard, and on it was portrayed one sole figure —Jesus, the Person. Christianity is Christ, and Christ is Christianity; and wherever there is a pulpit or a book which deals rather with doctrines than with Him who is the Fountain and Quarry of all doctrine, there is divergence from the primitive form of the Gospel.

I know, of course, that doctrines—which are only formal and orderly statements of principles involved in the facts—must flow from the proclamation of the person, Christ. I am not such a fool as to run amuck against theology, as some people in this day do. But what I wish to insist upon is that the first form of Christianity is not a theory, but a history, and that the revelation of God is the biography of a man. We must begin with the person, Christ, and preach Him. Would that all our preachers and all professing Christians, in their own personal religious life, had grasped this—that, since Christianity is not first a philosophy but a history, and its centre not an ordered sequence of doctrines but a living person, the act that makes a man possessor of Christianity is not the intellectual process of assimilating certain truths, and accepting them, but the moral process of clinging, with trust and love, to the person, Jesus.

But, further, if any of you consult the original, you will see that the order of the sentence is such as to throw a great weight of emphasis on that last word "crucified." It is not merely a person that is portrayed on the placard, but it is that person *upon the Cross*. Ah! brethren, Paul himself puts his finger, in the words of my text, on what, in his conception, was the throbbing heart of all his message, the vital point from which all its power, and all the gleam of its benediction, poured out upon humanity—"Christ crucified." If the placard is a picture of Christ in other attitudes and in other aspects, without the picture of Him crucified, it is an imperfect representation of the Gospel that Paul preached and that Christ was.

II. Now, think, secondly, of the fascinators that draw away the eyes.

Paul's question is not one of ignorance, but it is a rhetorical way of rebuking, and of expressing wonder. He knew, and the Galatians knew, well enough who it was that had bewitched them. The whole letter is a polemic worked in fire, and not in frost, as some argumentation is, against a very well-marked class of teachers—viz., those emissaries of Judaism who had crept into the Church, and took it as their special function to dog Paul's steps amongst the heathen communities that he had gathered together through faith in Christ, and used every means to upset his work.

I cannot but pause for a moment upon this original reference of my text, because it is very relevant to the present condition of things amongst us. These men whom Paul is fighting as if he were in a sawpit with them, in this letter, what was their teaching? This: they did not deny that Jesus was the Christ; they did not deny that faith knit a man to Him, but what they said was that the observance of the external rites of Judaism was necessary in order to entrance into the Church and to salvation. They did not in their own estimation detract from Christ, but they added to Him. And Paul says that to add is to detract, to say that anything is necessary except faith in Jesus Christ's finished work is to deny that that finished work, and faith in it, are the means of salvation; and the whole evangelical system crumbles into nothingness if once you admit that.

Now, is there anybody to-day that is saying the same things, with variations consequent upon change of external conditions? Are there no people within the limits of the Christian Church that are reiterating the old Jewish notion that external ceremonies—baptism and the Lord's Supper—are necessary to salvation and to connection with the Christian Church? And is it not true now, as it was then, that though they do not avowedly detract, they so represent these external rites as to detract, from the sole necessity of faith in the perfected work of Jesus Christ? The centre is shifted from personal union with a personal Saviour by a personal faith to participation in external ordinances. And I venture to think that the lava stream which, in this Epistle to the Galatians, Paul pours on the Judaisers of his day needs but a little deflection to pour its hot current over, and to consume, the sacramentarian theories of this day. "O foolish Galatians, who hath bewitched you?" Is it not like some malignant sorcery, that after the Evangelical revival of the last century and the earlier part of this, there should spring up again this old, old error, and darken the simplicity of the Gospel teaching, that Christ's work, apprehended by faith, without anything else, is the means, and the only means, of salvation?

But I need not spend time upon that original application. Let us rather come more closely to our own individual lives and their weaknesses. It is a strange thing, so strange that if one did not know it by one's own self, one would be scarcely disposed to believe it possible, that a man who has "tasted the good word of God and the powers of the world to come," and has known Jesus Christ as Saviour and Friend, should decline from Him, and turn to anything besides. And yet, strange and sad, and like some enchantment as it is, it is the experience at times and in a measure, of us all; and, alas! it is the experience, in a very tragical degree, of many who have walked for a little while behind the Master, and then have turned away and walked no more with Him. We may well wonder; but the root of the mischief is in no baleful glitter of a sorcerer's eye without us, but it is in the weakness of our own wills and the waywardness of our own hearts, and the wandering of our own affections. We often court the coming of the evil influence, and are willing to be fascinated and to turn our backs upon Jesus. Mysterious it is, for why should men cast away diamonds for paste? Mysterious it is, for we do not usually drop the substance to get the shadow. Mysterious it is, for a man does not ordinarily empty his pockets of gold in order to fill them with gravel. Mysterious it is, for a thirsty man will not usually turn away from the full, bubbling, living fountain, to see if he can find any drops still remaining, green with scum, stagnant and odorous, at the bottom of some broken cistern. But all these follies are sanity as compared with the folly of which we are guilty, times without number, when, having known the sweetness of Jesus Christ, we turn away to the fascinations of the world. Custom, the familiarity that we have with Him, the attrition of daily cares—like the minute grains of sand that are cemented on to paper, and make a piece of sandpaper that is strong enough to file an inscription off iron —the seductions of worldly delights, the pressure of our daily cares—all these are as a ring of sorcerers that stand round about us, before whom we are as powerless as a bird in the presence of a serpent, and they bewitch us and draw us away.

The sad fact has been verified over and over again on a large scale in the history of the Church. After every outburst of renewed life and elevated spirituality there is sure to come a period of reaction when torpor and formality again assert themselves. What followed the Reformation in Germany? A century of death. What followed Puritanism in England? An outburst of lust and godlessness.

So it has always been, and so it is with us individually, as we too well know. Ah! brethren, the seductions are omnipresent, and our poor eyes are very weak, and we turn away from the Lord to look on these misshapen monsters that are seeking by their gaze to draw us into destruction. I wonder how many professing Christians are in this audience who once saw Jesus Christ a great deal more clearly, and contemplated Him a great deal more fixedly, and turned their hearts to Him far more lovingly, than they do to-day? Some of the great mountain peaks of Africa are only seen for an hour or two in the morning, and then the clouds gather around them, and hide them for the rest of the day. It is like the experience of many professing Christians, who see Him in the morning of their Christian life far more vividly than they ever do after. "Who hath bewitched you?" The world; but the arch-sorcerer sits safe in our own hearts.

III. Lastly, keeping to the metaphor, let me suggest, although my text does not touch upon it, the Amulet.

One has seen fond mothers in Egypt and Palestine who hang on their babies' necks charms, to shield them from the influence of the Evil Eye; and there is a charm that we may wear if we will, which will keep us safe. There is no fascination in the Evil Eye if you do not look at it.

The one object that the sorcerer has is to withdraw our gaze from Christ; it is not illogical to say that the way to defeat the object is to keep our gaze fixed on Christ. If you do not look at the baleful glitter of the Evil Eye it will exercise no power over you; and if you will steadfastly look at Him, then, and only then, you will not look at it. Like Ulysses in the legend, bandage the eyes and put wax in the ears, if you would neither be tempted by hearing the songs, nor by seeing the fair forms, of the sirens on their island. To look fixedly at Jesus Christ, and with the resolve never to turn away from Him, is the only safety against these tempting delights around us.

But, brethren, it is the crucified Christ, looking to whom we are safe amidst all seductions and snares. I doubt whether a Christ who did not die for men has power enough over men's hearts and minds to draw them to Himself. The cords which bind us to Him are the assurance of His dying love which has conquered us. If only we will, day by day, and moment by moment, as we pass through the duties and distractions, the temptations and the trials, of this present life, by an act of will and thought turn ourselves to Him, then all the glamour of false attractiveness will disappear from the temptations around us, and we shall see that the sirens, for all their fair forms, end in loathly fishes' tails and sit amidst dead men's bones.

Brethren, "looking *off* unto Jesus" is the secret of triumph over the fascinations of the world. And if we will habitually so look, then the sweetness that we shall experience will destroy all the seducing power of lesser and earthly sweetness, and the blessed light of the sun will dim and all but extinguish the deceitful gleams, that tempt us into the swamps where we shall be drowned. Turn away, then, from these things; cleave to Jesus Christ; and though in ourselves we may be as weak as a humming-bird before a snake, or a rabbit before a tiger, He will give us strength, and the light of His face shining down upon us will fix our eyes and make us insensible to the fascinations of the sorcerers. So we shall not need to dread the question, "Who hath bewitched you?" but ourselves challenge the utmost might of the fascinators with the triumphant question, "Who shall separate us from the love of Christ?"

Help us, O Lord! we beseech Thee, to live near Thee. Turn away our eyes from beholding vanity, and enable us to set the Lord always before us that we be not moved.

PUTTING ON THE ARMOUR.*

"And the king of Israel answered and said, 'Tell him, Let not him that girdeth on his harness boast himself as he that putteth it off.'"— 1 KINGS xx. 11.

AHAB, King of Israel, was but a poor creature, and, like most weak characters, he turned out a wicked one, because he found that there were more temptations to do wrong than inducements to do right. Like other weak people, too, he was torn asunder by the influence of stronger wills. On the one side he had a termagant of a wife, stirring him up to idolatry and all evil, and on the other side Elijah thundering and lightning at him; so the poor man was often reduced to perplexity. Once in his lifetime he did behave like a king, with some flash of dignity. My text comes from that incident. His next neighbour, and, consequently, his continual enemy, was the King of Damascus. He had made a raid across the border and was dictating terms so severe as to invite even Ahab to courageous opposition. His back was at the wall, and he mustered up courage to say "No!" That provoked a bit of blustering bravado from the enemy, who sent back a message, "The gods do so unto me, and more also, if the dust of Samaria shall suffice for handfuls for all the people that follow me." And then Ahab replied in the words of our text. They

* Annual Sermon to the Young.

have a dash of contempt and sarcasm, all the more galling because of their unanswerable common-sense. "The time to crow and clap your wings is *after* you have fought. Samaria is not a heap of dust just yet. Threatened men live long." The battle began, and the bully was beaten; and for once Ahab tasted the sweets of success.

Now, I have nothing more to do with Ahab and the immediate application of his message, but I wish to apply it to my young friends, whom I have taken it upon me to ask to come and hear me say two or three homely words to them in this sermon.

You are beginning the fight; some of us old people are getting very near the end of it. And I would fain, if I could, see successors coming to take the places which we shall soon have to vacate. So my message to you, dear friends, young men and young women, is this, "Let not him that putteth on the harness boast himself as he that putteth it off."

I. Now, look for a moment at the general view of life that is implied in this saying thus understood.

There is nothing that the bulk of people are more unwilling to do than steadily to think about what life as a whole and in its deepest aspects, is. And that disinclination is strong, as I suppose, in the average young man or young woman. That comes, plainly enough, from the very blessings of your stage of life. Unworn health, a blessed inexperience of failures and limitations, the sense of undeveloped power within you, the natural buoyancy of early days, all tend to make you rather live by impulse than by reflection. And I should be the last man in the world to try to damp the noble, buoyant, beautiful enthusiasms with which Nature has provided that we should all begin our course. The world will do that soon enough; and there is no sadder sight than that of a bitter old man, who has outlived, and smiles sardonically at, his youthful dreams. But I do wish to press upon you all this question, Have you ever tried to think to yourself, "Now, what, after all, is this life that is budding within me and dawning before me—what is it, in its deepest character, and what am I to do with it?"

There are some of us to whom, so far as we have thought at all, life presents itself mainly as a shop, a place where we are to buy and sell, and get gain, and use our evenings, after the day's work is over, for such recreation as suits us. And there are young men among my hearers who, with the flush of their physical manhood upon them, and perhaps away from the restraints of home, and living in gloomy town lodgings, with nobody to look after them, are beginning to think that life after all is a kind of pigs' trough, with plenty of foul wash in it for whoso chooses to suck it up—a garden of not altogether pure delights, a place where a man may gratify the lusts of the flesh.

But, dear brethren, whilst there are many other noble metaphors under which we can set forth the essential character of this mysterious, tremendous life of ours, I do not know that there is one that ought to appeal more to the slumbering heroism, which lies in every human soul, and to the enthusiasms which, unless you in your youth cherish, you will be beggared indeed in your manhood, than that which this picture of my text suggests. After all, life is meant to be one long conflict. We are like the fellahin that one sometimes sees in Eastern lands, who cannot go out to plough in their fields, or reap their harvests, without a gun slung on their backs; for the condition under which we work in this world is that everything worth doing has to be done at the cost of opposition and antagonism, and that no noble service or building is possible without brave, continuous conflict. Even upon the lower levels of life that is so. No man learns a science or a trade without having to fight for it. But high above these lower levels, there is the one on which we all are called to walk, the high level of duty, and no man does what his conscience tells him, or refrains from that which his conscience sternly forbids, without having to fight for it. We are in the lists and compelled to draw the sword. And if we do not realise this, that all nobility, all greatness, all wisdom, all success, even of the lowest and most vulpine kind, are won by conflict, we shall never do anything in the world worth doing. You are a soldier, whether you will or not, and life is a fight, whether you understand the conditions or no.

So, standing at the beginning, do not fancy that there is opening before you a scene of enjoyment, or that you are stepping into a world in which you can take your ease, and come out successfully at the other end. It is not so; and you will find that out before long. Better that you should settle it in your minds at the beginning. When I was born I was enrolled on the roll-call of the regiment; and now I have to do a man's part in the battle.

II. Note the boastful temper which is sure to be beaten.

No doubt there is something inspiring in the spectacle of the young warrior standing there, chafing at the lists, eagerly pulling on his gauntlets, fitting on his helmet, and longing to be in the thick of the fight. No doubt, as I have already said, there is something in your early days which makes such buoyant hopes and anticipations of success natural, and which gives you, as a great gift, that expectation of victory. I do not wish to shatter any of your enthusiasms or ideals, but I do wish to suggest a consideration or two that may calm and sober them.

So I ask, have you ever estimated, are you now estimating rightly, what it is that you have to fight for? To make yourselves pure, wise, strong, self-governing, Christ-like men, such as God would have you to be. That is not a small thing for a man to set himself to do. You may go into the struggle for lower purposes, for bread and cheese, or wealth, or fame, or love, or the like, with a comparatively light heart; but if there once has dawned upon a young soul the whole majestic sweep of possibilities in each human life, then the battle assumes an aspect of solemnity and greatness that silences all boasting. Have you considered what it is that you have to fight for?

Have you considered the forces that are arrayed against you? " What act is all its thought had been?" Hand and brain are never paired. There is always a gap between the conception and its realisation. The painter stands before his canvas, and, while others may see beauty in it, he only sees what a small fragment of the radiant vision that floated before his eye his hand has been able to preserve. The author looks on his book and thinks what a poor, wretched transcript of the thoughts that inspired his pen it is. There is ever this same disproportion between the conception and accomplishment. Therefore, all we old people feel, more or less, that our lives have been failures. We set out as you do, thinking that we were going to build a tower whose top should reach to heaven, and we are contented if, at the last, we have scrambled together some little wooden shanty in which we can live. We thought as you do; you will come to think as we do. So you had better begin now, and not go into the fight boasting, or you will come out of it conscious of being beaten.

Have you realised how different it is to dream things and to do them? In our dreams we are, as it were, working *in vacuo*. When we come to acts, the atmosphere offers resistance. It is easy to imagine ourselves victorious in circumstances where things are all going rightly and are blending according to our own desires, but when we come to the grim world, where there are things that resist and people are not plastic, it is a very different matter. You do not yet understand, as you will some day, the fatal limitations of power that hem us all in, and the obstinate way that circumstances have of not falling in with our wishes. And you have not yet learned how completely and constantly failure accompanies success, like its shadow. The old Egyptians had no need to put a skeleton at the tables, nor the Romans to set a mocker behind the hero as he rode in triumph up to the Capitol. The world provides the skeleton at the banquet, and circumstances supply the mocker to add a dash of failure to all our triumphs.

Have you ever realised how certainly, into the brightest and most buoyant and successful lives, there will come crushing sorrows, blows as from an unseen hand in the dark, that fell a man? O friend! when one thinks of the miseries and the misfortunes, the sorrows and the losses, the broken and bleeding hearts that began life buoyant, elastic, hopeful, perhaps boasting, like you, there ought to be a sobering tint cast over our brightest visions.

I suppose that our colleges are full of students who are going to far outstrip their professors, that every life-school has a dozen lads, who have just begun to handle easel and brush, that are going to put Raffaelle in the shade. I suppose that every lawyer's office has a budding Lord Chancellor or two in it. And I suppose that that sharp criticism of us fumblers in the field, and half-expressed thought, " How much better I could do it," belong to youth by virtue of its youth. It is a crude form of undeveloped power, but it wants a great deal of sobering down, and I am trying now to let out a little of the blood, and to bring you to a clear conception of the very limited success which is likely to attend you. All of us old people, whose deficiencies and limitations you see so clearly, had the same dreams, impossible as it may appear to you, fifty years ago. We were going to be the men, and wisdom was going to die with us, and you see what we have made of it. You will not do much better.

Have you ever taken stock honestly of your own resources? "What king, going to make war against another king, sitteth not down first, and counteth the cost, whether with his ten thousand he can meet him that cometh against him with twenty thousand?" Boast if you like, but calculate first, and boast after that, if you can.

Your worst enemy is yourself. When you are counting your resources and saying, "I have this, that, and the other thing," do not forget to say, "I have a part of me, that it takes all the rest of me all its time to keep down and prevent from becoming master." You have traitors in the fortress who are in communication with the enemy outside, and may go over to him openly in the very crisis of the fight. You have to take that fact into account, and it ought to suppress boasting whilst you are putting on the harness.

You are not old enough to remember, as some of us do, the delirious enthusiasm with which, in the last Franco-German war, the emperor and the troops left Paris, and how, as the train steamed out of the station, shouts were raised, "À Berlin!" Ay! and they never got farther than Sedan, and there an emperor and an army were captured. Go into the fight bragging, and you will come out of it beaten.

III. Note the Confidence which is not boasting.

I can fancy some of you saying: "These gloomy views of yours will lead to nothing but absolute despair. You have been telling us that success is impossible; that we are bound to fight, and are sure to be beaten. What are we to do? Throw up the sponge, and say, 'Very well! then I may as well have my fling, and give up all attempts to be any better than my passions and my senses would lead me to be.'" And if there is nothing more to be said about the fight than has been already said, that *is* the conclusion. "Let us eat and drink," not only for to-morrow we die, but "for to-day we are sure to be beaten." But I have only been speaking about this self-distrust as preliminary to what is the main thing that I desire to urge upon you now, and it is this : You do not need to be beaten. There is no room for boasting, but there is room for absolute confidence. You, young men and women, standing at the entrance of the amphitheatre where the gladiators fight, may dash into the arena with the most perfect confidence that you will come out with your shield preserved and your sword unbroken.

There is one way of doing it. "Be of good cheer; I have overcome the world." That was not the boast of a man putting on the harness, but the calm utterance of the conquering Christ when He was putting it off. He has conquered that you may conquer. Remember how the Apostle, who has preserved for us that note of triumph at the end of Christ's life, has, like some musician with a favourite phrase, modulated and varied it in his letter written long after, when he says, "This is the victory that overcometh the world, even our faith." My dear young friends, distrust yourselves utterly, and trust Jesus Christ absolutely, and give yourself to Him, to be His servant and soldier till your life's end. Then you will not be beaten, for it is written of those who move in the light, wearing the victor's palm : "These are they who overcame by the blood of the Lamb, and by the word of His testimony." That blood secures our victory in a threefold fashion. By that great death of Jesus Christ all our past sins may be forgiven, and they no longer have power to tyrannise over us. In His sacrifice for us there are motives given to us for noble, grateful, God-like living, stronger than all the temptations that can arise from our own hearts, or from the evils around us. And if we put our humble trust in Him, then that faith opens the door for the entrance into our hearts, in simple reality, of a share in His conquering life which will make us victorious over the world, the flesh, and the devil.

"This is the victory that overcometh the world," and the youngest, feeblest Christian who lays his or her hand in Christ's strong hand, may look out upon all the embattled antagonisms that front them, and say, "He will cover my head in the day of battle, and teach my hands to war and my fingers to fight."

Dear young friends, people sometimes preach to you that you should be Christians, because life is uncertain and death is drawing near, and after death the Judgment. I preach that, too; but the Gospel that I seek to press upon you now is not merely a thing to die by, but it is *the* thing to live by; and it is the only power by which we shall be sure of overcoming the armies of the aliens. This confidence in Christ will take away from you no shred of your natural, youthful, buoyant elasticity, but it will save you from much transgression and from bitter regrets.

One last word. There is possible a triumph which is not boasting, for him who puts *off* the harness. The war-worn soldier has little heart for boasting, but he may be able to say, "I have not been beaten." The best of us, when we come to the end, will have to recognise in retrospect failures, deficiencies, palterings with evil, yieldings to temptation, sins of many sorts, that will put all boasting out of our thoughts. But, whilst that is so, there is sometimes granted to the man, who has been faithful in his adherence to Jesus Christ, a gleam of sunshine at eventime, which foretells Heaven's welcome and " well done " before it is uttered. He was no self-righteous braggart, but a very rigid judge of himself, who, close by the headsman's block that ended his life, said : " I have fought a good fight ; I have finished my course ; I have kept the faith." Put on the whole armour of God, and when the time comes to put it off you will have a peaceful assurance, as far removed from despair as it is from boasting. Distrust yourselves ; do not underestimate your enemies ; understand that life is warfare ; trust utterly to Jesus Christ, and He will see to it that you are not conquered, will give you the calm confidence of which we have been speaking here, and a share hereafter in the throne which He promises to him that overcometh. If you will trust yourselves to Him, and take service in His army, you cannot be too certain of victory. If you fling yourself into the fight in your own strength, with however high a hope, and fight without the Captain for your ally, you cannot escape defeat.

DYING MEN AND THE UNDYING WORD.

" Your fathers, where are they? and the prophets, do they live for ever? But My words and My statutes, which I commanded My servants the prophets, did they not take hold of your fathers?"—ZECH. i. 5, 6.

ZECHARIAH was the prophet of the Restoration. Some sixteen years before his date a feeble band of exiles had returned from Babylon, with high hopes of rebuilding the ruined temple. But their designs had been thwarted, and for long years the foundations stood unbuilded upon. The delay had shattered their hopes and flattened their enthusiasm; and when, with the advent of a new Persian king, a brighter day dawned, the little band was almost too dispirited to avail itself of it. At that crisis, two prophets " blew soul-animating strains," and, as the narrative says elsewhere, " the work prospered through the prophesying of Haggai and Zechariah."

My text comes from the first of Zechariah's prophecies. In it he lays the foundation for all that he has subsequently to say. He points to the past, and summons up the august figures of the great pre-Exilic prophets, and reminds his contemporaries that the words which they spoke had been verified in the experience of past generations. He puts himself in line with these, his mighty predecessors, and declares that, though the hearers and the speakers of that prophetic word had glided away into the vast unknown, the word remained, lived still, and on his lips demanded the same obedience as it had vainly demanded from the generation that was past.

It has sometimes been supposed that of the two questions in my text the first is the prophet's—" Your fathers, where are they ? " and that the second is the retort of the people—" The prophets, do *they* live for ever ? " " It is true that our fathers are gone, but what about the prophets that you are talking of ? Are *they* any better off ? Are they not dead, too ? " But though the separation of the words into dialogue gives vivacity, it is wholly unnecessary. And it seems to me that Zechariah's appeal is all the more impressive if we suppose that he here gathers the mortal hearers and speakers of the immortal word into one class, and sets over against them the eternal word, which lives to-day as it did then, and has new lessons for a new generation. So it is from that point of view that I wish to look at these words now, and try to gather from them some of the solemn and, as it seems to me, striking lessons which they inculcate. I follow with absolute simplicity the prophet's thoughts.

I. The mortal hearers and speakers of the abiding Word.

" Your fathers, where are they ? And the prophets, do they live for ever ? " It is all but impossible to invest that well-known thought with any fresh force ; but, perhaps, if we look at it from the special angle from which the prophet here regards it, we may get some new impression of the old truth. That special angle is to bring into connection the Eternal Word and the transient vehicles and hearers of it.

Did you ever stand in some roofless, ruined, cathedral or abbey-church, and try to gather round you the generations that had bowed and worshipped there? Did you ever step across the threshold of some ancient sanctuary, where the feet of vanished generations had worn down the sand-stone steps at the entrance? It is solemn to think of the fleeting series of men; it is still more striking to bring them into connection with that everlasting Word which once they heard, and accepted or rejected.

But let me bring the thought a little closer. There is not a sitting in our churches that has not been sat in by dead people. As I stand here and look round I can re-people almost every pew with faces that we shall see no more. Many of you, the older *habitués* of this place, can do the same, and can look and think, " Ah! *he* used to sit there; *she* used to be in that corner." And I can remember many mouldering lips that have stood in this place where I stand, of friends and brethren that are gone. " Your fathers, where are they?" " Graves under us, silent," are the only answer. " And the prophets, do they live for ever?" No memories are shorter-lived than the memories of the preachers of God's word.

Take another thought, that all these past hearers and speakers of the word had that word verified in their lives. " Took it not hold of your fathers?" Some of them neglected it, and its burdens were upon them, little as they felt them sometimes. Some of them clave to it, and accepted it, and its blessed promises were all fulfilled to them. Not one of them who, for the brief period of their earthly lives, came in contact with that Divine message, but realised, more or less consciously, some blessedly and some in darkened lives and ruined careers, the solemn truth of its promises and of its threatenings. The word may have been received, or it may have been neglected, by the past generations ; but whether the members thereof put out a hand to accept or withheld their grasp, whether they took hold of it or it took hold of them—wherever they are now, their earthly relation to that word is a determining factor in their condition. The syllables died away into empty air, the messages were forgotten, but the men that ministered them are eternally influenced by the faithfulness of their ministrations, and the men that heard them are eternally affected by the reception or rejection of that word. So, when we summon around us the congregation of the dead, which is more numerous than the audience of the living to whom I now speak, the lesson that their silent presence teaches us is, " wherefore we should give the more earnest heed to the things that we have heard."

II. Let us note the abiding Word, which these transient generations of hearers and speakers have had to do with.

It is maddening to think of the sure decay and dissolution of all human strength, beauty, wisdom, unless that thought brings with it immediately, like a pair of coupled stars, of which the one is bright and the other dark, the corresponding thought of that which does not pass, and is unaffected by time and change. Just as reason requires some unalterable substratum, below all the fleeting phenomena of the changeful creation—a God who is the Rock-basis of all, the staple to which all the links hang—so we are driven back and back and back, by the very fact of the transiency of the transient, to grasp, for a refuge and a stay, the permanency of the Permanent. "In the year that King Uzziah died I saw the Lord sitting upon a throne"—the passing away of the mortal shadow of sovereignty revealed the undying and true King. It is blessed for us when the lesson which the fleeting of all that *can* flee away reads to us is that, beneath it all, there is the Unchanging. When the leaves drop from the boughs of the trees that veil the face of the cliff, then the steadfast rock is visible; and when the generations, like leaves, drop and rot, then th rock background should stand out the more clearly.

Zechariah meant by the "word of God" simply the prophetic utterances about the destiny and the punishment of his nation. We ought to mean by the "word of God, which liveth and abideth for ever," not merely the written embodiment of it in the Old or New Testament, but the Personal Word, the Incarnate Word, the Everlasting Son of the Father, who came upon earth to be God's mouthpiece and utterance, and who is for us all *the* Word, the Eternal Word of the Living God. It is His perpetual existence rather than the continuous duration of the written word, declaration of Himself though it is, that is mighty for our strength and consolation when we think of the transient generations.

Christ lives. That is the deepest meaning of the ancient saying, "All flesh is grass. . . . The Word of the Lord endureth for ever." He lives; therefore we can front change and decay in all around calmly and triumphantly. It matters not though the prophets and their hearers pass away. Men depart; Christ abides. Luther was once surprised by some friends sitting at a table from which a meal had been removed, and thoughtfully tracing with his fingers upon its surface with some drop of water or wine the one word " Vivit "; He lives. He fell back upon that when all around was dark. Yes, men may go; what of that? Aaron may have to ascend to the summit of Hor, and put off his priestly garments and die there. Moses may have to climb Pisgah, and with one look at the land which he must never tread, die there alone by the kiss of God, as the Rabbis say. Is the host below leaderless? The Pillar of Cloud lies still over the Tabernacle, and burns steadfast and guiding in front of the files of Israel. " Your fathers, where are they? The prophets, do they live for ever?" " Jesus Christ is the same yesterday and to-day and for ever."

Another consideration to be drawn from this contrast is, since we have this abiding Word, let us not dread changes, however startling and revolutionary. Jesus Christ does not change. But there is a human element in the Church's conceptions of Jesus Christ, and still more in its working out of the principles of the Gospel in institutions and forms, which partakes of the transiency of the men from whom it has come. In such a time as this, when everything is going into the melting-pot, and a great many timid people are trembling for the Ark of God, quite unnecessarily as it seems to me, it is of prime importance for the calmness and the wisdom and the courage of Christian people, that they should grasp firmly the distinction between the Divine treasure which is committed to the Churches, and the earthen vessels in which it has been enshrined. Jesus Christ, the Man Jesus, the Divine Person, His Incarnation, His Sacrifice, His Resurrection, His Ascension, the gift of His Spirit to abide for ever with His Church—these are the permanent "things which cannot be shaken." And creeds and churches and formulas and forms—these are the human elements which are capable of variation, and which need variation from time to time. No more is the substance of that eternal Gospel affected by the changes, which are possible on its vesture, than is the stateliness of some cathedral touched, when the reformers go in and sweep out the rubbish and the trumpery which have masked the fair outlines of its architecture, and vulgarised the majesty of its stately sweep. Brethren, let us fix this in our hearts, that nothing which is of Christ can perish, and that nothing which is of man can or should endure. The more firmly we grasp the distinction between the permanent and the transient, in existing embodiments of Christian truth, the more calm shall we be amidst the surges of contending opinions. " He that believeth shall not make haste."

III. Lastly, the present generation and its relation to the abiding Word.

Zechariah did not hesitate to put himself in line with the mighty forms of Isaiah, and Jeremiah, and Ezekiel, and Hosea. He, too, was a prophet. We claim, of course, no such authority for present utterers of that eternal message, but we do claim for our message a higher authority than the authority of this ancient prophet. He felt that the word of God that was put into his lips was a new word, addressed to a new generation, and with new lessons for new circumstances, fitting as close to the wants of the little band of exiles as the former messages, which it succeeded, had fitted to the wants of their generation. We have no such change in the message, for Jesus Christ speaks to us all, speaks to all times and to all circumstances, and to every generation. And so, just as Zechariah based upon the history of the past his appeal for obedience and acceptance, the considerations which I have been trying to dwell upon bring with them stringent obligations to us who stand, however unworthy, in the place of the generations that are gone, as the hearers and ministers of the Word of God.

Let me put two or three very simple and homely exhortations. First, see to it, brother, that you accept that Word. By acceptance I do not mean a mere negative attitude, which is very often the result of lack of interest, the negative attitude of simply not rejecting; but I mean the opening not only of your minds but of your hearts to it. For if what I have been saying is true, and the Word of God has for its highest manifestation Jesus Christ Himself, then you cannot accept a person by pure head-work. You must open your hearts and all your natures, and let Him come in with His love, with His pity, with His inspiration of strength and virtue and holiness, and you must yield yourselves wholly to Him. Think of the generations that are gone. Think of their brief moment when the great salvation was offered to them. Think of how, whether they received or rejected it, that Word took hold upon them. Think of how they regard it now, wherever they are in the dimness; and be you wise in time and be not as those of your fathers who rejected the Word.

Hold it fast. In this time of unrest make sure of your grasp of the eternal, central core of Christianity, Jesus Christ Himself, the Divine-human Saviour of the world. There are too many of us whose faith oozes out at their finger-ends, simply because they have so many around them that question and doubt and deny. Do not let the floating icebergs bring down *your* temperature; and have a better reason for not believing, if you do not believe, than that so many and such influential and authoritative names have gone away. When Jesus asks, Will ye also go away? our answer should be, " Lord, to whom shall we go? Thou hast the words of eternal life."

Accept Him, hold Him fast, trust to His guidance in present-day questions. Zechariah felt that his message belonged to the generation to whom he spoke. It was a new message. We have no new message, but there are new truths to be evolved from the old message. The questionings and problems, social, economical, intellectual, moral—shall I say political?—of this day, will find their solution in that ancient Word, " God so loved the world, that He gave His only begotten Son, that whosoever believeth in Him should not perish." There is the key to all the problems. " In Him are hid all the treasures of wisdom and knowledge."

Zechariah pointed to the experiences of a past generation as the basis of his appeal. We can point back to eighteen centuries, and say that the experiences of these centuries confirm the truth that Jesus Christ is the Saviour of the world. The blessedness, the purity, the power, the peace, the hope which He has breathed into humanity, the subsidiary and accompanying material and intellectual prosperity and blessings that attend His message, its independence of human instruments, its adaptation to all varieties of class, character, condition, geographical position, its power of recuperating itself from corruptions and distortions, its undiminished adaptedness to the needs of this generation and of each of us—enforce the stringency of the exhortation, and confirm the truth of the assertion: "This is My beloved Son; hear ye Him!" "The voice said, Cry. And I said, What shall I cry? All flesh is grass, and all the goodliness thereof as the flower of the field: the grass withereth, and the flower thereof falleth away: but the Word of our God shall stand for ever." Three hundred years after Isaiah a triumphant Apostle added, "This is the Word which by the Gospel is preached unto you." Eighteen hundred years after Peter, we can echo his confident declaration, and, with the history of these centuries to support our faith, can affirm that the Christ of the Gospel and the Gospel of the Christ are in deed and in truth the Living Word of the Living God.

CITIZENSHIP IN HEAVEN.

"Only let your conversation be as it becometh the gospel of Christ . . . that ye stand fast in one spirit, with one mind striving together for the faith of the Gospel; and in nothing terrified by your adversaries."—PHIL. i. 27, 28.

WHEN our translation of the Scriptures was made, "conversation" meant manner of life. It has now dwindled to mean talk. But the rendering of our version was inadequate even when the word had its nobler and fuller meaning. For, though it then contained the substance of the Apostle's exhortation in a general fashion, it entirely obliterated the striking figure which, as many of you know, underlies the exhortation. Instead of "let your conversation be" we ought to read "play the citizen"; or, as the margin of the Revised Version has it, "behave as citizens, worthily of the Gospel of Christ."

Now, what led the Apostle to cast his exhortation into this remarkable form? Perhaps the answer will be found by remembering the note in the Acts of the Apostles about this same city of Philippi, that it was "a colony." Now, the connection between a Roman colony and Rome was a great deal closer than that between an English colony and England. The colonists and their children were Roman citizens. Their names were borne on the roll of the Roman tribes. They were not amenable to the provincial governor, but to their own magistrates ; and these administered, not the local codes, but the Roman law. If we remember all these things, they give special force to the form of the exhortation here. No doubt many of the Philippian Christians, like Paul himself, possessed these privileges. They lived in Philippi ; they belonged to Rome. And so Paul would have them do by their true mother city what, as colonists, they did by Rome : realise that they belonged to it, live by its laws, feel the unity of their citizenship, and fight for the extension of its territory. I do not venture to adopt the tone of command befitting an Apostle, but let me put his commandments into exhortations.

I. Let us behave as citizens of the great city.

My text does not mean, as it is sometimes quoted as if it meant, "act as citizens" of an earthly kingdom or community, in a manner becoming the Gospel ; though a good many of our citizens and statesmen would be all the better if they took that application of the words to heart. But the community to which we are to feel that we belong is the great mother city beyond the sea. We live in Philippi ; we belong to Rome. We are members of another polity than that which surrounds us. And, "sometimes, in calm weather," our souls can catch a sight from some height of its sparkling buildings, lying dreamlike on the opal waves and bathed in unsetting sunshine.

So, brethren, if we are Christian men and women, surely one of our first duties is to keep fresh and vivid in our souls the sense that " here we have no continuing city," not because that truth is bitterly bitten into our souls by the *aqua fortis* of Change, but because it is the happy result of our happy seeking after the city that is to come. To all you Christian people the words are applicable as to the verity of your true affinities and belongings, whether they are realised consciously or no : "ye are come into the city of the living God."

True, as in Rome and in London, and many another capital, a stream lies between the principal part, where the palaces of the King are, and the suburb on the other side. But the communities are one—

"Though now divided by the stream,
The narrow stream of death."

Brethren, there is nothing—or, let me not exaggerate—there are few things that the average Christianity of this day needs more than that note of unworldliness, of belonging to another community than that in which our lot in the present is cast, which my text prescribes for us. We must speak the language of the land in which we dwell, but we should speak it with a foreign accent. There should be something about us, even when we are doing the same things as other people do—and which we must to a large extent do—that tells that the same things are by us done from such different motives, that they become different from themselves, when done by the men whose cares, and interests, and hopes are "cribbed, cabined, and confined" by the triviality of the transient present.

And that wholesome detachment will enfeeble no work, will darken no joy, but it will take the poison out of many a sorrow, and it will make small things great, and to be greatly done. He that stands above his work can come down upon it with more efficient blows, and the man that is lifted above the things seen and temporal will be able to draw all the sweetness out of them, to recognise all the nobleness in them, and to work nobly upon them. You are the citizens of another community, therefore you are to work here worthily thereof.

Now, our Apostle in these words not only prescribes the duty of keeping fresh that consciousness of belonging to another order, but he points to the imperial law to which the colonists are to submit—"worthily of the Gospel of Christ." I said that the Roman colonist in Philippi was not governed by the law of Macedonia, but by that of Rome. We, if we are Christian people, are not to be ruled and directed by the maxims of the world, still less by the notions that are current in the society to which we happen to belong, but are to take our commandments at first hand. "I appeal unto Cæsar," and I get my law from his autocratic lips.

For the Gospel which we say we believe is not only a set of *credenda*—things to be believed—but a set of *agenda*—things to be done; and in Christ Himself, and in the principles which underlie His life and His manifestation, and which plainly flow from all His course and from His Cross, there lie the germs of all human duty, and principles which may be applied to the smallest and the greatest things. The least and the largest of duties come under the one law of obligation, and the manner of their discharge can be found in the one life and death of Jesus Christ and the truths that are wrapped up therein. We do not need a tangle of precepts. Our law has been codified, and it is contained in Him "who hath left us an example that we should follow in His steps."

Only let your citizenship be discharged worthily of the Gospel of Christ; there is the law, the all-sufficient law. The same law that holds together two invisible atoms binds the planets into a system; and "the most ancient heavens" in all their abysses "by it are fresh and strong." Here is the all-comprehensive commandment, large enough to dominate the mightiest, flexible enough to be applied to the most entangled, capable of being brought to bear on the minutest: "Only let your conversation be as it becometh the Gospel of Christ."

II. Let us steadfastly hold by the unity of the city.

One of the secrets of Rome's conquering power was that to every citizen the idea of the city had become a religion. And so, however there might be diversities of judgment in the Forum where they assembled together, they were as one man when the enemy was at the gates or when the eagles had to be carried afield. Therefore, though far inferior to the swift-minded Greek, whose quickness of spirit carried with it the fatal gift of divisiveness, they, by their steadfastly linked power, overthrew a world. Paul would have us, in our degree and fashion, follow such an example, standing fast "in the unity of the spirit."

Now, it may be a question whether we should spell "spirit" here with a capital or a little letter. In the one case the reference would be directly to the Divine Spirit; in the other case it would be to the Christian spirit, actuated by that Divine Spirit. Substantially the meaning comes to be the same in either case. A

Christian man's spirit is always regarded in the New Testament as working under, and operated on by, that Divine Spirit which is given to every man that believes in Jesus Christ. And it is the unity, that is brought about by the operation of that one Spirit working in the spirits of all the citizens, that is suggested in our text. There is a deeper region in human nature than the intellect that works by reasoning, and that formulates its conclusions in propositions, and it is by the participation of that deeper element in us all in the one Spirit of God that our oneness is realised. Translate that into modern language, and it just comes to this, that our unity does not lie in identity of opinion, or in the adoption of like forms or methods, but it lies in the participation in a common life. "We are one bread," says Paul, "because we all partake of that one bread." And Christian men and women will never be brought together into anything but an illusive, external, frozen unity, unless we dig deep down beneath the region of opinion, and come to the region where the secrets of the life lie, and be one because the life of the one Lord is in us all.

But the exhortation of my text suggests for us that there are divisive tendencies which we have to resist; and it suggests, too, that the realisation of common citizenship, and, therein, of unity, supplies a powerful aid to steadfastness, and is the firm ground on which we can stand firm. Isolated, we may be overwhelmed; linked, we are strong. The legionaries had hooks on their shields, which fitted into eyes on their neighbours' bucklers; and thus linked together they made a wall of steel. Half a dozen men, with their arms interlocked in each others', can resist an ugly rush that would sweep them away singly. If we realise our unity in the Spirit we shall stand fast in one spirit. Each of us rooting himself in the Vine, we shall be close to each other.

III. Lastly, let us fight for the faith.

"In *one mind* striving together for the faith of the Gospel." The unity of spirit, which is realised in the depths of the nature, will, to a large extent, well up into the more superficial elements of humanity, and will bring about a competent oneness of mind. Churches have too often reversed the process, and thought they would begin by making all their members think alike, and then they would all feel alike. Paul says, begin by feeling alike, and you will come in reasonable measure to think alike. Let there be the one spirit, and there will be as much of the one mind as is necessary for union.

"In one mind striving together for the *faith* of the Gospel." The word "faith" seems here to be used abnormally, in its later common ecclesiastical signification, by which it means not the act of belief but the sum and contents of the thing believed. Though, perhaps, even here we might see the more frequent sense as still in force; "striving together for the faith of the Gospel" may mean striving together that faith may rule in our own hearts and in those of others; but I think the other meaning is perhaps the more probable —viz., that the body of Christian truth which Paul had delivered to the Philippians is by him here designated the faith, the things believed. And to strive for that is our business, Christian people, in this world. What has God made us Christians for? For our own well-being and elevation? Yes! For our own well-being and salvation *only*? No, but that the leaven might spread from each leavened particle to the unleavened one that lies next it, and God's grace fructify through us to all.

Rome had an expedient, which Russia in later ages copied, of setting on the frontiers military colonies whose one business was to keep the marches and to push forward the boundaries. You and I are set here for that purpose, to see to it that not one inch be encroached upon, but rather that continuously, with a pressure that is as irresistible, though it may be as slow, as that of a glacier, the territory of the Lord Christ be pushed forward in the world. We, as well as Nansen's men, ought to feel that the name of the ship that we are on is the *Fram*—" The Forward "—and should take the dying word of the Roman Catholic martyr-missionary saint for ours, " Amplius! Amplius! " further, further afield. " Striving for the faith of the Gospel."

My text adds the temper in which this striving should be carried on. " In nothing terrified by your adversaries." The metaphor is taken from the shying of a horse at some obstacle. Now, horses shy partly from nervousness and partly from dim sight. And the latter, as well as the former, is a reason for a great deal of the downcast pessimist talk of weak-hearted Christians in this generation. There is nothing to be afraid about. A great deal will change; a great deal that some of us think very sacred will go. The removing of the things that are shakeable and " shaken " takes place that " the things which cannot be shaken may remain." And they will remain. The Ark is quite safe. I do not say as much about the cart that carries it, but the Ark is safe enough; which, being interpreted, is this: Jesus Christ, His life, His death, His redemption, His salvation, His Spirit, His Church endure, and will endure. So, "in nothing terrified by your adversaries."

That courage fulfils itself—"which is to them an evident token of perdition, and to you of salvation." That courageous confidence is based upon personal experience: "We have heard Him ourselves, and know that this is the Saviour of the world." It is based on nineteen centuries, and it is based upon a sure hope. The striking metaphor of my text is once again employed by Paul in this letter. The other use of it bears upon that subject of the hope of the militant Christians; for he says, in another part of the epistle, "our citizenship is in heaven, from whence also we look for the Lord Jesus Christ as Saviour." The fight is at its sorest, and "through the long-tormented air" are heard the bugles of an advancing force. Down on to the field comes as Saviour the Captain of the Lord's host; and His onset scatters the enemy, and the colonists who were fighting at the outpost fall in behind Him, and swell His train, and partake of His triumphal entry into the City of the Living God.

A FATHER'S DISCIPLINE.

"For they verily for a few days chastened us after their own pleasure; but He for our profit, that we might be partakers of His holiness."—HEB. xii. 10.

FEW words of Scripture have been oftener than these laid as a healing balm on wounded hearts. They may be long unnoticed on the page, like a lighthouse in calm sunshine, but sooner or later the stormy night falls, and then the bright beam flashes out and is welcome. They go very deep into the meaning of life as discipline; they tell us how much better God's discipline is than that of the most loving and wise of parents, and they give that superiority as a reason for our yielding more entire and cheerful obedience to Him than we do to such.

Now, to grasp the full meaning of these words, we have to notice that the earthly and the heavenly disciplines are described in four contrasted clauses, which are arranged in what students call inverted parallelism—that is to say, the first clause corresponds to the fourth, and the second to the third. "For a few days" pairs off with "that we might be partakers of His holiness." Now, that does not seem a contrast at first sight; but notice that the "for" in the former clause is not the "for" of duration, but of direction. It does not tell us the space during which the chastisement or discipline lasts, but the end towards which it is pointed. The earthly parent's discipline trains a boy or girl for circumstances, pursuits, occupations, professions, all of which terminate with the brief span of life. God's training is for an eternal day. It would be quite irrelevant to bring in here any reference to the length of time during which an earthly father's discipline lasts, but it is in full consonance with the writer's intention to dwell upon the limited scope of the one, and the wide and eternal purpose of the other.

Then, as for the other contrast—" for their own pleasure," or, as the Revised Version reads it, "as seemed good to them"—" but He for our profit." Elements of personal peculiarity, whim, passion, limited and possibly erroneous conceptions of what is the right thing to do for the child, enter into the training of the wisest and most loving amongst us; and we often make a mistake and do harm when we think we are doing good. But God's training is all from a simple and unerring regard to the benefit of His child. Thus, the guiding principle of the two disciplines are contrasted in the two central clauses.

Now, these are very threadbare, commonplace, and old-fashioned thoughts; but, perhaps, they are so familiar that they have not their proper power over us; and I wish to try in this sermon, if I can, to get more into them, or to get them more into us, by one or two very plain remarks.

I. I would ask you to note, first, the grand, deep, general conception, here firmly laid hold of, of life as only intelligible when it is regarded as education or discipline.

He corrects, chastens, trains, educates. That is the deepest word about everything that befalls us. Now, there are involved in that two or three very obvious thoughts, which would make us all calmer and nobler and stronger, if they were vividly and vitally present to us day by day.

The first is that all which befalls us has a will behind it and is co-operant to an end. Life is not a heap of unconnected incidents, like a number of links flung down on the ground, but the links are a chain, and the chain has a staple. It is not a law without a law-giver that shapes men's lives. It is not a blind, impersonal Chance that presides over it. Why, these very meteors that astronomers expect in Autumn to be flying and flashing through the sky in apparent wild disorder, all obey law. Our lives, in like manner, are embodied thoughts of God's, in as far as the incidents which befall in them are concerned. We may mar, may fight against, may contradict the presiding Divine purpose; but yet, behind the wild dance of flashing and transitory lights that go careering all over the sky, there guides, not an impersonal Power, but a living, loving Will. *He*, not *it*; He, not *they*—men, circumstances, what people call second causes—*He* corrects, and He does it for a great purpose.

Ah! if we believed that, and not merely said it, from the teeth outwards, but if it were a living conviction with us, do you not think our lives would tower up into a nobleness, and settle themselves down into a tranquillity all strange to them to-day?

But, then, further, there is the other thought to be grasped, that all our days we are here in a state of pupilage. The world is God's nursery. There are many mansions in the Father's house; and this earth is where He keeps the little ones. That is the true meaning of everything that befalls us. It is education. Work would not be worth doing if it were not. Life is given to us to teach us how to live, to exercise our powers, to give us habits and facilities of working. We are like boys in a training ship that lies for most of the time in harbour, and now and then goes out upon some short and easy cruise; not for the sake of getting anywhere in particular, but for the sake of exercising the lads in seamanship. There is no meaning worthy of *us*—to say nothing of God—in anything that we do, unless it is looked upon as schooling. We all say we believe that. Alas! I am afraid very many of us forget it.

But that conception of the meaning of each event that befalls us carries with it the conception of the whole of this life, as being an education towards another. I do not understand how any man can bear to live here, and to do all his painful work, unless he thinks that by it he is getting ready for the life beyond; and that "nothing can bereave him of the force he made his own, being here." The rough ore is turned into steel by being

> "Plunged in baths of hissing tears,
> And heated hot with hopes and fears,
> And battered with the shocks of doom."

And then—what then? Is an instrument, thus fashioned and tempered and polished, destined to be broken and "thrown as rubbish into the void"? Certainly not. If this life is education, as is obvious upon its very face, then there *is* a place where we shall exercise the facilities that we have acquired here, and manifest in loftier forms the characters which here we have made our own.

Now, brethren, if we carry these thoughts with us habitually, what a difference it will make upon everything that befalls us! You hear men often maundering and murmuring about the mysteries of the pain and sorrow and suffering of this world, wondering if there is any loving Will behind it all. That perplexed questioning goes on the hypothesis that life is meant mainly for enjoyment or for material good. If we once apprehended in its all-applicable range this simple truth, that life is a discipline, we should have less difficulty in understanding what people call the mysteries of Providence. I do not say it would interpret everything, but it would interpret an immense deal. It would make us eager, as each event came, to find out its special mission and what it was meant to do for us. It would dignify trifles, and bring down the overwhelming magnitude of the so-called great events, and would make us lords of ourselves, and lords of circumstances, and ready to wring the last drop of possible advantage out of each thing that befell us. Life is a Father's discipline.

II. Note the guiding principle of that discipline.

"They . . . as seemed good to them." I have already said that, even in the most wise and unselfish training by an earthly parent, there will mingle subjective elements, peculiarities of view and thought, and sometimes of passion and whim and other ingredients, which detract from the value of all such training. The guiding principle for each earthly parent can only be his conception of what is for the good of his child, even at the best; and oftentimes that is not purely the guide by which the parent's discipline is directed. So the text turns us away from all these incompletenesses, and tells us, "He for our profit"—with no sidelong look to anything else, and with an entirely wise knowledge of what is best for us, so that the result will be always and only for our good. This is the point of view from which every Christian man ought to look upon all that befalls him.

What follows? This, plainly: there is no such thing as evil except the evil of sin. All that comes is good—of various sorts and various complexions, but all generically the same. The inundation comes up over the fields, and men are in despair. It goes down; and then, like the slime left from the Nile in flood, there is better soil for the fertilising of our fields. Storms keep sea and air from stagnating. All that men call evil, in the material world, has in it a soul of good.

That is an old, old commonplace; but, like the other one, of which I have been speaking, it is more often professed than realised, and we need to be brought back to the recognition of it more entirely than we ordinarily are. If it be that all my life is paternal discipline, and that God makes no mistakes, then I can embrace whatever comes to me, and be sure that in it I shall find that which will be for my good.

Ah, brethren, it is easy to say so when things go well; but, surely, when the night falls is the time for the stars to shine. That gracious word should shine upon some of us in to-day's perplexities, and pains, and disappointments, and sorrows—"He for our profit."

Now, that great thought does not in the least deny the fact that pain and sorrow, and so-called evil, are very real. There is no false stoicism in Christianity. The mission of our troubles would not be effected unless they did trouble us. The good that we get from a sorrow would not be realised unless we did sorrow. "Weep for yourselves," said the Master, "and for your children." It is right that we should writhe in pain. It is right that we should yield to the impressions that are made upon us by calamities. But it is not right that we should be so affected as that we should fail to discern in them this gracious thought—"for our profit." God sends us many love-tokens, and amongst them are the great and the little annoyances and pains that beset our lives, and on each of them, if we would look, we should see written, in His own hand, this inscription: "For your good." Do not let us have our eyes so full of tears that we cannot see, or our hearts so full of regrets that we cannot accept, that sweet, strong message.

The guiding principle of all that befalls us is God's unerring knowledge of what will do us good. That will not prevent, and is not meant to prevent, the arrow from wounding, but it does wipe the poison off the arrow, and diminish the pain, and should diminish the tears.

III. Lastly, here we see the great aim of all the discipline.

The earthly parent trains his son, or her daughter, for earthly occupations. These last a little while. God trains us for an eternal end: "that we should be partakers of His holiness." The one object which is congruous with a man's nature, and is stamped on his whole being, as its only adequate end, is that he should be like God. Holiness is the Scriptural shorthand expression for all that in the Divine nature which separates God from, and lifts Him above, the creature; and in that aspect of the word the gulf can never be lessened nor bridged between us and Him. But it also is the expression for the moral purity and perfection of that Divine nature which separates Him from the creatures far more really than do the metaphysical attributes that belong to His infinitude and eternity; and in that aspect the great hope that is given to us is that we may rise nearer and nearer to that perfect whiteness of purity, and though we cannot share in His essential, changeless being, may "*walk*"—as befits our limited and changeful natures—" in the light, as He "—as befits His boundless and eternal being—"*is* in the light." That is the only end which it is worthy of a man, being what he is, to propose to himself as the issue of his earthly experience. If I fail in that, whatever else I have accomplished, I fail in everything. I may have made myself rich, cultured, learned, famous, refined, prosperous; but if I have not at least begun to be like God in purity, in will, in heart, then my whole career has missed the purpose for which I was made, and for which all the discipline of life has been lavished upon me. Fail there, and, wherever you succeed, you are a failure. Succeed there, and, wherever you fail, you are a success.

That great and only worthy end may be reached by the ministration of circumstances and the discipline through which God passes us. These are not the only ways by which He makes us partakers of His holiness, as we well know. There is the work of that Divine Spirit who is granted to every believer to breathe into him the holy breath of an immortal and incorruptible life. To work along with these there is the influence that is brought to bear upon us by the circumstances in which we are placed and the duties which we have to perform. These may all help us to be nearer and liker to God.

That is the intention of our sorrows. They will wean us; they will refine us; they will blow us to His breast, as a strong wind might sweep a man into some refuge from itself. I am sure that among my hearers there are some who can thankfully attest that they were brought nearer to God by some short, sharp sorrow than by many long days of prosperity. What Absalom, in his wayward, impulsive way, did with Joab is like what God sometimes does with His sons. Joab would not come to Absalom's palace, so Absalom set his corn on fire; and then Joab came. So God sometimes burns our harvests that we may go to Him.

But the sorrow that is meant to bring us nearer to Him may be in vain. The same circumstances may produce opposite effects. I daresay there are people listening to me now who have been made hard, and sullen, and bitter, and paralysed for good work, because they have some heavy burden or some wound that life can never heal, to be carried or to ache. Ah, brethren, we are often like shipwrecked crews, of whom some are driven by the danger to their knees, and some are driven to the spirit-casks. Take care that you do not waste your sorrows; that you do not let the precious gifts of disappointment, pain, loss, loneliness, ill-health, or similar afflictions that come in your daily life, mar you instead of mending you. See that they send you nearer to God, and not that they drive you farther from Him. See that they make you more anxious to have the durable riches and righteousness which no man can take from you, than to grasp at what may yet remain of fleeting earthly joys.

So, brethren, let us try to school ourselves into the habitual and operative conviction that life is discipline. Let us yield ourselves to the loving will of the unerring Father, the perfect Love. Let us beware of getting no good from what is charged to the brim with good. And let us see to it that out of the many fleeting circumstances of life we gather and keep the eternal fruit of being partakers of His holiness. May it never have to be said of any of us that we wasted the mercies which were judgments too, and found no good in the things that our tortured hearts felt to be also evils; lest God should have to wail over any of us, " In vain have I smitten your children; they have received no correction!"

AHAB AND MICAIAH.

"And Jehoshaphat said, Is there not here a prophet of the Lord besides, that we might inquire of him? And the king of Israel said unto Jehoshaphat, There is yet one man, Micaiah the son of Imlah, by whom we may inquire of the Lord: but I hate him; for he doth not prophesy good concerning me, but evil."—1 KINGS xxii. 7, 8.

AN ill-omened alliance had been struck up between Ahab of Israel and Jehoshaphat of Judah. The latter, who would have been much better in Jerusalem, had come down to Samaria to join in an assault on the kingdom of Damascus; but, like a great many other people, Jehoshaphat first made up his mind without asking God, and then thought that it might be well to get some kind of varnish of a religious sanction for his decision. So he proposes to his ally to inquire of the Lord about this matter. One would have thought that that should have been done before, and not after, the determination was made. Ahab does not at all see the necessity for such a thing, but, to please his scrupulous ally, he sends for his priests. They came, four hundred of them, and they all played the tune, of course, that Ahab called for. It is not difficult to get prophets to pat a king on the back, and tell him, "Do what you like."

But Jehoshaphat was not satisfied yet. Perhaps he

thought that Ahab's clergy were not exactly God's prophets, but at all events he wanted an independent opinion ; and so he asks if there is not in all Samaria a man that can be trusted to speak out. He gets for answer the name of this " Micaiah the son of Imlah." Ahab had had experience of him, and knew his man ; and the very name leads him to an explosion of passion, which, like other explosions, lays bare some very ugly depths. "I hate him ; for he doth not prophesy good concerning me, but evil."

That is a curious mood, is it not? that a man should know another to be a messenger of God, and therefore know that his words are true, and that if he asked his counsel he would be forbidden to do the thing that he is dead set on doing, and would be warned that to do it was destruction ; and so, like a fool, he will not ask the counsel, and never dreams of dropping the purpose, but simply bursts out in a passion of puerile rage against the counsellor, and will have none of his reproofs. Very curious ! But there are a great many of us that have something of the same mood in us, though we do not speak it out as plainly as Ahab did. It lurks more or less in us all ; and, dear friends, it largely determines the attitude that some of you take to Christianity and to Christ. So I wish to say a word or two about it.

I. My text suggests the inevitable opposition between a message from God and man's evil.

No doubt, God is love ; and just because He is, it is absolutely necessary that what comes from Him, and is the reflex and cast, so to speak, of His character, should be in stern and continual antagonism to that evil which is the worst foe of men, and is sure to lead to their death. It is because God is love, that "to the froward He shows Himself froward," and opposes that which, unopposed and yielded to, will ruin the man that does it. So this is one of the characteristic marks of all true messages from God, that men who will not part with their evil call them "stern," "rigid," "gloomy," "narrow." Yes, of course, because God must look upon godless lives with disapprobation, and must desire by all means to draw men away from that which is drawing them away *from* Him and *to* their death.

Now, I suppose I need not spend time in enumerating or describing the points in the attitude of Christianity towards the solemn fact of human sin, which correspond to Ahab's complaint that the prophet spake always "not good concerning him, but evil." The "Gospel" of Jesus Christ proves its name to be true, and that it *is* "good news," not only by its graciousness, its promises, its offers, and the rich blessings of eternal life with which its hands are full, but by its severity, as men call it. One characteristic of the Gospel is the altogether unique place which the fact of sin fills in it. There is no other religion on the face of the earth that has so grasped and made prominent this thought : "All have sinned and come short of the glory of God." There is none that has painted human nature as it is in such dark colours, because there is none that knows itself to be able to change human nature into such radiance of glory and purity. The Gospel has, if I might so say, on its palette a far greater range of pigments than any other system. Its blacks are blacker; its whites are whiter; its golds are more lustrous than those of other painters of human nature as it is and as it may become. It is a mark of its Divine origin that it unfalteringly looks facts in the face, and will not say smooth things about men as they are.

Side by side with that characteristic of the dark picture which it draws of us, as we are of ourselves, is its unhesitating restraint or condemnation of deep-seated desires and tendencies. It does not come to men with the smooth words on its lips, "Do as thou wilt." It does not seek for favour by relaxing bonds, but it rigidly builds up a wall on either side of a narrow path, and says, "Walk within these limits and thou art safe. Go beyond them a hair's-breadth, and thou perishest." It may suit Ahab's prophets to fling the reins on the neck of human nature; God's prophet says, "Thou shalt not." That is another of the tests of Divine origin, that there shall be no base compliance with inclinations, but rigid condemnation of many of our deep desires.

Side by side with these two, there is a third characteristic that the Word, which is the outcome and expression of the Divine love, is distinguished by its plain and stern declarations of the bitter consequences of evil-doing. I need not dwell upon these, brethren. They seem to me to be far too solemn to be spoken of by a man to men in other words than Scripture's. But I beseech you to remember that this, too, is the characteristic of Christ's message. So a man may say, when he thinks of the dark and solemn things that the Old Testament partially, and the New Testament more clearly, utter as to the death which is the outcome of sin, that these are indeed the very voice of infinite love pleading with us all. Brother, do not so misapprehend facts as to think that the restraints and threatenings and dark pictures which Christ and His servants have drawn are anything but the utterance of the purest affection.

II. Now, secondly, let me ask you to look for a moment at the strange dislike which this attitude of Christianity kindles.

I have said that Ahab's mental condition was a very odd one. Strange as it is, it is, as I have already remarked, in some degree a very frequent one. There are in us all, as we see in many regions of life, the beginnings of the same kind of feeling. Here, for example, is a course that I am quite sure, if I pursue it, will land me in evil. Does the drunkard take a glass the less, because he knows that if he goes on he will have a drunkard's liver and die a miserable death? Does the gambler ever take away his hand from the pack of cards or the dice-box, because he knows that play means, in the long run, poverty and disgrace? When a man sets his will upon a certain course, he is like a bull that has started in its rage. Down goes the head, and, with eyes shut, he will charge a stone wall or an iron door, though he knows it will smash his skull. Men are very foolish animals; and there is no greater mark of their folly than the conspicuous and oft-repeated fact that the clearest vision of the consequences of a course of conduct is powerless to turn a man from it, when once his passions, or his will, or, worse still, his weakness, or, worst of all, his habits, have bound him to it.

Take another illustration. Do we not all know that honest friends have sometimes fallen out of favour, perhaps with ourselves, because they have persistently kept telling us what our consciences and common-sense knew to be true, that if we go on by that road we shall be suffocated in a bog? A man makes up his mind to a course of conduct. He has a shrewd suspicion that his honest friend will condemn, and that the condemnation will be right. What does he do, therefore? He never tells his friend, and if by chance that friend should say what was expected of him, he gets angry with his adviser and goes his road. I suppose we all know what it is to treat our consciences in the style in which Ahab treated Micaiah. We do not listen to them because we know what they will say before they have said it; and we call ourselves sensible people! Martin Luther once said: "It is neither safe nor *wise* to do anything against conscience." But Ahab put Micaiah in prison; and we shut up our consciences in a dungeon, and put a gag in their mouths, and a muffler over the gag, that we may hear them say no word, because we know that what we are doing, and we are doggedly determined to do, is wrong.

But the saddest illustration of this infatuation is to be found in the attitude that many men take in regard to Christianity. There is a great craving to-day, more perhaps than there has been in some other periods of the world's history, for a religion which shall adorn, but shall not restrain; for a religion which shall be toothless, and have no bite in it; for a religion that shall sanction anything that it pleases our sovereign mightiness to want to do. We should all like to have God's sanction for our actions. But there are a great many of us that will not take the only way to secure that—viz., to do the actions which He commands, and to abstain from those which He forbids. Popular Christianity is a very easy-fitting garment; it is like an old shoe, that you can slip off and on without any difficulty. But a religion which does not put up a strong barrier between you and many of your inclinations is not worth anything. The mark of a message from God is that it restrains and coerces and forbids and commands. And some of you do not like it because it does.

There is a great tendency in this day to cut out of the Old and New Testaments all the pages that say things like this, "The soul that sinneth it shall die"; or things like this, "This is the condemnation, that light is come into the world, and men love darkness rather than light"; or things like this, "Then shall the wicked go away into outer darkness." Brethren, men being what they are, and God being what He is, there can be no Divine message without a side of what the world calls threatening, or what Ahab called "prophesying evil." I beseech you, do not be carried away by the modern talk about Christianity being gloomy and dark, or fancy that it is a blot and an excrescence upon the pure religion of the Man of Nazareth, when we speak of the death that follows sin, and of the darkness into which unbelief carries a man.

III. Once more, let me say a word about the intense folly of such an attitude.

Ahab hated Micaiah. Why? Because Micaiah told him what would come to him as the fruit of his own actions. That was foolish. It is no less foolish for people to take up a position of dislike, and to turn away from the Gospel of Jesus Christ because it speaks in like manner. I said that men are very foolish animals; there is surely nothing in all the annals of human stupidity more stupid than to be angry with the word that tells you the truth about what you are bringing down upon your heads. It is absurd, because Micaiah did not make the evil, but Ahab made it; and Micaiah's business was only to tell him what he was doing. It is absurd, because the only question to be asked is, Are the warnings true? are the threatenings representations of what really will come? are the prohibitions reasonable? And it is absurd, because, if these things are so—if it is true that the soul that sinneth dies, and will die; if it is true that you, who have heard the name and the salvation of Jesus Christ over and over again, and have turned away from it, will, if you continue in that negligence and unbelief, reap bitter fruits here and hereafter therefrom—if these things are true, surely the man that tells you, and the Gospel that tells you, deserve better treatment than Ahab's petulant hatred or your stolid indifference and neglect.

Would you think it wise for a sea-captain to try to take the clapper out of the bell that floats and tolls above a shoal on which his ship will be wrecked, if it strikes? Would it be wise to put out the lighthouse lamps, and then think that you had abolished the reef? Does the signalman with his red flag make the danger that he warns of, and is it not like a baby to hate and to neglect the message that comes to you and says, "Turn ye, turn ye, why will ye die?"

IV. So, lastly, I notice the end of this foolish attitude. Ahab was told in plain words by Micaiah, before the interview closed, that he would never come back again in peace. He ordered the bold prophet into prison, and rode away gaily, no doubt, to his campaign. Weak men are very often obstinate, because they are not strong enough to rise to the height of changing a purpose when reason urges. This weak man was always obstinate in the wrong place, as so many of us are. So away he went, down from Samaria, across the plain, down to the fords of the Jordan. But when he had crossed to the other side, and was coming near his objective point, the memories of Micaiah in prison at Samaria began to sit heavy on his soul.

So he tried to dodge Divine judgment, and got up an ingenious scheme by which his ally was to go into the field in royal pomp, and he to slip into it disguised. A great many of us try to dodge God, and it does not answer. The man who "drew the bow at a venture" had his hand guided by a higher hand. Ahab was plated all over with iron and brass, but there is always a crevice through which God's arrow can find its way; and, where God's arrow finds its way, it kills. When the night fell he was lying dead on his chariot floor, and the host was scattered, and Micaiah, the prisoner, was avenged; and his word took hold on the despiser of it.

So it always will be. So it will be with us, dear brethren, if we do not take heed to our ways and listen to the word which may be bitter in the mouth, but, taken, turns sweet as honey. Nailing the index of the barometer to "set fair" will not keep off the thunderstorm, and no negligence or dislike of Divine threatenings will arrest the slow, solemn march, inevitable as destiny, of the consequence of our doings. Things will be as they will be; believed or unbelieved, the avalanche will come.

Dear brethren, there is one way to get Micaiah on our side. Listen to him, and then he will speak good to you, and not what you foolishly call evil. Let God's word convince you of sin. Let it bring you to the Cross for pardon. Jesus Christ addresses each of us in the Apostle's words: "Am I therefore become your enemy because I tell you the truth?" The sternest "threatenings" in the Bible come from the lips of that infinite Love. If you will listen to Him, if you will yield yourselves to Him, if you will take Him for your Saviour and your Lord, if you will cast your confidence and anchor your love upon Him, if you will let Him restrain you, if you will consult Him about what He would have you do, if you will accept His prohibitions as well as His permissions, then His word and His act to you, here and hereafter, will be only good and not evil, all the days of your life.

Remember Ahab lying dead on the floor of his chariot in a pool of his own blood, and bethink yourselves of what despising the threatenings, and turning away from the rebukes and prohibitions of the Divine word come to. These threatenings are spoken that they may never need to be put in effect; if you give heed to them they will never be put in effect in regard to you. If you neglect them and "will none of" God's "reproof," they will come down on you like a mighty rock loosed from the mountain, and will grind you to powder.

THE ROYAL JUBILEE.*

"He that ruleth over men must be just, ruling in the fear of God. And he shall be as the light of the morning, when the sun riseth, even a morning without clouds; as the tender grass springing out of the earth, by clear shining after rain."—2 SAM. xxiii. 3, 4.

ONE of the Psalms ascribed to David sounds like the resolves of a new monarch on his accession. In it the Psalmist draws the ideal of a king, and says such things as, "I will behave myself wisely, in a perfect way. I will set no wicked thing before mine eyes. I hate the work of them that turn aside. Mine eyes shall be upon the faithful of the land, that they may dwell with me." That psalm we may regard as the first words of the king, when, after long, weary years, the promise of Samuel's anointing was fulfilled, and he sat on the throne.

My text comes from what purports to be the last words of the same king. He looks back, and again the ideal of a monarch rises before him. The psalm, for it is a psalm, though it is not in the Psalter, is compressed to the verge of obscurity; and there may be many questions raised about its translation and its bearing.

* Preached on the occasion of Her Majesty's "Diamond Jubilee."

These do not need to occupy us now, but the words which I have selected for my text, may, perhaps, best be represented to an English reader in some such sentence as this—"If (or, when) one rules over men justly, ruling in the fear of God, then it shall be as the light of the morning when the sun riseth, even a morning without clouds." With such a monarch all the interests of his people will prosper. His reign will be like the radiant dawn of a cloudless day, and his land like the spring pastures, when the fresh, green grass is wooed out of the baked earth by the combined influence of rain and sunshine. David's little kingdom was surrounded by giant empires, in which brute force, wielded by despotic will, ground men down, or squandered their lives recklessly. But the King of Israel had learnt, partly by the experience of his own reign, and partly by Divine inspiration, that such rulers were not true types of a monarch after God's own heart. This ideal king is neither a warrior nor a despot. Two qualities mark him, Justice and Godliness. Pharaoh, and his like, oppressors, were as the lightning which blasts and scorches. The true king was to be as the sunshine that vitalises and gladdens. "He shall come down like rain upon the mown grass, and as showers that water the earth."

We do not need to ask the question here, though it might be very relevant on another occasion, whether this portraiture is a mere ideal, floating *in vacuo*, or whether it is a direct prophecy of that expected Messianic king who was to realise the Divine ideal of sovereignty. At all events we know that, in its highest and deepest significance, the picture of my text has lived, and breathed human breath, in Jesus Christ, who, both in His character and in His influence on the world, fulfilled the ideal that floated before the eyes of the aged king.

I do not need to follow the course of thought in this psalm any farther. You will have anticipated my motive for selecting this text now. It seems to me to gather up, in vivid and picturesque form, the thoughts and feelings which to-day are thrilling through an empire, to which the most extended dominion of these warrior kings of old was but a speck. On such an occasion as this I need not make any apology, I am sure, for diverging from the ordinary topics of pulpit address, and associating ourselves with the many millions who to-day are giving thanks for Queen Victoria.

My text suggests two lines along which the course of our thoughts may run. The one is the personal character of this ideal monarch; the other is its effects on his subjects.

I. Now, with regard to the former, the pulpit is, in my judgment, not the place either for the discussion of current events or the pronouncing of personal eulogiums. But I shall not be wandering beyond my legitimate province, if I venture to try to gather into a few words the reasons, in the character and public life of our Queen, for the thankfulness of this day. Our text brings out, as I have said, two great qualities as those on which a throne is to be established, Justice and Godliness. Now, the ancient type of monarch was the fountain of justice, in a very direct sense; inasmuch as it was his office, not only to pronounce sentence on criminals, but to give decisions on disputed questions of right. These functions have long ceased to be exercised by our monarchs, but there is still room for both of those qualities—the Justice which holds an even balance between parties and strifes, the righteousness which has supreme regard to the primary duties that press alike upon prince and pauper, and the godliness which, as I believe, is the root from which all righteousness, as between man and man, and as between prince and subject, must ever flow. Morality is the garb of religion; religion is the root of morality. He, and only he, will hold an even balance and discharge his obligations to man, whose life is rooted in, and his acts under the continual influence of, the fear of God, which has in it no torment, but is the parent of all things good.

We shall not be flatterers if we thankfully recognise in our Sovereign Lady the presence of both these qualities. I have spoken of the first inaugural words of the King of Israel, and the resolutions that he made. It is recorded that when, to the child of eleven years of age, the announcement was made that she stood near in the line of succession to the throne, the tremulous young lips answered, " It is a great responsibility; but I will be good." And all round the world to-day her subjects attest that the aged monarch has kept the little maiden's vow. Contrast that life with the lives of the other women that have sat on the throne of England. Think of the brilliant Queen, whose glories our greatest poets were not ashamed to sing, with the Tudor masterfulness in her, and not a little of the Tudor grossness and passion, and of the blots that stained her glories. Think of her sister, the morbidly melancholy tool of priests, who goes down to the ages branded with an epithet only too sadly earned. Think of another woman that ruled over England in name, the weak instrument of base intrigues. And then turn to this life which we are looking upon to-day. Think of the nameless scandals, the hideous immorality of the reigns that preceded hers, and you will not wonder that every decent man and every modest woman was thankful that, with the young girl, there came a breath of purer air into the foul atmosphere. I am old enough to remember hearing, as a boy, the talk of my elders as to the probabilities of insurrection if, instead of our Queen, there had come to the throne the brother of her two predecessors. The hopes of those early days have been more than fulfilled.

It is not for us to determine the religious character of others, and that is too sacred a region for us to enter, but this we may say that in all these sixty years of diversified trial, there has been no act known to us outsiders inconsistent with the highest motive, the fear of the Lord; and some of us who have worshipped in the humble Highland church where she has bowed have felt that on the throne of England sat a Christian.

Nor need we forget how, from that root of fear of God, there has come that wondrous patience and faithfulness to duty, the form of "Justice" which is possible for a constitutional monarch. We have little notion of how pressing and numerous and continual the Royal duties must necessarily be. They have been discharged, even when the blow that struck all sunshine out of life left an irrepressible shrinking from pageantry and pomp. Joys come; joys go. Duties abide, and they have been done.

Nor can we forget, either, how the very difficult position of a constitutional monarch, with the semblance of power and the reality of narrow restrictions, has been discharged. Our Sovereign has never set herself against the will of the people, expressed by its legitimate representatives, even when that will may have imposed upon her the sanction of changes which she did not approve. And that is much to say. We have seen young despots whose self-will has threatened to wreck a nation's prosperity.

Nor can we forget how all the immense influence of position and personality have been thrown on the side of purity and righteousness. Even we outsiders know how, more than once or twice, she has steadfastly set her face against the admission to her presence of men and women of evil repute, and has in effect repeated David's proclamation against vice and immorality at his accession : " He that worketh wickedness shall not dwell within my house."

Nor must we forget, either, the simplicity, the beauty, the tenderness of the wedded and family life, the love of rural quiet, and of wholesome communion with Nature, and the eagerness to take her people into her confidence, as set forth in the book which, whatever its literary merits, speaks of her earnest appreciation of Nature and her wish for the sympathy of her subjects.

Then came the bolt from the blue, that sudden crash that wrecked the happiness of a life. Many of us, I have no doubt, remember that dreary December Sunday morning when, while the nation was standing in expectation of another calamity from across the Atlantic, there flashed through the land the news of the Prince's death; thrilling all hearts, and bringing all nearer to her, the lonely widow, than they had ever been in her days of radiant happiness. How pathetically, silently, nobly, devoutly, that sorrow has been borne, it is not for us to speak. She has become one of the great company of sad and lonely hearts, and in her sadness has shown an eager desire to send messages of sympathy to all whom she could reach, who were in like darkness and sorrow.

Brethren, I have ventured to diverge so far from the ordinary run of pulpit ministrations because I feel that to-day we all of us, whatever may be our political or ecclesiastical relationships and proclivities, are one in thanking God for the monarch whose life has been without a stain, and her reign without a blot.

II. Now let me say a word as to the other line of thought which my text suggests, the effect of such a reign on the condition of the subject.

Now, of course, in the narrowly limited domain of that strange creation, a constitutional monarchy, there is far less opportunity for the Sovereign's direct influence on the Subject, than there was in the ancient kingdoms of which David was thinking in his psalm. The marvellous progress of England during these sixty years is due, not to our Sovereign, but to a multitude of strenuous workers and earnest thinkers in a hundred different departments, as well as to the evolution of the gifts that come down to us from our ancient inheritance of freedom. But we shall much mistake if, for that reason, we set aside the monarch's character and influence as of no account in the progress.

A supposition, which is a violent one, may be made

which will set this matter in clearer light. Suppose that during these sixty years we had had kings on the throne of England like some of the kings we have had. The sentiment of loyalty now is not of such a character as that it will survive a vicious sovereign. If we had had such a monarch as I have hinted at, the loyalty of the good would for all these years have been suffering a severe strain, and the forces that make for evil would have been disastrously strengthened. Dangers escaped are unnoticed, but one twelvemonth of the reign of a profligate would shake the foundations of the monarchy, and would open the flood gates of vice; and we should then know how much the nation owed to the Queen whose life was pure, and who cast all her influence on the side of "things that are lovely and of good report."

Take another supposition. Suppose that during these years of wonderful transition, when the whole aspect of English politics and society has been transformed, we had had a king like George III., who set his opinion against the nation's will constitutionally expressed. Then no man knows with what storm and tumult, with what strife and injury, the inevitable transition would have been effected. Be sure of this, that the wise self-effacement of our Sovereign during these critical years of change is largely the reason why they have been years of peace, in which the new has mingled itself with the old without revolution or disturbance. It is due to her in a very large degree that

"Freedom broadens slowly down
From precedent to precedent."

I need not dilate on the changed England that she

looks out upon and rules to-day. I need not speak—there will be many voices to do that, in not altogether agreeable notes, for there will be a dash of too much self-complacency in them—about progress in material wealth, colonial expansion, the increase of education, the gentler manners, the new life that has been breathed over art and literature, the achievements in science and philosophy, the drawing together of classes, the bridging over of the great gulf between rich and poor by some incipient and tentative attempts at sympathy and brotherhood.

Nor need I dwell upon the ecclesiastical signs of the times, in which, mingled as they are, there is at least this one great good, that never since the early days have so large a proportion of Christian men been "seeking after the things that make for peace," and realising the oneness of all believers who hold the Head.

All this review falls more properly into other hands than mine. Only I would put in a caution—do not let us mingle self-conceit with our congratulations; and, above all, do not let us "rest and be thankful." There is much to be done yet. Listening ears can catch on every side vague sounds that tell of unrest and of the stirrings into wakefulness of

> "The spirit of the years to come,
> Yearning to mix itself with life?"

I seem to hear all around me the rushing in the dark of a mighty current that is bearing down upon us. Great social questions are rapidly coming to the front—the questions of distribution of wealth, abolition of privilege, the relations of labour and capital, and many others are clamant to be dealt with at least, if not solved. There is much to be done before Jesus Christ is throned as King of England. War has to be frowned down; the brotherhood of man has to be realised, temperance has to be much more largely practised than it is.

I need not go over the catalogue of *desiderata*, of *agenda*, things that have to be done—in the near future. Only this I would say—Christian men and women are the last people who should be ready to " rest and be thankful," for the principles of the Gospel that we profess, which have never been applied to the life of nations as they ought to be, will solve the questions which make the despair of so many in this generation. We shall best express our thankfulness for these past sixty years by each of us taking our part in the great movement which, in the inevitable drift of things to democracy, is going to " cast the kingdom old into another mould," and which will, I pray, make our people more of what John Milton long ago called them, " God's Englishmen." We have taught the nations many things. This land is called the mother of Parliaments. It is

> "The land where, girt with friends or foes,
> A man may say the thing he will."

It has taught the nations a tempered freedom, and that a monarchy may be a true republic. May we rise to the height of our privileges and responsibilities, and teach our subject peoples, not only mechanics, science, law, free trade, but a loftier morality, and the name of Him by whom kings reign and princes decree justice!

We, members of the free Churches of England, come seldom under the notice of Royalty, and have little acquaintance with courts, but we yield to none in our recognition of the virtues and in our sympathy with the sorrows of the Sovereign Lady, the good woman, who rules these lands, and we all heartily thank God for her to-day, and pray that for long years still to come the familiar letters V.R. may stand, as they have stood to two generations, as the symbol of womanly purity and of the faithful discharge of queenly duty.

"THE SPIRIT OF BURNING."

"He shall baptize you with the Holy Ghost, and with fire."—MATT. iii. 11.

THERE is something extremely beautiful and pathetic in John the Baptist's clear discernment of his limitations, and of the imperfection of his work. His immovable humility is all the more striking because it stands side by side with as immovable a courage in confronting evil-doers, whether of low or high degree. To him to efface himself and be lost in the light of Christ was no trial, but brought joy like that of the friend of the Bridegroom. He saw that the spiritual deadness and moral corruption of his generation was such that a crash must come. The axe was "laid at the root of the trees," and there was impending a mighty hewing and a fierce conflagration. There are periods when the only thing to be done with the present order is to burn it.

But John saw, too, that there was a great deal more needed than he could give; and so, with a touch of sadness, he symbolises the incompleteness of his work in the words preceding my text, by reference to his baptism. He baptised with water that cleansed the outside, but did not go deeper. It was cold, negative.

It brought no new impulses ; and he recognised that something far other than it was wanted, and that He who was to come, before whom his whole spirit prostrated itself in joyful submission, was to plunge into a holy fire, which would cleanse in another fashion than water could do. So my text goes very deep into the heart of Christ's work, and may well occupy our thoughts on Whitsunday, when so many Churches are commemorating the great event which began to fulfil John's prophecy.

I. Let me ask you to look, then, at this fiery Spirit.

Now, you will observe, I daresay, the singular solemnity of the triple refrain at the close of three contiguous verses, each of which ends with "fire." But there are fires and fires. The rotten tree "is cast into the fire," the empty chaff "is burned with unquenchable fire." But there is another kind of fire, into which it is not destruction but blessedness for a man to be flung. "He shall baptize you with the Holy Ghost and with fire." That is promise, not threatening ; and the two fires are set in contrast. Strange that superficial readers should so often have omitted to notice the significance of this threefold repetition of the one word.

Now, I suppose that no one who looks at the passage carefully can doubt that the fire in my text is the symbol of the Divine Spirit. I would point to another instance of precisely the same collocation, in reference to the same subject, of the reality and the figure which expresses it, in our Lord's words, about being born of water and of the Spirit. Just as there the water is the symbol of the cleansing influences of the Spirit and has no reference whatsoever to the water of baptism, so here the fire is a symbol, in another form, of the same cleansing and hallowing operation.

I need not remind you that this metaphor is one of frequent occurrence; in the Old Testament occasionally, and in the New Testament habitually. I need only recall to you our Lord's own words, so full of yearning, longing, and conscious hindrances: "I am come to send fire upon the earth, and how I wish it was already kindled;" and I need only remind you, in passing, of the fiery tongues that sat upon the heads of the disciples on the Day of Pentecost.

So, then, if we take this symbol as expressive of the operations of that Divine Spirit which Christ brings, it may suggest to us some thoughts as to what He does for human nature, and what He is willing to do for us all. Let me just try to work out very briefly the force of this symbolical representation.

That fire gives life. That seems a paradox, but put your hands or your lips on the cheek of the beloved corpse, and you know the shock of icy coldness. Put them on the living flesh that holds the spirit that you love, and you know the electric glow of warmth. Heat is life; death is cold. And so, not only in the word "spirit," whether you take it as meaning breath or as meaning an immaterial personality, there is conveyed the promise of life, but in the symbol of "fire" it is no less conveyed. For though there is a fire that destroys, there is a warmth that vivifies.

I, for my part, believe that modern Evangelicalism has, to a large extent, failed in "prophesying according to the proportion of faith," and that it has fixed its gaze far too exclusively on forgiveness and acceptance, and the escape from the penal consequences of sin, as being the gifts of Christ to the world, and as making up the notion of Christ's salvation, and has not sufficiently given weight and proportionate prominence to the thought that these gifts—the barring out of penalty, forgiveness, and acceptance with God ; the transference into the condition of friends and children from that of enemies and aliens—are but the preliminaries to the true, central, deepest gift which Christ has to bestow, according to His own great words, " I am come that they might have life." It is the gift of life which the wholesome mysticism of Christianity insists upon as the highest that He can give. Do not go away with the notion that it is a metaphor, or a piece of rhetorical embellishment of some simple fact. The very centre of Christ's work for man is that He breathes into the dead spirit, dead because it lives in self, the germ of a new nature, and imparts a spiritual life, without which we are dead while we live. That life is given us by the Spirit of life in Christ Jesus, which "makes us free from the law of sin and death."

Have you been quickened by that indwelling Spirit? Is the life that you now live in the flesh not your life, but the life of Christ that lives in you ? " He shall baptize with the . . . fire " that gives life.

Again, this fire kindles emotion. We all know the common use of that metaphor in language. We speak about ardent desires, warm feelings, fervid emotions, burning love, and the like. The great gift which Christ brings to men is in one aspect the heightening and hallowing of the emotions. Ancient moralists did not know what to do with them. They tried to suppress them, and looked upon all the play of feeling as being disturbing to the loftier reason and will. Jesus Christ puts holy fire into the emotions, and heightens and sanctifies them, and makes love, which the world regards as a weakness, and often handles so as to make it a sin, the basis of all goodness, and the productive soil in which everything that is of good report will grow.

The fire kindles men's love. Think what a strange, new thing, when Christ came into the world, it was for men to love God. Judaism had very partially grasped that idea. The selectest of the psalmists had had glimpses of it, but for the nation at large there was no emotion in their religion, no warmth of feeling in their prayers, no love to God in their hearts. Christ came, and everything became different; and men poured out the treasures of their hearts like water at His feet, and felt that He, and He only, was the adequate object of all their emotions, and that all were glorified and ennobled when they were fixed on Him.

Religion is worth nothing unless it is warm. There is nothing more irrational than that people should; as a great many of us do, believe in a way the truths of Christianity, and feel next door to nothing about them. Its truths are so solemn, so certain, so tremendous, that not to be stirred to the very depths of our being by them, and yet to believe them, or say we do, is sheer insanity. Some of you will remember that in the original preface to the " Christian Year," a book about which I would speak with all admiration, the writer commits himself to the statement that " next to a sound creed there is nothing of so much importance as a sober standard of feeling in matters of practical religion." Well, I do not think so.

It seems to me that "a sober standard of feeling" is only a fine name for what Jesus Christ designated as "neither cold nor hot," and that, instead of sober feeling, what we want is the burning enthusiasm, of which one sees so little in Christians round about one and feels so little in one's own heart.

Oh, brethren, not to be all aflame is madness, if we believe our own creed. Isaiah says, in one of his gigantic metaphors, "The Lord's fire is in Zion, and His furnace in Jerusalem." Does that apply to most of our Churches, Nonconformist or Episcopalian? A fire and a furnace—does that describe this church? An ice-house would be a better illustration of the facts, in a great many cases. "He shall baptize you with . . . fire"; and if it does anything it will kindle emotion.

Again, that fire cleanses by kindling. John's water-baptism washed the outside. There is a better way of making things clean than that. Fire purifies, either by melting down the obstinate ore and bringing the scum up to the top, from whence it may be skimmed, leaving the residue clear, or it cleanses by dissipating the cause of the foulness, and, as it passes off, the stain melts from the surface of the disfigured clay. The great glory of the Gospel is to cleanse men's hearts by raising their temperature, making them pure because they are made warm, and that separates them from their evils. It is slow work to take mallet and chisel and try to chip off the rust, speck by speck, from a row of railings, or to punch the specks of iron ore out of the ironstone. Pitch the whole thing into the furnace, and the work will be done—which, being translated, is—the true way for a man to be purged of his weaknesses, his meannesses, his passions, his lusts, sins, is to submit himself to the cleansing fire of that Divine Spirit.

II. And now let me say a word about the baptism with the fiery Spirit.

Now, you all know that I am a Baptist; and you also all know that I do not obtrude my views upon that subject, as an ordinary thing, upon my congregation. And so you will not suppose me to be trying to bring anything in by a side wind, or to be seeking for proselytes, if I, purely as a Biblical critic, make a plain observation. The American Revisers who worked along with our Revision Committee, made a suggestion, which you will find printed at the end of the Revised New Testaments, to the effect that in all cases after the word "baptism" or "baptised," the "with" of the text, and the "in" of the margin, should change places. Our more conservative Revision Committee did not see their way to that, but they preserved the recommendation. And there can be no question—I speak now, not from my own denominational standpoint, but as voicing the opinion of the majority of students—there can be no question that here the *literal* rendering is the accurate rendering, and that fire is not the instrument *with* which, but the element *in* which, the person is baptised. Neither can there be any question that the primitive form of baptism is part of the significance of the symbol here—viz., a total immersion in the element.

Now, that being so, let me just suggest, for your time will not allow of my doing more, how, from this symbol, there comes a very solemn and impressive thought and appeal to all professing Christian people. John's prophecy, which was God's promise, is that a man shall be plunged into, immersed over head and ears in, this fiery Spirit. What can that mean less than a complete influence exercised over all a man's faculties, desires, and capabilities? What can it mean less than a complete bestowment of that sanctifying Spirit?

The same completeness is suggested by other sayings of Scripture upon the same subject; when we read, for instance, of Christ's promise to the Apostles that before long they should be "clothed with power from on high," as if with a vesture enveloping the whole body; or, as when we read about being "filled with the Spirit," as a vessel charged to the brim with some precious wine. If that is God's ideal, if that is God's desire, if that complete subjection to, and reception of, the Divine influences is possible through Jesus Christ, what shall we say of the fragmentary, the partial, the broken operations of that hallowing Spirit upon the best and highest of us? There are but points in a row, with long gaps between, when there ought to be one straight line, without variation and without interruption. Dear friends, let us try ourselves by that image of a complete immersion in the fire of the Spirit, and ask ourselves why is it that, with such a possibility, the reality of my life is as earth-bound as it is.

III. Lastly, we have here the Administrator of the baptism with the Spirit of fire.

"He shall baptize you." I need not, I suppose, remind you of how, in many places, our Lord claimed that same power. You remember the passage that I have already quoted: "I am come to fling fire upon the earth," and the more gracious aspect of the same promise given to the sorrowing company in the upper chamber: "I will send Him unto you." I need not remind you of what a tremendous claim that is to be made by a man sitting among men, nor what it involves about Him that made it. Nor is there time, here and now, to enter upon the deep thoughts that are suggested, by this glimpse into the administration of the revelation, in regard to the relations of the Divine nature within itself. The revelation in the life and death of Jesus Christ had to be completed, before the fulness of the operations of the cleansing Spirit could be realised. He had been brooding over the earth from the beginning, and, in lands far away from revelation, had been touching men's hearts and consciences. But until the Son of man was glorified, that Spirit in its perfection could not be given. It is no mere arbitrary limitation, but one inherent in the nature of the gift and in the nature of man, that it can only be bestowed upon those that have received Christ by faith.

So we come back to the old central truth, that Christ, the Administrator of the baptism with the fiery Spirit, must be clung to by simple faith, ere we can pass into the blessed possession of the highest gift from Him. Trust Him, and He bestows His Spirit upon us ; refrain from trusting Him, and we never possess it.

I cannot close without just recurring, in one word, to that solemn refrain to which I have already referred, as occurring in these adjacent verses. It comes like the triple tolling of some great bell : "Fire ! fire ! fire ! " One kind of fire is for the barren tree and the empty chaff, another kind of fire is for the man that believes in Christ. Yes ; the choice is before each of us—to be plunged into the fire which cleanses and quickens, or to be cast into the fire that destroys. Like the three Jews in Babylon, we may walk in that fiery furnace and be glad to feel the flames curling round our limbs and consuming our bonds. You have to make your choice of which of these fires you will have experience.

"SEEK YE."—"I WILL SEEK."

"When Thou saidst, Seek ye My face, my heart said unto Thee, Thy face, Lord, will I seek. Hide not Thy face far from me."—Ps. xxvii. 8, 9.

WE have here a report of a brief dialogue between God and a devout soul. The psalmist tells us of God's invitation and of his acceptance, and on both he builds the prayer that the face which he had been bidden to seek, and had sought, may not be hid from him. The correspondence between what God said to him and what he said to God is even more emphatically expressed in the original than in our version. In the Hebrew the sentence is dislocated, at the risk of being obscure, for the sake of bringing together the two voices. It runs thus, "My heart said to Thee," and then, instead of going on with his answer, the psalmist interjects God's invitation "Seek ye My face," and then, side by side with that, he lays his response, "Thy face, Lord, will I seek." The completeness and swiftness of his answer could not be more vividly expressed. To hear was to obey: as soon as God's merciful call sounded, the psalmist's heart responded, like a harp-string thrilled into music by the vibration of another tuned to the same note. Without hesitation, and in entire correspondence with the call, was his response. So swiftly, completely, resolutely should we respond to God's voice, and our ready "I will" should answer His commandment, as the man at the wheel repeats the captain's orders whilst he carries them out. Upon such acceptance of such an invitation we, too, may build the prayer, " Hide not Thy face far from me."

Now, there are three things here that I desire to look at—God's merciful call to us all; the response of the devout soul to that call ; and the prayer which is built upon both.

I. We have God's merciful call to us all.

"Thou saidst, Seek ye My face." Now, that expression, "the face of God," though highly metaphorical, is perfectly clear and defined in its meaning. It corresponds substantially to what the Apostle Paul calls, in speaking of the knowledge of God beyond the limits of Revelation, "that which may be known of God"; or, in more modern language, the side of the Divine nature which is turned to man ; or, in plainer words still, God, in so far as He is revealed. It means substantially the same thing as the other Scriptural expression, "the name of the Lord." Both phrases draw a broad distinction between what God is, in the infinite fulness of His incomprehensible being, and what He is as revealed to man ; and both imply that what is revealed is knowledge, real and valid, though it may be imperfect.

This, then, being the meaning of the phrase, what is the meaning of the invitation : " Seek ye My face " ? Have we to search for that, as if it were something hidden, far off, lost, and only to be recovered by our effort ? No : a thousand times no. For the seeking, to which God mercifully invites us, is but the turning of the direction of our desires to Him, the recognition of the fact that His face is more than all else to men, the recognition that whilst there are many that say, " Who will show us any good?" and put the question impatiently, despairingly, vainly, they that turn the seeking into a prayer, and ask, "Lord! lift Thou the light of Thy countenance upon us," will never ask in vain. To seek is to desire, to turn the direction of thought and will and affection to Him, and to take heed that the ordering of our daily lives is such as that no mist rising from them shall come between us and that brightness of light, or hide from us the vision splendid. They who seek God by desire, by the direction of thought and will and love, and by the regulation of their daily lives in accordance with that desire, are they who obey this commandment.

Next we come to that great thought that God is ever sounding out to all mankind this invitation to seek His face. By the revelation of Himself He bids us all sun ourselves in the brightness of His countenance. One of the New Testament writers, in a passage which is mistranslated in our Authorised Version, says that God "calls us by His own glory and virtue." That is to say, the very manifestation of the Divine Being is such that there lies in it a summons to behold Him, and an attraction to Himself. So fair is He, that He but needs to withdraw the veil, and men's hearts rejoice in that countenance, which is as the sun shining in his strength; "nor know we anything more fair than is the smile upon His face." If we see Him as He really is, we cannot choose but love. By all His works He calls us to seek Him, not only because the intellect demands that there shall be a personal will behind all these phenomena, but because they in themselves proclaim His name, and the proclamation of His name is the summons to behold.

By the very make of our own spirits He calls us to Himself. Our restlessness, our yearnings, our movings about as aliens in the midst of things seen and visible, all these bid us turn to Him in whom alone our capacities can be satisfied, and the hunger of our souls appeased. You remember the old story of the Saracen woman who came to England seeking her lover, and passed through these foreign cities, with no word upon her tongue that could be understood of those that heard her except his name whom she sought. Ah! that is how men wander through the earth, strangers in the midst of it. They cannot translate the cry of their own hearts, but it means, " God—my soul thirsteth for Thee "; and the thirst bids us seek His face.

He summons us by all the providences and events of our changeful lives. Our sorrows by their poignancy, our joys by their incompleteness and their transiency, alike call us to Him ;in whom alone the sorrows can be soothed and the joys made full and remain. Our duties, by their heaviness, call us to turn ourselves to Him, in whom alone we can find the strength to fill the *rôle* that is laid upon us, and to discharge our daily tasks.

But, most of all, He summons us to Himself by Him who is the angel of His face, " the effulgence of His glory, and the express image of His person." In the face of Jesus Christ, " the light of the knowledge of the glory of God" beams out upon us, as it never shone on this psalmist of old. He saw but a portion of that countenance, through a thick veil which thinned as faith gazed, but was never wholly withdrawn. The voice that he heard calling him was less penetrating and less laden with love than the voice that calls us. He caught some tones of invitation sounding in providences and prophesies, in ceremonies and in law; we hear them more full and clear from the lips of a brother. They sound to us from the Cradle and the Cross, and they are wafted down to us from the Throne. God's merciful invitation to us poor men never has taken, nor will, nor can, take a sweeter and more attractive form than in Christ's version of it: "Come unto Me, all ye that labour and are heavy laden, and I will give you rest." Friend! that summons comes to us; may we deal with it as the psalmist did!

II. That brings me to note, secondly, the devout soul's response to the loving call from God.

I have already pointed out how beautifully and vividly the contrast between the two is expressed in our text. "Seek ye My face"—"Thy face will I seek." The psalmist takes the general invitation and converts it into an individual one, to which he responds. God's "ye" is met by his "I." The psalmist makes no hesitation or delay—"*When* thou saidst . . . my heart said to Thee." The psalmist gathers himself together in a concentrated resolve of a fixed determination—"Thy face *will* I seek." That is how we ought to respond.

Make the general invitation thy very own. God summons all, because He summons each. He does not cast His invitations out at random over the heads of a crowd, as some rich man might fling coppers into a mob, but He addresses every one of us singly and separately, as if there were not another soul in the universe to hear His voice but our very own selves. It is for us not to lose ourselves in the crowd, since He has not lost us in it; but to appropriate, to individualise, to make our very own, the universality of His call to the world. It matters nothing to you what other men do; it matters nothing to you how many others may be invited, and whether they may accept or may refuse. When that "Seek ye" comes to my heart, life or death depends on my answering, "Whatsoever others may do, as for me, I will seek Thy face." We preachers that have to stand and address a multitude sound out the invitation, and it loses in power, the more there are to listen to us. If I could get you one by one, the poorest words would have more weight with you than the strongest have when spoken to a crowd. Brother, God individualises us, and God speaks to thee, "Wilt thou behold My face?" Answer, "As for me, I will."

Again, the psalmist "made haste, and delayed not, but made haste" to respond to the merciful summons. Ah! how many of us, in how many different ways, fall into the snare "by-and-by"! "not now"; and all these days, that slip away whilst we hesitate, gather themselves together to be our accusers hereafter. Friend, why should you limit the blessedness that may come into your life to the fag end of it when you have got tired and satiated, or tired and disappointed with the world and its good? "Seek ye the Lord while He may be found, call ye upon Him while He is near." It is poor courtesy to show to a merciful invitation from a bountiful host if I say: "After I have looked to the oxen I have bought, and tested them, and measured the field that I have acquired; after I have drunk the sweetness of wedded life with the wife that I have married, then I will come. But, for the present, I pray thee, have me excused." And that is what many are doing, more or less.

The psalmist gathered himself together in a fixed resolve, and said, "I *will*." That is what we have to do. A languid seeker will not find; an earnest one will not fail to find. But if half-heartedly, now and then, when we are at leisure in the intervals of more important and pressing daily business, we spasmodically bethink ourselves, and for a little while seek for the light of God's felt presence to shine upon us, we shall not get it. But if we lay a masterful hand, as we ought to do, on these divergent desires that draw us asunder, and bind ourselves, as it were, together, by the strong cord of a resolved purpose carried out throughout our lives, then we shall certainly not seek in vain.

Alas! how strange and how sad is the reception which this merciful invitation receives from so many of us! Some of you never hear it at all. Standing in the very focus where the sounds converge, you are deaf, as if a man behind the veil of the falling water of Niagara, on that rocky shelf there, should hear nothing. From every corner of the universe that voice comes; from all the providences and events of our lives that voice comes; from the life and death of Jesus Christ that voice comes; and not a sound reaches your ears. "Having ears, they hear not." And some of us might take the psalmist's answer, with one sad word added, as ours—

"When Thou saidst, Seek ye My face, my heart said unto Thee, Thy face, Lord, will I *not* seek."

Brethren, it is heaven on earth to say, "Thou dost call, and I answer. Speak, Lord, for Thy servant heareth." Yet you shut yourselves up to, and with, misery and vanity, if you so deal with God's merciful summons as some of us are dealing with it, so that He has to say, "I called, and ye refused; I stretched out My hand, and no man regarded."

III. Lastly, we have here a prayer built upon both the invitation and the acceptance.

"Hide not Thy face far from me." That prayer implies that God will not contradict Himself. His promises are commandments. If He bids us seek He binds Himself to show. His veracity, His unchangeableness, are pledged to this, that no man who yields to His invitation will be baulked of his desire. He does not hold out the gift in His hand, and then twitch it away when we put out encouraged and stimulated hands to grasp it. You have seen children flashing bright reflections from a mirror on to a wall, and delighting to direct them away to another spot, when a hand has been put out to touch them. That is not how God does. The light that He reveals is steady, and whosoever turns his face to it will be irradiated by its brightness.

The prayer builds itself on the assurance that, because God will not contradict Himself, therefore every heart seeking is sure to issue in a heart finding. There is only one region where that is true, brethren; there is only one tract of human experience in which the promise is always and absolutely fulfilled:—"Ask, and ye shall receive; seek, and ye shall find." We hunt after all other good, and at the best we get it in part or for a time, and, when possessed, it is not as bright as when it shone in the delusive colours of hope and desire. If you follow other good, and are drawn after the elusive lights that dance before you, and only show how great is the darkness, you will not reach them, but will be mired in the bog. If you follow after God's face, it will make a sunshine in the shadiest places of life here. You will be blessed because you walk all the day long in the light of His countenance, and when you pass hence it will irradiate the darkness of death, and thereafter, "His servants shall serve Him, and shall see His face," and, seeing, shall be made like Him, for "His name shall be in their foreheads."

Brethren, we have to make our choice whether we shall see His face here on earth, and so meet it hereafter as that of a long-separated and long-desired friend ; or whether we shall see it first when He is on His throne, and we at His bar, and so shall have to call on the rocks and the hills to fall on us, and cover us from the face of Him who is our judge.

SOUND DOCTRINE OR HEALTHY TEACHING.

"Hold fast the form of sound words, which thou hast heard of me, in faith and love which is in Christ Jesus."—2 TIM. i. 13.

ANY great author or artist passes, in the course of his work, from one manner to another; so that a person familiar with him can date pretty accurately his books or pictures as being in his "earlier" or "later" style. So there is nothing surprising in the fact that there are great differences between Paul's last writings and his previous ones. The surprising thing would have been if there had not been such differences. The peculiarities of the so-called three pastoral Epistles (the two to Timothy, and the one to Titus) are not greater than can fairly be accounted for by advancing years, changed circumstances, and the emergence of new difficulties and enemies.

Amongst them there are certain expressions, very frequent in these letters and wholly unknown in any of Paul's other work. These have been pounced upon as disproving the genuineness of these letters, but they only do so if you assume that a man, when he gets old, must never use any words that he did not use when he was young, whatever new ideas may have come to him. Now, in this text of mine is one of these phrases peculiar to these later letters—" sound words." That phrase and its parallel one, "sound doctrine," occur in all some half-dozen times in these letters, and never anywhere else. The expression has become very common among us. It is more often used than understood; and the popular interpretation of it hides its real meaning and obscures the very important lessons which are to be drawn from the true understanding of it, lessons which, I take leave to think, modern Christianity stands very sorely in need of. I desire now to try to unfold the thoughts and lessons contained in this phrase.

I. What does Paul mean by a "form of sound words"?

I begin the answer by saying that he does not mean a doctrinal formula. The word here rendered "form" is the same which he employs in the first of the letters to Timothy, when he speaks of himself and his own conversion as being "a pattern to them that should hereafter believe." The notion intended here is not a cut-and-dried creed, but a body of teaching which shall not be compressed within the limits of an iron form, but shall be a pattern for the lives of the men to whom it is given. The Revised Version has "the pattern," and not "the form." I take leave to think that there were no creeds in the Apostolic time, and that the Church would probably have had a firmer grasp of God's truth if there had never been any. At all events, the idea of a cast-iron creed, into which the whole magnificence of the Christian faith is crushed, is by no means Paul's idea in the word here. Then, with regard to the other part of the phrase—"sound words"—we all know how that is generally understood by people. Words are supposed to be "sound," when they are in conformity with the creed of the critic. A sound High Churchman is an entirely different person from a sound Nonconformist. Puritan and Sacramentarian differ with regard to the standard which they set up, but they use the word in the same way, to express theological statements in conformity with that standard. And we all know how harshly the judgment is sometimes made, and how easy it is to damn a man by a solemn shake of the head or a shrug of the shoulders, and the question whether he is sound.

Now, all that is clean away from the Apostolic notion of the word in question. If we turn to the other form of this phrase, which occurs frequently in these letters, "sound doctrine," there is another remark to be made. "Doctrine" conveys to the ordinary reader the notion of an abstract, dry, theological statement of some truth. Now, what the Apostle means is not "doctrine" so much as "teaching"; and if you will substitute "teaching" for "doctrine" you will get much nearer his thought; just as you will get nearer it, if, for "sound," with its meaning of conformity to a theological standard, you substitute what the word really means, "healthy," wholesome, health-giving, healing. All these ideas run into each other. That which is in itself healthy is health-giving as food, and as a medicine is healing. The Apostle is not describing the teaching that he had given to Timothy by its conformity with any standard, but is pointing to its essential nature as being wholesome, sound in a physical sense; and to its effect as being healthy and health-giving. Keep hold of that thought and the whole aspect of this saying changes at once.

There is only one other point that I would suggest in

this first part of my sermon, as to the Apostolic meaning of these words, and it is this : " healing " and " holy " are etymologically connected, they tell us. The healing properties of the teaching to which Paul refers are to be found entirely in this—its tendency to make men better, to produce a purer morality, a loftier goodness, a more unselfish love, and so to bring harmony and health into the diseased nature. The one healing for a man is to be holy ; and, says Paul, the way to be holy is to keep a firm hold of that body of teaching which I have presented.

Now, that this tendency to produce nobler manners and purer conduct and holier character is the true meaning of the word " sound " here, and not " orthodox," as we generally take it, will be quite clear, I think, if you will notice how, in another part of these same letters, the Apostle gives a long catalogue of the things which are contrary to the health-giving doctrine. If the ordinary notion of the expression were correct, that catalogue ought to be a list of heresies. But what is it? A black list of vices—" deceivers," " ungodly," " sinners," " unholy," " profane," " murderers," " man-slayers," " whoremongers," " man-stealers," " liars," " perjured " persons. Not one of these refers to aberration of opinion ; all of them point to divergencies of conduct, and these are the things that are contrary to the healing doctrine. But they are not contrary, often, to sound orthodoxy. For there have been a great many imitators of that King of France, who carried little leaden images of saints and the Virgin in his hat and the devil in his heart. " The form of sound words " is the pattern of healing teaching, which proves itself healing because it makes holy. Now, that is my first question answered.

II. Where Paul thought these healing words were to be found.

He had no doubt whatever as to that. They were in the message that he preached of Jesus Christ and His salvation. There and there only, in his estimation and inspired teaching, are such words to be found. The truth of Christ, His incarnation, His sacrifice, His resurrection, His ascension, the gift of His Divine Spirit, with all the mighty truths on which these great facts rest, and all which flow from these great facts, these, in the aggregate, are the health-giving words for the sickly world.

Now, historically, it is proved to be so. I do not need to defend, as if it were in full conformity with the dictates and principles of Christianity, the life and practice of any generation of Christian people. But this I do venture to say, that the world has been slowly lifted, all through the generations, by the influence, direct and indirect, of the great truths of Christianity, and that to-day the very men who, in the name of certain large principles which they have learned from the Gospel, are desirous of brushing aside the old-fashioned Gospel, are kicking down the ladder by which they climbed, and that, with all the imperfections, for which we have to take shame to ourselves before God; still the reflection of the perfect Image which is cast into the world from the mirror of the collective Christian conduct and character, though it be distorted by many a flaw in the glass, and imperfect by reason of many a piece of the reflecting medium having dropped away, is still the fairest embodiment of character that the world has ever seen. Why, what is the meaning of the sarcasms that we have all heard, till we are wearied of them, about "the Nonconformist conscience"? The adjective is wrong; it should be "the *Christian* conscience." But with that correction I claim the sarcasms as unconscious testimony to the fact that the Christian ideal of character and conduct set forth, and approximately realised, by religious people, is far above the average morality of even a so-called Christian nation. And all that is due to the "pattern of health-giving words."

Now, the historical confirmation of Paul's claim that these health-giving words were to be found in his Gospel is no more than is to be expected, if we look at the contents of that Gospel to which he thus appeals. For there never has been such an instrument for regenerating individuals and society as lies in the truths of Christianity, firmly grasped and honestly worked out. Their healing power comes, first, from their giving the sense of pardon and acceptance. Brethren, there is nothing, as I humbly venture to affirm, that will go down to the fountain and origin of all the ills of man, except that teaching "God was in Christ reconciling the world to Himself, not imputing unto them their trespasses." That reality of guilt, that schism and alienation between man and God, must be dealt with first before you can produce high morality. Unless you deal with that central disease you do very little. Something you do; but the cancer is deep-seated, and the world's remedies for it may cure pimples on the surface, but are powerless to extirpate the malignant tumour that has laid hold of the vitals. You must begin by dealing with the disease of sin, not only in its aspect as habit, but in its consequence of guilt and responsibility and separation from God, before you can bring health to the sick man.

And then, beyond that, I need but remind you of how a higher and more wholesome morality is made possible by these health-giving words, inasmuch as they set forth for us the perfect example of Jesus Christ, inasmuch as they bring into operation love, the mightiest of all powers to mould a life, inasmuch as they open up for us, far more solemnly and certainly than ever else has been revealed, the solemn thought of judgment, and of every man giving account of himself to God, and the assurance that "whatsoever a man soweth here, that," a thousand-fold increased in the crop, "shall he also reap" in the eternities. In addition to the example of perfection in the beloved Christ, the mighty motive of love, the solemn urgency of judgment and retribution, the health-giving words bring to us the assurance of a Divine power dwelling within us, to lift us to heights of purity and goodness to which our unaided feet can never, never climb. And for all these reasons the message of Christ's incarnation and death is the health-giving word for the world.

But, further, let me remind you that, according to the Apostolic teaching, these healing and health-giving effects will not be produced except by that Gospel. Some of you, perhaps, may have listened to the first part of my sermon with approbation, because it seemed to fit in with the general disparagement of doctrine prevalent in this day. Will you listen to this part too? I venture to assert that, although there are many men apart from Christ who have as clear a conception of what they ought to be and to do as any Christian, and some men apart from Christ who do aim after high and pure, noble lives, not altogether unsuccessfully, yet on the whole, on the wide scale, and in the long run, if you change the "pattern of health-giving words," you lower the health of the world. It seems to me that this generation is an object-lesson in that matter. Why is it that these two things are running side by side in the literature of these closing years of the century—viz., a rejection of the plain laws of morality, especially in regard of the relations of the sexes, and a rejection of the old-fashioned Gospel of Jesus Christ? I venture to think that the two things stand to each other very largely in the relation of cause and effect, and that, if you want to bring back the world to Puritan morality, you will have to go back in the main to Puritan theology. I do not mean to insist upon any pinning of faith to any theological system, but this I am bound to say, and I beseech you to consider, that if you strike out from the "pattern of health-giving words" the truth of the Incarnation, the sacrifice on the Cross, the Resurrection, the Ascension, and the gift of the Spirit, the "health-giving words," that you have left are not enough to cure a fly.

III. Lastly, notice what Paul would have us do with these "health-giving words."

"Hold the form . . . in faith and love, which is in Christ Jesus."

Now, that exhortation includes three things. Your time will not allow me to do more than just touch them. First it applies to the understanding. " Hold fast the teaching" by letting it occupy your minds. Brethren, I am unwillingly bound to acknowledge my suspicion that a very large number of Christian people scarcely ever occupy their thoughts with the facts and principles of the Gospel, and that they have no firm and intelligent grasp of these, either singly or in their connection. I would plead for less newspaper and more Bible; for less novel and more Gospel. I know how hard it is for busy men to have spare energy for anything beyond their business and the necessary claims of society, but I would even venture to advise a little less of what is called Christian work, in order to get a little more Christian knowledge. "Come ye yourselves apart into a solitary place," said the Master; and all busy workers need that. "Hold fast the health-giving words" by meditation, a lost art among so many Christians.

The exhortation applies next to the heart. "Hold . . . in faith and love." If that notion of the expression, which I have been trying to combat, were the correct one, there would be no need for anything beyond familiarising the understanding with the bearings of the doctrinal truths. But Paul sees need for a great deal more. The understanding brings to the emotions that on which they fasten and feed. Faith—which is more than credence, being an act of the will—casts itself on the truth believed, or rather on the person revealed in the truth; and love, kindled by faith, and flowing out in grateful response and self-abandonment, are as needful as orthodox belief, in order to hold fast the health-giving words.

The exhortation applies, finally, to character and conduct. Emotion, even when it takes the shape of faith and love, is as little the end of God's revelation as is knowledge. He makes Himself known to us in all the greatness of His grace and love in Jesus Christ, not that we may know, and there an end, nor even that knowing, we may feel, and there an end, though a great many emotional Christians seem to think that is all ; but that knowing, we may feel, and knowing and feeling, we may be and do what He would have us do and be. We have the great river flowing past our doors. It is not only intended that we should fill our cisterns by knowledge, nor only bathe our parched lips by faith and love, but that we should use it to drive all the wheels of the mill of life. Not he that understands, nor he that glows, but he that does, is the man that holds fast the pattern of sound, health-giving words.

The world is like that five-porched pool in which were gathered a great multitude of sick folks. Its name is the " House of Mercy," for so Bethesda means, tragically as the title seems to be contradicted by the condition of the cripples and diseased lying there. But this fountain once moved gushes up for ever ; and whosoever will may step into it, and immediately be made whole of whatsoever disease he has.

TRUE GREATNESS.

"He shall be great in the sight of the Lord."—LUKE i. 15.

SO spake the angel who foretold the birth of John the Baptist. "In the sight of the Lord"—then men are not on a dead level in His eyes. Though He is so high and we are so low, the country beneath Him that He looks down upon is not flattened to Him, as it is to us from an elevation, but there are greater and smaller men in His sight, too. No epithet is more misused and misapplied than that of "a great man." It is flung about indiscriminately as ribbons and orders are by some petty State. Every little man that makes a noise for awhile gets it hung round his neck. Think what a set they are that are gathered in the world's Valhalla, and honoured as the world's great men! The mass of people are so much on a level, and that level is so low, that an inch above the average looks gigantic. But the tallest blade of grass gets mown down by the scythe, and withers as quickly as the rest of its green companions, and goes its way into the oven as surely. There is the world's false estimate of greatness and there is God's estimate. If we want to know what the elements of true greatness are, we may well turn to the life of this man, of whom the prophecy went before him that he should be "great in the sight of the Lord." That is gold that will stand the test.

We may remember, too, that Jesus Christ, looking back on the career to which the angel was looking forward, endorsed the prophecy and declared that it had become a fact, and that "of them that were born of woman there had not arisen a greater than John the Baptist." With the illumination of His eulogium we may turn to this life, then, and gather some lessons for our own guidance.

I. First, we note in John unwavering and immovable firmness and courage.

"What went ye out into the wilderness for to see? A reed shaken with the wind?" Nay! an iron pillar that stood firm whatsoever winds blew against it. This, as I take it, is in some true sense the basis of all moral greatness—that a man should have a grip which cannot be loosened, like that of the cuttle-fish with all its tentacles round its prey, upon the truths that dominate his being and make him a hero. "If you want me to weep," said the old artist-poet, "there must be tears in your own eyes." If you want me to believe, you yourself must be aflame with conviction which has penetrated to the very marrow of your bones. And so, as I take it, the first requisite either for power upon others, or for greatness in a man's own development of character, is that there shall be this unwavering firmness of grasp of clearly-apprehended truths, and unflinching boldness of devotion to them.

I need not remind you how magnificently, all through the life of our typical example, this quality was stamped upon every utterance and every act. It reached its climax, no doubt, in his bearding Herod and Herodias. But moral characteristics do not reach a climax unless there has been much underground building to bear the lofty pinnacle; and no man, when great occasions come to him, develops a courage and an unwavering confidence which are strange to his habitual life. There must be the underground building; and there must have been many a fighting down of fears, many a curbing of tremors, many a rebuke of hesitations and doubts in the gaunt, desert-loving prophet, before he was man enough to stand before Herod and say, " It is not lawful for thee to have her."

No doubt there is much to be laid to the account of temperament, but whatever their temperament may be, the way to this unwavering courage, and firm, clear ring of indubitable certainty, is open to every Christian man and woman; and it is their own fault, their own sin, and their own weakness, if they do not possess these qualities. Temperament! What on earth is the good of our religion if it is not to modify and govern our temperament? Has a man a right to jib on one side, and give up the attempt to clear the fence, because he feels that in his own natural disposition there is little power to take the leap? Surely not. Jesus Christ came here for the very purpose of making our weakness strong, and if we have a firm hold upon Him, then, in the measure in which His love has permeated our whole nature, will be our unwavering courage, and out of weakness we shall be made strong.

Of course the highest type of this undaunted boldness and unwavering firmness of conviction is not in John and his like. He presented strength in a lower form than did the Master from whom his strength came. The willow has a beauty as well as the oak. Firmness is not obstinacy ; courage is not rudeness. It is possible to have the iron hand in the velvet glove, not of etiquette-observing politeness, but of a true considerateness and gentleness. They who are likest Him that was "meek and lowly in heart" are surest to possess the unflinching resolve, which set His face like a flint, and enabled Him to go unhesitatingly and unrecalcitrant to the Cross itself.

Do not let us forget, either, that John's unwavering firmness wavered ; that over the clear heaven of his convictions there *did* steal a cloud ; that he from whom no violence could wrench his faith felt it slipping out of his grasp when his muscles were relaxed in the dungeon ; and that he sent "from the prison"—which was the excuse for the message—to ask the question, After all, *art* Thou He that should come ?

Nor let us forget that it was that very moment of tremulousness which Jesus Christ seized, in order to pour an unstinted flood of praise for the firmness of his convictions, on the wavering head of the Forerunner. So, if we feel that though the needle of our compass points true to the pole, yet when the compass-frame is shaken, the needle sometimes vibrates away from its true direction, do not let us be cast down, but believe that a merciful allowance is made for human weakness. This man was great ; first, because he had such dauntless courage and firmness that, over his headless corpse in the dungeon at Machærus, might have been spoken what the Regent Murray said over John Knox's coffin, "Here lies one that never feared the face of man."

II. Another element of true greatness that comes nobly out in the life with which I am dealing is its clear elevation above worldly good.

That was the second point that our Lord's eulogium signalised. "What went ye out into the wilderness for to see? A man clothed in soft raiment?" But you would have gone to a palace, if you had wanted to see that, not to the reed-beds of Jordan. As we all know, in his life, in his dress, in his food, in the aims that he set before him, he rose high above all regard for the debasing and perishable sweetnesses that appeal to flesh, and are ended in time. He lived conspicuously for the Unseen. His asceticism belonged to his age, and was not the highest type of the virtue which it expressed. As I have said about his courage, so I say about his self-denial—Christ's is of a higher sort. As the might of gentleness is greater than the might of such strength as John's, so the asceticism of John is lower than the self-government of the Man that came eating and drinking.

But whilst that is true, I seek, dear brethren, to urge this old threadbare lesson, always needed, never needed more than amidst the senselessly luxurious habits of this generation, needed in few places more than in a great commercial centre like that in which we live, that one indispensable element of true greatness and elevation of character is that, not the prophet and the preacher alone, but every one of us, should live high above these temptations of gross and perishable joys, should

"Scorn delights and live laborious days."

No man has a right to be called "great" if his aims are small. And the question is, not as modern idolatry of intellect, or, still worse, modern idolatry of success, often makes it out to be, has he great capacities? or has he won great prizes? but, has he greatly used himself and his life? If your aims are small you will never be great; and if your highest aims are but to get a good slice of this world's pudding—no matter what powers God may have given you to use—you are essentially a small man.

I remember a vigorous and contemptuous illustration of St. Bernard's, who likens a man that lives for these perishable delights which John spurned, to a spider spinning a web out of his own substance, and catching in it nothing but a wretched prey of poor little flies. Such a one has surely no right to be called a great man. Our aims rather than our capacity determine our character, and they who greatly aspire after the greatest things within the reach of men, which are faith, hope, charity, and who, for the sake of effecting these aspirations, put their heels upon the head of the serpent and suppress the animal in their nature, these are the men "great in the sight of the Lord."

III. Another element of true greatness, taught us by our type, is fiery enthusiasm for righteousness.

You may think that that has little to do with greatness. I believe it has everything to do with it, and that the difference between men is very largely to be found here, whether they flame up into the white heat of enthusiasm for the things that are right, or whether the only things that can kindle them into anything like earnestness and emotion are the poor, shabby things of personal advantage. I need not remind you how, all through John's career, there burnt unflickering and undying that steadfast light; how he brought to the service of the plainest teaching of morality a fervour of passion and of zeal almost unexampled and magnificent. I need not remind you how Jesus Christ Himself laid His hand upon this characteristic, when He said of him that "he was a light kindled and shining." But I would lay upon all our hearts the plain, practical lesson that, if we keep in that tepid region of lukewarmness which is the utmost approach to tropical heat that moral and religious questions are capable of raising in many of us, good-bye to all chance of being "great in the sight of the Lord." "We hear a great deal about the blessings of moderation," the "dangers of fanaticism," and the like. I venture to think that the last thing which the moral consciousness of England wants to-day is a refrigerator, and that what it needs a great deal more than that is, that all Christian people should be brought face to face with this plain truth—that their religion has, as an indispensable part of it, "a spirit of burning," and that if they have not been baptised in fire, there is little reason to believe that they have been baptised with the Holy Ghost.

I long that you and myself may be aflame for goodness, may be enthusiastic over plain morality, and may show that we are so by our daily life, by our rebuking the opposite, if need be, even if it took us into Herod's chamber, and made Herodias our enemy for life.

IV. Lastly, observe the final element of greatness in this man—absolute humility of self-abnegation before Jesus Christ.

There is nothing that I know in biography anywhere more beautiful, more striking, than the contrast between the two halves of the character and demeanour of the

Baptist; how, on the one side, he fronts all men undaunted and recognises no superior, and how neither threats nor flatteries nor anything else will tempt him to step one inch beyond the limitations of which he is aware, nor to abate one inch of the claims which he urges ; and, on the other hand, like some tall cedar, touched by the lightning's hand, he falls prone before Jesus Christ and says, " He must increase, and I must decrease : " " a man can receive nothing except it be given him of God." He is all boldness on one side ; all submission and dependence on the other.

You remember how, in the face of many temptations, that attitude was maintained The very message which he had to carry was full of temptations to a self-seeking man to assert himself. You remember the almost rough "No!" with which, reiteratedly, he met the suggestions of the deputation from Jerusalem, that sought to induce him to say that he was more than he knew himself to be, and how he stuck by that infinitely humble and beautiful saying, "I am a voice" —that is all. You remember how the whole nation was in a kind of conspiracy to tempt him to assert himself, and was ready to break into a flame if he had dropped a spark, for "all men were musing in their heart whether he was the Christ or not," and all the lawless and restless elements would have been only too glad to gather round him, if he had declared himself the Messiah. Remember how his own disciples came to him, and tried to play upon his jealousy and to induce him to assert himself : " Master, He whom thou didst baptize,"—and so didst give Him the first credentials that sent men on His course,—has outstripped thee, and "all men are coming to Him." And you remember the lovely answer that opened such depths of unexpected tenderness in the rough nature : "He that hath the bride is the bridegroom : the friend of the bridegroom heareth the voice ; and that is enough to fill my cup with joy to the very brim."

And what conceptions of Jesus Christ had John, that he thus bowed his lofty crest before Him, and softened his heart into submission almost abject? He knew Him to be the coming Judge, with the fan in His hand, who could baptise with fire, and he knew Him to be "the Lamb of God which taketh away the sin of the world." Therefore he fell before Him.

Brethren, we shall not be "great in the sight of the Lord" unless we copy that example of utter self-abnegation before Jesus Christ. Thomas à Kempis says somewhere, "He is truly great who is small in his own sight, and thinks nothing of the giddy heights of worldly honour." You and I know far more of Jesus Christ than John the Baptist did. Do we bow ourselves before Him as he did? The Source from which he drew his greatness is open to us all.

Let us begin with the recognition of the Lamb of God that takes away the world's sin, and with it ours. Let the thought of what He is, and what He has done for us, bow us in unfeigned submission. Let it shatter all dreams of our own importance or our own desert. The vision of the Lamb of God, and it only, will crush in our hearts the serpent's eggs of self-esteem and self-regard.

Then, let our closeness to Jesus Christ, and our experience of His power, kindle in us the fiery enthusiasm with which He baptises all His true servants, and let it, because we know the sweetnesses that excel, deprive us of all liability to be tempted away by the vulgar and coarse delights of earth and of sense. Let us keep ourselves clear of the babble that is round about us, and be strong because we grasp Christ's hand.

I have been speaking about no characteristic which may not be attained by any man, woman, or child amongst us. "The least in the Kingdom of Heaven" may be greater than John. It is a poor ambition to seek to be *called* " great." It is a noble desire to *be* " great in the sight of the Lord." And if we will keep ourselves close to Jesus Christ that will be attained. It will matter very little what men think of us, if at last we have praise from the lips of Him who poured such praise on His servant. We may, if we will. And then it will not hurt us though our names on earth be dark and our memories perish from among men.

"Of so much fame in heaven expect the meed."

GREATNESS IN THE KINGDOM.

"He that is least in the kingdom of God is greater than he."—
LUKE vii. 28.

WE were speaking in the preceding sermon about the elements of true greatness, as represented in the life and character of John the Baptist. As we remarked then, our Lord poured unstinted eulogium upon the head of John, in the audience of the people, at the very moment when he showed himself weakest. "None born of women" were, in Christ's eyes, "greater than John the Baptist." The eulogium, authoritative as it was, was immediately followed by a depreciation as authoritative, from Christ's lips: "The least in the kingdom is greater than he." Greatness depends, not on character, but on position. The contrast that is drawn is between being *in* and being *out* of the kingdom. And this man, great as he was among them "that are born of women," stood but upon the threshold. Therefore, and only therefore, and in that respect, was he "less than the least" who was safely in.

Now, there are two things to notice by way of introduction, in these great words of the Lord's. One is the calm assumption which He makes of authority to marshal men, to stand above the greatest of them, and to allocate their places, because He knows all about them ; and the other is the equally calm and strange assumption of authority which He makes, in declaring that the least within the kingdom is greater than the greatest without. For the kingdom is embodied in Him, its King, and He claimed to have opened the door of entrance into it. "The Kingdom of God," or of heaven—an old Jewish idea—means, whatever else it means, an order of things in which the will of God is supreme. Jesus Christ says, "I have come to make that real reign of God, in the hearts of men, possible and actual." So He presents Himself in these words as infinitely higher than the greatest within, or the greatest without, the kingdom, and as being Himself the sovereign arbiter of men's claims to greatness. Greater than the greatest is He, the King; for if to be barely across the threshold stamps dignity upon a man, what shall we say of the conception of His own dignity which He formed who declared that He sat on the throne of that kingdom, and was its Monarch?

I. The first thought that I suggest is the greatness of the little ones in the kingdom.

As I have said, our Lord puts the whole emphasis of His classification on men's position. Inside all are great, greater than any that are outside. The least in the one order is greater than the greatest in the other. So, then, the question comes, How does a man step across that threshold? Our Lord evidently means the expression to be synonymous with His true disciples. We may avail ourselves, in considering how men come to be in the kingdom, of His own words. Once He said that unless we *received* it as little children, we should never be *within* it. There the blending of the two metaphors adds force and completeness to the thought. The kingdom is without us, and is offered to us; we must receive it as a gift, and it must come into us before we can be in it. The point of comparison between the recipients of the kingdom and little children does not lie in any sentimental illusions about the innocence of childhood, but in its dependence, in its absence of pretension, in its sense of clinging helplessness, in its instinctive trust. All these things in the child are natural, spontaneous, unreflecting, and therefore of no value. You and I have to think ourselves back to them, and to work ourselves back to them, and to fight ourselves back to them, and to strip off their opposites which gather round us in the course of our busy, effortful life. Then they become worth infinitely more than their instinctive analogues in the infant. The man's absence of pretension and consciousness of helplessness and dependent trust are beautiful and great, and through them the Kingdom of God, with all its lights and glories, pours into his heart, and he himself steps into it, and becomes a true servant and subject of the King.

Then there is another word of the Master's, equally illuminative, as to how we pass into the kingdom, when He said to the somewhat patronising Pharisee that came to talk to Him by night, and condescended to give the young Rabbi a certificate of approval from the Sanhedrim, "We know that Thou art a Teacher come from God." Christ's answer was, in effect, "Knowing will not serve your turn. There is something more than that wanted: 'except a man be born of water, and of the Spirit, he cannot enter into the Kingdom of God.'" So, another condition of entering the kingdom—that is, of coming for myself into the attitude of lowly, glad submission to God's will—is the reception into our natures of a new life-principle, so that we are not only, like the men whom Christ compared with John, "born of women," but by a higher birth are made partakers of a higher life, and born of "the Spirit of God." These are the conditions: on our side the reception with humility, helplessness, dependent trust like those of children; on God's side the imparting, in answer to that dependence and trust, of a higher principle of life;—these are the conditions on which we can pass out of the realm of darkness into the kingdom of the Son of His love.

This being so, then we come to consider the greatness that belongs to the least of those who thus have crossed the threshold, and come to exercise joyous submission to the will of God. The highest dignity of human nature, the loftiest nobility of which it is capable, is to submit to God's will. "Man's chief end is to glorify God." There is nothing that leads life to such sovereign power as when we lay all our will at His feet, and say, "Break, bend, mould, fashion it as Thou wilt." We are in a higher position when we are in God's hand, His tools and the pawns on His board, than we are when we are seeking to govern our lives at our pleasure. Dignity comes from submission, and they who keep God's commandments are the aristocracy of the world.

Then, further, there comes the thought that the greatness that belongs to the least of the little ones within the kingdom springs from their closer relation to the Saviour, whose work they more clearly know and more fully appropriate. It is often said that the Sunday-school child that can repeat the great text, "God so loved the world that He gave His only begotten Son, that whosoever believeth in Him should not perish, but have everlasting life," stands far above prophet, righteous man, and John himself. This is not exactly true, for knowledge of the truth is not what introduces into the kingdom; but it is true that the weakest, the humblest, the most ignorant amongst us, who grasps that truth of the God-sent Son whose death is the world's life, and who lives, therefore, nestling close to Jesus Christ, walks in a light far brighter than the twilight that shone upon the Baptist, or the yet dimmer rays that reached prophets and righteous men of old. It is not a question of character; it is a question of position. True greatness is regulated by closeness to Jesus Christ, and by apprehension and appropriation of His work to myself. The dwarf on the shoulders of the giant sees further than the giant; and "the least in the kingdom," being nearer to Jesus Christ than the men of old could ever be, because possessing the fuller revelation of God in Him, is greater than the greatest without. They who possess, even in germ, that new life-principle, which comes in the measure of a man's faith in Christ, thereby are lifted above saints and martyrs and prophets of old. The humblest Christian grasps a fuller Christ, and therein possesses a fuller spiritual life, than did the ancient heroes of the faith. Christ's classification here says nothing about individual character. It says nothing about the question as to the possession of true religion or of spiritual life by the ancient saints, but it simply declares that because we have a completer revelation, we therefore, grasping that revelation, are in a more blessed

GREATNESS IN THE KINGDOM.

position, "God having provided some better thing for us, that they without us should not be made perfect." The lowest in a higher order is higher than the highest in a lower order. As the geologist digs down through the strata, and, as he marks the introduction of new types, declares that the lowest specimen of the mammalia is higher than the highest preceding of the reptiles or of the birds, so Christ says, " he that is lowest in the Kingdom of Heaven is greater than he."

Brethren, these thoughts should stimulate and should rebuke us that having so much we make so little use of it. We know God more fully, and have mightier motives to serve Him, and larger spiritual helps in serving Him, than had any of the mighty men of old. We have a fuller revelation than Abraham had; have we a tithe of his faith? We have a mightier Captain of the Lord's host with us than stood before Joshua; have we any of his courage? We have a tenderer and fuller revelation of the Father than had psalmists of old; are our aspirations greater after God, whom we know so much better, than were theirs in the twilight of revelation? A savage with a shell and a knife of bone will make delicate carvings that put our workers, with their modern tools, to shame. A Hindoo, weaving in a shed, with bamboos for its walls and palm-leaves for its roof, and a rough loom, the same as his ancestors used three thousand years ago, will turn out muslins that Oldham machinery cannot rival. We are exalted in position, let us see to it that Abraham, and Isaac, and Jacob, and all the saints, do not put us to shame, lest the greatest should become the guiltiest, and exaltation to heaven should lead to dejection to hell.

II. Notice the littleness of the great ones in the kingdom.

Our Lord here recognises the fact that there will be varieties of position, that there will be an outer and an inner court in the Temple, and an aristocracy in the kingdom. " In a great house there are not only vessels of gold and silver, but of wood and of clay." When a man passes into the territory, it still remains an open question how far into the blessed depths of the land he will penetrate. Or, to put away the figure, if as Christian people we have laid hold of Jesus Christ, and in Him have received the kingdom and the new life-power, there still remains the question, how much and how faithfully we shall utilise the gifts, and what place in the earthly experience and manifestation of His kingdom we shall occupy. There are great and small within it.

So it comes to be a very important question for us all, how we may not merely be content, as so many of us are, with having scraped inside and just got both feet across the boundary line, but may become great in the kingdom. Let me answer that question in three sentences. The little ones in Christ's kingdom become great by the continual exercise of the same things which admitted them there at first. If greatness depends on position in reference to Jesus Christ, the closer we come to Him and the more we keep ourselves in loving touch and fellowship with Him, the greater in the kingdom we shall be. Again, the little ones in Christ's kingdom become great by self-forgetting service. " He that will be great among you, let him be your minister." Self-regard dwarfs a man, self-oblivion magnifies him. If ever you come across, even in the walks of daily life, traces in people of thinking much of themselves, and of living mainly for themselves, down go these men in your estimation at once. Whether you have a beam of the same sort in your eye or not, you can see the mote in theirs, and you lower your appreciation of them immediately. It is the same in Christ's kingdom, only in an infinitely loftier fashion. There, to become small is to become great. Again, the little ones in Christ's kingdom become great, not only by cleaving close to the source of all greatness, and deriving thence a higher dignity by the suppression and crucifixion of self-esteem and self-regard, but by continual obedience to their Lord's commandment. As He said in the Sermon on the Mount, "Whoso shall do and teach one of the least of these commandments shall be called great in the Kingdom of Heaven." The higher we are, the more we are bound to punctilious obedience to the smallest injunction. The more we are obedient to the lightest of His commandments, the greater we become. Thus the least in the kingdom may become the greatest there, if only, cleaving close to Christ, he forgets himself, and lives for others, and does the Father's will.

III. Lastly, I travel for a moment beyond my text, and note the perfect greatness of all in the perfected kingdom.

The very notion of a Kingdom of God established in reality, however imperfectly here on earth, demands that somewhere, and some time, and somehow, there should be an adequate, a universal and an eternal manifestation and establishment of it. If, here and now, dotted about over the world, there are men who, with much hindrance and many breaks in their obedience, are still the subjects of that realm, and trying to do the Will of God, unless we are reduced to utter bewilderment intellectually, there must be a region in which that Will shall be perfectly done, shall be continually done, shall be universally done. The obedience that we render to Him, just because it is broken by so much rebellion, slackened by so much indifference, hindered by so many clogs, hampered by so many limitations, points, by its attainments and its imperfections alike, to a region where the clogs and limitations and interruptions shall have all vanished, and the Will of the Lord shall be the life and the light thereof.

So there rises up before us the fair prospect of that heavenly kingdom, in which all that here is interrupted and thwarted tendency shall have become realised effect.

That state must necessarily be a state of continual advance. For if greatness consists in apprehension and appropriation of Christ and His work, there are no limits to the possible expansion and assimilation of a human heart to Him, and the wealth of His glory is absolutely boundless. An infinite Christ to be assimilated, and an indefinite capacity of assimilation in us, make the guarantee that eternity shall see the growing progress of the subjects of the kingdom, in resemblance to the King.

If there is this endless progress, which is the only notion of heaven that clothes with joy and peace the awful thought of unending existence, then there will be degrees there too, and the old distinction of "least" and "greatest" in the kingdom will subsist to the end. The army marches onwards, but they are not all abreast.

They that are in front do not intercept any of the blessings or of the light that come to the rearmost files ; and they that are behind are advancing, and envy not those who lead the march.

Only let us remember, brother, that the distinction of least and great in the kingdom, in its imperfect forms on earth, is carried onwards into the kingdom in its perfect form into heaven. The highest point of our attainment here is the starting-point of our progress yonder. "An entrance shall be ministered ; " it may be " ministered abundantly," or we may be " saved yet so as by fire." Let us see to it that, being least in our own eyes, we belong to the greatest in the kingdom. And, that we may, let us hold fast by the source of all greatness, Christ Himself, and so we shall be launched on a career of growing greatness through the ages of eternity. To be joined to Him is greatness, however small the world may think us. To be separate from Him is to be small, though the hosannas of the world may misname us great.

"THE MATTER OF A DAY IN ITS DAY."

"At all times, as the matter shall require."—1 KINGS viii. 59.

I HAVE ventured to diverge from my usual custom, and take this fragment of a text because, in the forcible language of the original, it carries some very important lessons. The margin of our Bible gives the literal reading of the Hebrew; the sense, but not the vigorous idiom, of which is conveyed in the paraphrase in our version. "At all times, as the matter shall require," is, literally, "the thing of a day in its day"; and that is the only limitation which this prayer of Solomon places upon the petition that God would maintain the cause of His servants and of His people Israel. The kingly suppliant got a glimpse of very great, though very familiar, truths, and at that hour of spiritual illumination, the very high-water mark of his relations to God—for I suppose he was never half as good a man afterwards—he gave utterance to the great thought that God's mercies come to us day by day, according to the exigencies of the moment.

Now, I think in the words "the matter of a day in its day" we may see both a principle in reference to God's gifts and a precept in reference to our actions. Just let us look at these two things.

I. A principle in reference to God's gifts.

Of course, obviously—and I need not say more than a word about that—we find it so in regard to the outward blessings that are poured into our lives. We are taught, if the translation of the New Testament is correct, to ask, " Give us this day our daily bread," and to let to-morrow alone. Life comes to us pulsation by pulsation, breath by breath, by reason of the continual operation, in the material world, of the present God's present giving. He does not start us, at the beginning of our days, with a fund of physical vitality upon which we thereafter draw, but moment by moment He opens His hand, and lets life and breath and all things flow out to us moment by moment, so that no creature would live for an instant except for the present working of a present God. If we only realised how the slow pulsation of the minutes is due to the touch of His finger on the pendulum, and how everything that we have, and the existence of us who have it, are results of the continuous welling out from the fountain of life, of ripple after ripple of the waters, everything would be sacreder, and solemner, and fuller of God than, alas! it is.

But the true region in which we may best find illustrations of this principle in reference to God's gifts is the region of the spiritual and moral bestowments that He in His love pours upon us. He does not flood us with them; He filters them drop by drop, for great and good reasons. I only mention three various forms of this one great thought.

God gives us gifts adapted to the moment. " The matter of a day," the thing fitted for the instant, comes. In deepest reality, it is all one gift, for in truth what

God gives to us is Himself ; or, if you like to put it so, His grace. That little word "grace" is like a small window that opens out on to a great landscape, for it gathers up into one encyclopædical expression the whole infinite variety of beneficences and bestowments which come showering down upon us. That one gift is, as the Apostle puts it in one of his eloquent epithets, "the *manifold* grace of God," which word in the original is even more rich and picturesque, because it means the "many-variegated grace"—like some rich piece of embroidery glowing with all manner of dyes and gold. So the one gift comes to us manifold, rich in its adaptation to, and its exquisite fitness for the needs of the moment. The rabbis had a tradition that the manna in the wilderness tasted to every man just what each man needed or wished most. You might go into some imperial city on a day of rejoicing, and find a fountain in the market-place pouring out, according to the wish of the people, various costly wines and refreshing drinks. God's gift comes to us with like variety— the " matter of the day in its day."

He never gives us the wrong medicine. Whatever variety of circumstances we stand in, there, in that one infinitely simple and yet infinitely complex gift, is what we specially want at the moment. Am I struggling ? He extends a hand to steady me. Am I fighting ? He is my "sword and shield, my buckler, and the horn of my salvation, and my high tower." Am I anxious ? He comes into my heart, and brings with Him a great peace, and all waves cease to toss, and smooth themselves into a level plain. Am I glad ? He comes to heighten the gladness by some touch of holier joy. Am I perplexed in mind? If I look to Him, "His coming shall be as the morning," and illumination will be granted. Am I treading a lonely path? There is One by my side who will neither change, nor fail, nor die. Whatever any man needs, at the moment that he needs it that one great Gift shall supply "the matter of a day in its day."

God gives punctually. Many of us may have sometimes sent Christmas presents to India or Australia some weeks before. Some will arrive in time and some will be too late. God's gifts never reach us before the day, and they never come after the day. "The Lord shall help her, and that right early," said the grand psalm. What the psalmist was thinking about was, I suppose, that miraculous intervention when the army of Sennacherib was smitten in a night. Timid and faithless souls in Jerusalem, as they looked over the walls and saw the encircling lines of the fierce foes drawing closer and closer round the doomed city, must have said, "Our Lord delayeth His coming," and could not stand the test of their faith and patience, involved in God's apparent indifference to the need of His people. To-morrow the assault is to be delivered. To-night "the Angel of Death spread his wings on the blast, And breathed on the face of the foe as he passed"; and the would-be assailants, when that to-morrow dawned, were lying stiff and stark in their tents. God's help comes, not too soon, lest we should not know the blessedness of trusting in the dark; and not too late, lest we should know the misery of trusting in vain.

Peter is lying in prison. Herod intends, after the Passover, to bring him out to the people. The scaffolding is ready. The first watch of the night passes, and the second. If once it is fairly light, escape is impossible. But in the grey dawn the angel touches the sleeper. He wakes while his guards sleep. There is no need for hurry. He who has God for his deliverer has no occasion to " go out with haste." So, with strange and majestic leisureliness, the escaping prisoner is bid to put on his shoes and gird himself. No doubt, he cast many a scrutinising glance at the four sleeping legionaries whom a heedless movement might have wakened. When all is ready, he is led forth through all the wards, each being a separate peril, and all made safe to him. The first gate opens, and the second gate opens, and the iron gate that leads into the city opens, and quietly he and the angel go down the street. It is light enough for him to see his way to the house where the brethren are assembled. He gets safe behind Mary's door before it is light enough for the gaolers to discover his absence, and the pursuers to be started in their search. The Lord did help him, and that right early—" the matter of a day in its day."

We shall find, if we leave our times in His hand, that the old simple faith has yet a talismanic power to quiet us. His time is best, so be patient, and be trustful in your patience.

Again, God gives gifts enough, and not more than enough. He serves out our rations for spirit as for body, as they do on ship-board, where the sailors have to take their pots and plates to the galley every day and every meal, and get enough to help them over the moment's hunger. The manna fell morning by morning. "He that gathered much had nothing over, he that gathered little had no lack." So all the variety of our changeful conditions, besides its purpose of disciplining ourselves and of making character, has also the purpose of affording a theatre for the display, if I may use such cold language—or rather let me say affording an opportunity for the bestowment—of the infinitely varied, exquisitely adapted, punctual, and sufficient grace of God.

II. But now, secondly, a word about the text as containing a precept for our action.

Let me put what I have to say in three plain sentences. First, take short views of the future.

Of course, we have to look ahead, and in reference to many things to take prudent forecasts, but how many of us there are who weaken ourselves and spoil to-day by being "over-exquisite to cast the fashion of uncertain evils!" It is a great piece of practical philosophy, and I am sure it has a great deal to do with our getting the best out of the present moment, that we should either take very short or very long views of the future. Either

"Let the unknown to-morrow
Bring with it what it may,"

or look beyond the last of the days into the unseen light of an unsetting sun. If I must anticipate, let me anticipate the ultimate, the changeless, the certain; and let me not condemn my faculty of picturing that which is to come, to look along the low ranges of earthly life, and torture myself by imagining all the possibilities of evil that my condition admits of, as being turned into certainties to-morrow. Take the matter of a day *in* its day. "Sufficient unto the day is the evil thereof." Let us make the minute what it ought to be; God will make the whole what it ought to be.

Again I say, let us fill each day with discharged duties. If you and I do not do the matter of the day in its day, the chances are that no to-morrow will afford an opportunity of doing it. So there will come upon us all, if we are unfaithful to this portioning out of tasks to times, that burden of an irrevocable past, and of the omitted duties that will stand reproving and condemning before us, whensoever we turn our eyes to them. "It might have been, and it is not"; does a sadder speech than that fall from human lips? Brethren, the day, though it is short, is elastic; and nobody knows how much of discharged service and accomplished tasks and fulfilled responsibilities can be crammed into its hours, until he has earnestly tried to fill each moment with the task which belongs to the moment. "The sluggard will not plough by reason of the cold; therefore shall he beg in harvest and have nothing." If our day is not filled full of work, some to-morrow will be filled full, in retrospect, of thorns and stings. Life is short; the night cometh when no man can work. "I must work the works of Him that sent me while it is day."

Lastly, I would say, keep open a continual communion with God, that day by day you may get what day by day you need. There are hosts of people who call themselves, and, in some kind of surface way, are, Christian people, who seem to think that they get all that they need of the grace of God in a lump, at the beginning of their Christian career, and who are living upon past communications and the memory of these, and are forgetting that they can no more live and be nourished upon past gifts of God's grace than upon the dinner that they ate this day last year. We must hang continually upon Him, if we are continually to receive from His hand. No past blessing will avail for present use.

Dear friends, the purpose of this principle, which I have been trying to illustrate in God's way of dealing with us, is that we shall be content to be continually dependent, and consciously as well as continually dependent, upon Him. In the measure in which we keep our hearts open for the perpetual influx of His grace, in that measure shall we be ready for each day as it comes; for its trials and its joys, for its possibilities and its duties.

This, too, must be remembered—that the days bolted together make months; and the months, years; and the years, life; and that life as a whole is "a day"; and that there is a matter of that day which can only be done in its day. Oh that none of us may be the subjects of that sad wail from a Saviour's heart and a Saviour's lips, which lamented, "If thou hadst known, at least, in this thy day, the things that belong to thy peace; but now"—the night has come, and the darkness of the night and—" they are hid from thine eyes!"

THE FOUNDER AND FINISHER OF THE TEMPLE.

"The hands of Zerubbabel have laid the foundation of this house; his hands shall also finish it."—ZECH. iv. 9.

I AM afraid that Zerubbabel is very little more than a grotesque name to most Bible-readers ; so I may be allowed a word of explanation as to him and as to the original force of my text. He was a prince of the blood royal of Israel, and the civil leader of the first detachment of returning exiles. With Joshua, the high priest, he came, at the head of a little company, to Palestine, and there pathetically attempted with small resources, to build up some humble house that might represent the vanished glories of Solomon's Temple. Political enmity on the part of the surrounding tribes stopped the work for nearly twenty years. During all that time, the hole in the ground where the foundations had been dug, and a few courses of stones laid, gaped desolate, a sad reminder to the feeble band of the failure of their hopes. But with the accession of a new Persian king, new energy sprang up, and new, favourable circumstances developed themselves. The prophet Zechariah came to the front, although quite a young man, and became the mainspring of the renewed activity in building the temple. The words of my text are, of course, in

THE FOUNDER AND FINISHER OF THE TEMPLE. 265

their plain, original meaning, the prophetic assurance that the man, grown an old man by this time, who had been honoured to take the first spadeful of soil out of the earth should be the man "to bring forth the headstone with shoutings of Grace, grace unto it!"

But whilst that is the original application, and whilst the words open to us a little door into long years of constrained suspension of work and discouraged hope, I think we shall not be wrong, if we recognise in them something deeper than a reference to the prince of David's line, concerning whom they were originally spoken. I take them to be, in the true sense of the term, a Messianic prophecy; and I take it that, just because Zerubbabel, a member of that royal house from which the Messiah was to come, was the builder of the temple, he was a prophetic person. What was true about him primarily is thereby shown to have a bearing upon the greater Son of David who was to come thereafter, and who was to build the Temple of the Lord. In that aspect I desire to look at the words now : "His hands have laid the foundation of the house, and His hands shall also finish it."

I. There is, then, here a large truth as to Christ, the true Temple-builder.

It is the same blessed message which was given from His own lips long centuries after, when He spoke from heaven to John in Patmos, and said, "I am Alpha and Omega, the First and the Last." The first letter of the Greek alphabet, and the last letter of the Greek alphabet, and all the letters that lie between, and all the words that you can make out of the letters—they are all from Him, and He underlies everything.

Now that is true about creation, in the broadest and in the most absolute sense. For what does the New Testament say, with the consenting voice of all its writers? "In the beginning was the Word, and the Word was with God, and the Word was God. Without Him was not anything made that was made." His hands laid the foundations of this great house of the universe, with its "many mansions." And what says Paul? "He is the beginning, in Him all things consist"—"that in all things He might have the pre-eminence." And what says He, Himself, from heaven? "I am the First and the Last." So, in regard of everything in the universe, Christ is its origin, and Christ is its goal and its end. He "has laid the foundation, and His hands shall also finish it."

But, further, we turn to the application which is the more usual one, and say that He is the beginner and finisher of the work of redemption, which is His only from its inception to its accomplishment, from the first breaking of the ground for the foundations of the Temple to the triumphant bringing forth of the last stone that crowns the corner and gleams on the topmost pinnacle of the completed structure. There is nothing about Jesus Christ, as it seems to me, more manifest, unless our eyes are blinded by prejudice, than that the Carpenter of Nazareth, who grew up amidst the ordinary conditions of infant manhood, was trained as other Jewish children, increased in wisdom, spoke a language that had been moulded by man, and inherited His nation's mental and spiritual equipment, yet stands forth on the pages of these four Gospels as a perfectly original man, to put it on the lowest ground, and as owing nothing to any predecessor, and not as merely one in a series, or naturally accounted for by reference to His epoch or conditions. He makes a new beginning; He presents a perfectly fresh thing in the history of human nature. Just as His coming was the introduction into the heart of humanity of a new type, the second Adam, the Lord from heaven, so the work that He does is all His own. He does it all Himself, for all that His servants do in carrying out the purposes dear to His heart is done by His working in and through them, and, though we are fellow-labourers with Him, His hands alone lay every stone of the Temple.

Not only does my text, in its highest application, point to Jesus Christ as the author of redemption from its very beginning, but it also declares that all through the ages His hand is at work. "Shall also finish it"—then He is labouring at it now; and we have not to think of a Christ who once worked, and has left to us the task of developing the consequences of His completed activity, but of a Christ who is working on and on, steadily and persistently. The builders of some great edifice, whilst they are laying its lower courses, are down upon our level, and as the building rises the scaffolding rises, and sometimes the platform where they stand is screened off by some frail canvas stretched round it, so that we cannot see them as they ply their work with trowel and mortar. So Christ came down to earth to lay the courses of His Temple that had to rest upon earth, but now the scaffolding is raised and He is working at the top stories. Though out of our sight, He is at work as truly and energetically as He was when He was down here. You remember how strikingly one of the

Evangelists puts that thought in the last words of his Gospel—if, indeed they are his words. "He was received up into heaven, and sat at the right hand of God. They went everywhere, preaching the word." Well, that looks as if there was a sad separation between the Commander and the soldiers that He had ordered to the front, as if He was sitting at ease, on a hill overlooking the battle-field from a safe distance and sending His men to death. But the next words bring Him and them together—"the Lord also working with them, and confirming the word with signs following." And so, brethren, a work begun, continued, and ended by the same immortal hand, is the work on which the redemption of the world depends.

II. Notice, secondly, that we have here the assurance of the triumph of the Gospel.

No doubt, in the long-forgotten days in which my text was spoken, there were plenty of over-prudent calculators in the little band of exiles who said, "What is the use of our trying to build in face of all this opposition and with these poor resources of ours?" They would throw cold water enough on the works of Zerubbabel, and on Zechariah who inspired them. But there came the great word of promise to them, "He shall bring forth the headstone with shoutings." The text is the cure for all such calculations by us Christian people, and by others than Christian people. When we begin to count up resources, and to measure these against the work to be done, there is little wonder if good men and bad men sometimes concur in thinking that the Gospel of Jesus Christ has very little chance of conquering the world. And that is perfectly true,

THE FOUNDER AND FINISHER OF THE TEMPLE. 269

unless you take Him into the calculation, and then the probabilities look altogether different. We are but like a long row of cyphers, but put one significant figure in front of the row of cyphers and it comes to be of value. And so, if you are calculating the probabilities of the success of Christianity in the world and forget to start with Christ, you have left out the principal factor in the problem. Churches lose their fervour, their members die and pass away. He renews and purifies the corrupted Church, and He liveth for ever. Therefore, because we may say, with calm confidence, "His hands have laid the foundation of the house, and His hands are at work on all the courses of it as it rises," we may be perfectly sure that the Temple which He founded, at which He still toils, shall be completed, and not stand a gaunt ruin, looking on which passers-by will mockingly say, "This man began to build and was not able to finish." When Brennus conquered Rome, and the gold for the city's ransom was being weighed, he clashed his sword into the scale to outweigh the gold. Christ's sword is in the scale, and it weighs more than the antagonism of the world and the active hostility of hell. "His hands have laid the foundation; His hands shall also finish it."

III. Still further, here is encouragement for despondent and timid Christians.

Jesus Christ is not going to leave you half way across the bog. That is not His manner of guiding us. He began; He will finish. Remember the words of Paul which catch up this same thought: "Being confident of this very thing, that He which hath begun a good work in you will perfect the same until the day of

Jesus Christ." Brethren, if the seed of the kingdom is in our hearts, though it be but as a grain of mustard seed, be sure of this, that He will watch over it and bless the springing thereof. So, although when we think of ourselves, our own slowness of progress, our own feeble resolutions, our own wayward hearts, our own vacillating wills, our many temptations, our many corruptions, our many follies, we may well say to ourselves, " Will there ever be any greater completeness in this terribly imperfect Christian character of mine than there is to-day?" let us be of good cheer, and not think only of ourselves, but much rather of Him who works on and in and for us. If we lift up our hearts to Him, and keep ourselves near Him, and let Him work, He will work. If we do not—like the demons in the old monastic stories, who every night pulled down the bit of walling that the monks had in the daytime built for their new monastery—by our own hands pull down what He, by His hand, has built up, the structure will rise, and we shall be " builded together for a habitation of God through the Spirit." Be of good cheer, only keep near the Master, and let Him do what He desires to do for us all. God is " faithful who hath called us to the fellowship of His Son," and He also will do it.

IV. Lastly, here is a striking contrast to the fate which attends all human workers.

There are very few of us who even partially seem to be happy enough to begin and finish any task, beyond the small ones of our daily life. Authors die, with half-finished books, with half-finished sentences sometimes, where the pen has been laid down. No man starts an entirely fresh line of action ; he inherits much from his past. No man completes a great work that he undertakes; he leaves it half-finished, and coming generations, if it is one of the great historical works of the world, work out its consequences for good or for evil. The originator has to be contented with setting the thing going and handing on unfinished tasks to his successors. That is the condition under which we live. We have to be contented to do our little bit of work, that will fit in along with that of a great many others, like a chain of men who stand between a river and a burning house, and pass the buckets from end to end. How many hands does it take to make a pin? How many did it take to make the cloth of our dress? The shepherd out in Australia, the packer in Melbourne, the sailors on the ship that brought the wool home, the railway men that took it to Bradford, the spinner, the weaver, the dyer, the finisher, the tailor—they all had a hand in it, and the share of none of them was fit to stand upright by itself, as it were, without something on either side of it to hold it up.

So it is in all our work in the world, and eminently in our Christian work. We have to be contented with being parts of a mighty whole, to do our small piece of service, and not to mind though it cannot be singled out in the completed whole. What does that matter, as long as it is there? The waters of the brook are lost in the river, and it, in turn, in the sea. But each drop is there, though indistinguishable.

Multiplication of joy comes from division of labour. "One soweth and another reapeth," and the result is that there are two to be glad over the harvest instead of one—"that he that soweth and he that reapeth may rejoice together." So it is a good thing that the hands that laid the foundations so seldom are the hands that finish the work; for thereby there are more admitted into the social gladness of the completed results. The navvy that lifted the first spadeful of earth in excavating for the railway line, and the driver of the locomotive over the completed track, are partners in the success and in the joy. The forgotten bishop who, I know not how many centuries ago, laid the foundations of Cologne Cathedral, and the workmen who, a few years since, took down the old crane that had stood for long years on the spire, and completed it to the slender apex, were partners in one work that reaches through the ages.

So let us do our little bit of work, and remember that whilst we do it, He for whom we are doing it is doing it in us, and let us rejoice to know that at the last we shall share in the "joy of our Lord," when He sees of the travail of His soul and is satisfied. Though He builds all Himself, yet He will let us have the joy of feeling that we are labourers together with Him. "Ye are God's building"; but the Builder permits us to share in His task and in His triumph.

PETER'S DELIVERANCE FROM PRISON.

"Peter therefore was kept in prison: but prayer was made earnestly of the Church unto God for him."—ACTS xii. 5.

THE narrative of Peter's miraculous deliverance from prison is full of little vivid touches which can only have come from himself. The whole tone of it reminds us of the Gospel according to St. Mark, which is in like manner stamped with peculiar minuteness and abundance of detail. One remembers that at a late period in the life of the Apostle Paul, Mark and Luke were together with him; and no doubt in those days in Rome, Mark, who had been Peter's special companion and is called by one of the old Christian writers his "interpreter," was busy in telling Luke the details about Peter which appear in the first part of this book of the Acts.

The whole story seems to me to be full of instruction as well as of picturesque detail; and I desire to bring out the various lessons which appear to me to lie in it.

I. The first of them is this; the strength of the helpless.

Look at that eloquent "but" in the verse that I have taken as a starting-point: "Peter therefore was kept in the prison, *but* prayer was made without ceasing of the Church unto God for him." There is another similarly eloquent "but" at the end of the chapter:

"Herod . . . was eaten of worms, and gave up the ghost, *but* the Word of God grew and multiplied." Here you get, on the one hand, all the pompous and elaborate preparations—" four quaternions of soldiers " —four times four is sixteen—sixteen soldiers, two chains, three gates with guards at each of them, Herod's grim determination, the people's malicious expectation of having an execution as a pleasant sensation to wind up the Passover Feast with. And what had the handful of Christian people? Well, they had prayer; and they had Jesus Christ. That was all, and that is more than enough. How ridiculous all the preparation looks when you let the light of that great " but " in upon it! Prayer, " earnest prayer, was made of the Church unto God for him." And evidently, from the place in which that fact is stated, it is intended that we should say to ourselves that it was *because* prayer was made for him that what came to pass did come to pass. It is not jerked out as an unconnected incident; it is set in a logical sequence. " Prayer was made without ceasing of the Church unto God for him"—and so when Herod would have brought him forth, behold, the angel of the Lord came, and the light shined into the prison. It is the same sequence of thought that occurs in that grand theophany in the eighteenth Psalm, " My cry entered into His ears; then the earth shook and trembled; " and there came all the magnificence of the thunderstorm, and the earthquake, and the Divine manifestation; and this was the purpose of it all— " He sent from above, He took me, He drew me out of many waters." The whole energy of the Divine nature is set in motion, and comes swooping down from highest heaven to the trembling earth. And of that fact the one end is one poor man's cry, and the other end is his deliverance. The moving spring of the Divine manifestation was an individual's prayer; the aim of it was the individual's deliverance. A teaspoonful of water is put into a hydraulic ram at one point, and the outcome is the lifting of tons. So the helpless men that can only pray are stronger than Herod and his quaternions and his chains and his gates. "Prayer was made," therefore all that happened was brought to pass, and Peter was delivered.

Peter's companion, James, was killed off, as we read in a verse or two before. Did not the Church pray for him? Surely they did. Why was their prayer not answered, then? God has not any step-children. James was as dear to God as Peter was. One prayer was answered; was the other left unanswered? It was the Divine purpose that Peter, being prayed for, should be delivered; and we may reverently say that, if there had not been the many in Mary's house praying, there would have been no angel in Peter's cell.

So here are revealed the strength of the weak, the armour of the unarmed, the defence of the defenceless. If the Christian Church in its times of persecution and affliction had kept itself to the one weapon that is allowed it, it would have been more conspicuously victorious. And if we, in our individual lives—where, indeed, we have to do something else besides pray—would remember the lesson of that eloquent "but," we should be less frequently brought to perplexity and reduced to something bordering on despair. So my first lesson is the strength of the weak.

II. My next is the delay of deliverance.

Peter had been in prison for some days, at any rate, and the praying had been going on all the while, and there was no answer. Day after day "of the unleavened bread" and of the festival was slipping away. The last night had come ; " and the same night" the light shone, and the angel appeared. Why did Jesus Christ not hear the cry of these poor suppliants sooner ? For their sakes ; for Peter's sake ; for our sakes ; for His own sake. For the eventual intervention, at the very last moment, and yet at a sufficiently early moment, tested faith. And look how beautifully all bore the test. The man that was to be killed to-morrow is lying quietly sleeping in his cell. Not a very comfortable pillow he had to lay his head upon, with a chain on each arm and a legionary on each side of him. But he slept ; and whilst he was asleep Christ was awake, and the brethren were awake. Their faith was tested, and it stood the test, and thereby was strengthened. And Peter's patience and faith, being tested in like manner and in like manner standing the test, were deepened and confirmed. Depend upon it, he was a better man all his days, because he had been brought close up to Death and looked it in the fleshless eye-sockets, unwinking and unterrified. And I daresay if, long after, he had been asked, " Would you not have liked to have escaped those two or three days of suspense, and to have been let go at an earlier moment ? " he would have said, " Not for worlds ! For I learned in those days that my Lord's time is the best. I learned patience "—a lesson which Peter especially needed—" and I learned trust."

Do you remember another incident, singularly parallel

in spirit, though entirely unlike in circumstances, to this one? The two weeping sisters at Bethany send their messenger across the Jordan, grudging every moment that he takes to travel to the far-off spot where Christ is. The message sent is only this: "He whom Thou lovest is sick." What an infinite trust in Christ's heart that form of the message showed! They would not say "Come"; they would not ask Him to do anything; they did not think it was needful; they were quite sure that what He would do would be right.

And how was the message received? "Jesus loved Martha and Mary and Lazarus." Well, did that not make Him hurry as fast as He could to the bedside? No; it rooted Him to the spot. "He abode, *therefore*" —because He loved them—"two days still in the same place where He was," to give him plenty of time to die, and the sisters plenty of time to test their confidence in Him. Their confidence does not seem to have stood the test altogether. "Lord, if Thou hadst been here my brother had not died." "And why wast Thou *not* here?" is implied. Christ's time was the best time. It was better to get a dead brother back to their arms and to their house than that they should never have lost him for those dreary four days. So delay tests faith, and makes the deliverance, when it comes, not only the sweeter, but the more conspicuously Divine. So, brother, "men ought always to pray, and not to faint"—always to trust that "the Lord will help them, and that right early."

III. The next lesson that I would suggest is the leisureliness of the deliverance.

A prisoner escaping might be glad to make a bolt for

it, dressed or undressed, anyhow. But when the angel comes into the cell, and the light shines, look how slowly and, as I say, leisurely, he goes about it. "Put on thy shoes." He had taken them off, with his girdle and his upper garment, that he might lie the less uncomfortably. " Put on thy shoes ; lace them ; make them all right. Never mind about these two legionaries ; they will not wake. Gird thyself ; tighten thy girdle. Put on thy garment. Do not be afraid. Do not be in a hurry; there is plenty of time. Now, are you ready? Come." Now it would have been as easy for the angel to have whisked him out of the cell and put him down at Mary's door ; but that was not to be the way. Peter was led past all the obstacles—" the first ward," and the soldiers at it; " the second ward," and the soldiers at *it* ; " and the third gate that leads into the city," which was no doubt bolted and barred. There was a leisurely procession through the prison.

Why? Because Omnipotence is never in a hurry, and God, not only in His judgments but in His mercies, very often works slowly, as becomes His majesty. " Ye shall not go out with haste ; nor go by flight, for the Lord will go before you ; and the God of Israel shall be your rereward." We are impatient, and hurry our work over ; God works slowly ; for He works certainly. That is the law of the Divine working in all regions ; and we have to regulate the pace of our eager expectation so as to fall in with the slow, solemn march of the Divine purposes, both in regard to our individual salvation and the providences that affect us individually, and in regard to the world's deliverance from the world's evils. " An inheritance may be gotten hastily in the beginning, but the end thereof shall not be blessed." "He that believeth shall not make haste."

IV. We see here, too, the delivered prisoner left to act for himself as soon as possible.

As long as the angel was with Peter, he was dazed and amazed. He did not know—and small blame to him—whether he was sleeping or waking; but he gets through the gates, and out into the empty street, glimmering in the morning twilight, and the angel disappears, and the slumbering city is lying around him. When he is *left* to himself, he *comes* to himself. He could not have passed the wards without a miracle, but he can find his way to Mary's house without one. He needed the angel to bring him as far as the gate and down into the street, but he did not need him any longer. So the angel vanished into the morning light, and then he felt himself, and steadied himself, when responsibility came to him. That is the thing to sober a man. So he stood in the middle of the unpeopled street, and "he considered the thing," and found in his own wits sufficient guidance, so that he did not miss the angel. He said to himself "I will go to Mary's house." Probably he did not know that there was any one praying there, but it was near, and it was, no doubt, convenient in other respects that we do not know of. The economy of miraculous power is a remarkable feature in Scriptural miracles. God never does anything for us that we could do for ourselves. Not but that our doing for ourselves is, in a deeper sense, His working on us and in us, but He desires us to take the share that belongs to us in completing the deliverance which must begin by supernatural intervention of a Mightier than the angel, even the Lord of angels.

And so this little picture of the angel leading Peter through the prison, and then leaving him to his own common-sense and courage as soon as he came out into the street, is just a practical illustration of the great text, "Work out your own salvation with fear and trembling, for it is God that worketh in you."

V. Now the last lesson is the unbelieving astonishment of the believing men who pray, at the answer to their prayer.

They "prayed earnestly"; and when Rhoda, with fine feminine illogicalness, was *so* glad that she left Peter standing out there in the street, in danger of falling into the hands of Herod's men, in order to tell the wonderful story that he was there, the brethren, when they heard her outpoured narrative, did not believe that their prayer had been answered. They were prepared rather to believe either of two far more unlikely alternatives than to accept the fact that their cry had been heard. In the first place, rather than suppose that it had, they were ready to think that the poor child was mad; and then, when that notion was disposed of, they hit on the other hypothesis : " It is his angel." A great many of us have a touch of unbelief in our most earnest petitions, and would be surprised at nothing so much as that the answer should stand there before us.

Then come two more of Luke's vivid touches ; " Peter continued knocking." No wonder ; it was like him, and it was very warrantable in the circumstances, that he should persist in hammering at the door, whilst they were discussing inside whether he was there or not.

And then it dawned upon some of them that perhaps the best way to settle the debate would be to open the door and see. But this time they do not send Rhoda—perhaps she was too frightened to go back—so we read "*they* opened the door." The whole body of them seem to have flocked out to keep each other in company and courage. "They opened the door, and they were"—what? "Astonished." Then they all began, in Eastern fashion, to talk at once; so Peter "beckoned with his hand to them" to be quiet and did away with the astonishment; for "he told them how the Lord had delivered him."

Well, do not let us pray like them, with unbelief streaking our earnestness and faith. Expect an answer to your prayer; and do not be surprised when it comes, and do not be ready to adopt any hypothesis, however ridiculous, rather than the plain, Christian one that God has answered your prayer.

"Lord, I believe, help Thou mine unbelief!" said another man, whose prayer was a strange mixture of faith and distrust; and Christ helped him. But we are more sure to be helped and to get the answer, if we do not doubt, but believe in our hearts that when we stand praying, we receive the things that we ask, and then we shall have them.

A PAIR OF FRIENDS.

"Can two walk together, except they be agreed?"—AMOS. iii. 3.

THEY do not need to be agreed about everything. They must, however, wish to keep each other's company, and they must be going by the same road to the same place. The application of the parable is very plain, though there are differences of opinion as to the bearing of the whole context, which need not concern us now. The "two" whom the prophet would fain see walking together are God and Israel, and his question suggests not only the companionship and communion with God, which are the highest form of religion and the aim of all forms and ceremonies of worship, but also the inexorable condition on which alone that height of communion can be secured and sustained. Two *may* walk together, though the one be God in heaven and the other be I in England. But they have to be agreed thus far, at any rate, that both shall wish to be together, and both be going the same road.

I. So I ask you to look, first, at that possible blessed companionship which may cheer a life.

There are three phrases in the Old Testament, very like each other, and yet presenting different facets or aspects of the same great truth. Sometimes we read about "walking before God," as Abraham was bid to do. That means ordering the daily life under the continual sense that we are "ever in the great Taskmaster's eye." Then there is "walking after God," and that means conforming the will and active efforts to the rule that He has laid down, setting our steps firm on the paths that He has prepared that we should walk in them, and accepting His providences. But also, high above both these conceptions of a devout life is the one which is suggested by my text, and which, as you remember, was realised in the case of the patriarch Enoch—walking "with God." For to walk before Him may have with it some tremor, and may be undertaken in the spirit of the slave, who would be glad to get away from the jealous eye that rebukes his slothfulness ; and "walking after Him" may be a painful and partial effort to keep His distant figure in sight; but to "walk with Him" implies a constant, quiet sense of His Divine presence which forbids that I should ever be lonely, which guides and defends, which floods my soul and fills my life, and in which, as the companions pace along side by side, words may be spoken by either, or blessed silence may be eloquent of perfect trust and rest.

But, dear brother, far above us as such experience seems to sound, such a life is a possibility for every one of us. We *may* be able to say, as truly as our Lord said it, " I am not alone, for the Father is with me." It is possible that the dreariest solitude of a soul, such as is not realised when the body is removed from men, but is felt most in the crowded city, where there is none that loves or fathoms and sympathises, may be turned into blessed fellowship with Him. Yes, but that solitude will not be so turned unless it is first painfully felt. As Daniel said, "I was left alone, and I saw the great vision." We need to feel in our deepest hearts that loneliness on earth before we walk with God.

If we are so walking, it is no piece of fanaticism to say that there will be mutual communications. Do you not believe that God knows His way into the spirits that He has endowed with conscious life? Do you believe that He speaks now to people as truly as He did to prophets and Apostles of old—as truly; though the results of His speech to us of to-day be not of the same authority for others, as the words that He spoke to a Paul or a John. The belief in God's communications as for ever sounding in the depths of the Christian spirit does not at all obliterate the distinction between the kind of inspiration which produced the New Testament and that which is realised by all believing and obedient souls. High above all our experience of hearing the words of God in our hearts stands that of those holy men of old who heard God's message whispered in their ears, that they might proclaim it on the house tops to all the world through all generations. But, though they and we are on a different level and God spoke to them for a different purpose, He speaks in our spirits, if we will comply with the conditions, as truly as He did in theirs. As really as it was ever true that the Lord spoke unto Abraham, or Isaiah, or Paul, it is true that He now speaks to the man that walks with Him. Frank speech on both sides beguiles many a weary mile, when lovers or friends foot it side by side; and this pair of friends, of whom our text speaks, have mutual intercourse. God speaks with His servant now, as of old, "as a man speaketh with his friend"; and we on our parts, if we are truly walking with Him, shall feel it natural to speak frankly to God. As two friends on the road will interchange remarks about trifles, and, if they love each other, the remarks about the trifles will be weighted with love, so we can tell our smallest affairs to God; and, if we have Him for our Pilgrim-Companion, we do not need to lock up any troubles or concerns of any sort, big or little, in our hearts, but may speak them all to our Friend who goes with us.

The two *may* walk together. That is the end of all religion. What are creeds for? What are services and sacraments for? What is theology for? What is Christ's redeeming act for? All culminate in this true, constant fellowship between men and God. And unless, in some measure, that result is arrived at in our cases, our religion, let it be as orthodox as you like; our faith in the redemption of Jesus Christ, let it be as real as you will; our attendances on services and sacraments, let them be as punctilious and regular as may be, are all "sounding brass and tinkling cymbal." Get side by side with God. That is the purpose of all these, and fellowship with Him is the climax of all religion.

It is also the secret of all blessedness, the only thing that will make a life absolutely sovereign over sorrow, and fixedly unperturbed by all tempests, and invulnerable to all "the slings and arrows of outrageous fortune." Hold fast by God, and you have an amulet against every evil, and a shield against every foe, and a mighty power that will calm and satisfy your whole being. Nothing else, nothing else will do so. As Augustine said, "O God! Thou hast made us for Thyself, and in Thyself only are we at rest." If the Shepherd is with us we will fear no evil.

II. Now, a word, in the next place, as to the sadly incomplete reality, in much Christian experience, which contrasts with this possibility.

I am afraid that very, very few so-called Christian people habitually feel, as they might do, the depth and blessedness of this communion. And sure I am that only a very small percentage of us have anything like the continuity of companionship which my text suggests as possible. There may be, and therefore there should be, running unbroken through a Christian life one long, bright line of communion with God and happy inspiration from the sense of His presence with us. Is it a line in *my* life, or is there but a dot here, and a dot there, and long breaks between? The long embarrassed pauses in a conversation between two who do not know much of, or care much for, each other are only too like what occurs in many professing Christians' intercourse with God. Their communion is like those time-worn inscriptions that archæologists dig up, with a word clearly cut and then a great gap, and then a letter or two, and then another gap, and then a little bit more legible, and then the stone broken, and all the rest gone. Did you ever read the meteorological reports in the newspapers and observe a record like this, "Twenty minutes' sunshine out of a possible eight hours"? Do you not think that such a state of affairs is a little like the experience of a great many Christian people in regard to their communion with God? It is broken at the best, and imperfect at the completest, and shallow at the deepest. Oh, dear brethren, rise to the height of your possibilities, and live as close to God as He lets you live, and nothing will much trouble you.

III. And now, lastly, a word about the simple explanation of the failure to realise this continual presence.

"Can two walk together except they be agreed?" Certainly not. Our fathers, in a sterner and more religious age than ours, used to be greatly troubled how to account for a state of Christian experience, which they supposed to be due to God's withdrawing of the sense of His presence from His children. Whether there is any such withdrawal or not, I am quite certain that that is not the cause of the interrupted communion between God and the average Christian man. I make all allowance for the ups and downs, and changing moods which necessarily affect us, in this present life, and I make all allowances, too, for the pressure of imperative duties and distracting cares which interfere with our communion, though, if we were as strong as we might be, they would not wile us away from, but drive us to, our Father in heaven.

But when all such allowances have been made, I come back to my text as *the* explanation of interrupted communion. The two are *not* agreed; and that is why they are not walking together. The consciousness of God's presence with us is a very delicate thing. It is like a very sensitive thermometer, which will drop when an iceberg is a league off over the sea, and scarcely visible. We do not wish His company, or we are not in harmony with His thoughts, or we are not going His road, and therefore, of course, we part. At bottom there is only one thing that separates a soul from God, and that is sin—sin of some sort, like tiny grains of dust that get between two polished plates in an engine, that ought to move smoothly and closely against each other. The obstruction may be invisible, and yet be powerful enough to cause friction, which hinders the working of the engine and throws everything out of gear. A light cloud that we cannot see may come between us and a star, and we shall only know it is there, because the star is *not* visibly there. Similarly, many a Christian, quite unconsciously, has something or other in his habits, or in his conduct, or in his affections, which would reveal itself to him, if he would look, as being wrong, because it blots out God.

Let us remember that very little divergence will, if the two paths are prolonged far enough, part their other ends by a world. Our way may go off from the ways of the Lord at a very acute angle. There may be scarcely any consciousness of parting company at the beginning. Let the man travel on upon it far enough, and the two will be so far apart that he cannot see God or hear Him speak. Take care of the little divergencies which are habitual, for their accumulated results will be complete separation. There must be absolute surrender if there is to be uninterrupted fellowship.

Such, then, is the direction in which we are to look for the reasons for our low and broken experiences of communion with God. Oh, dear friends, when we do as we sometimes do, wake with a start, like a child that all at once starts from sleep and finds that its mother is gone—when we wake with a start to feel that we are alone, then do not let us be afraid to go straight back. Only be sure that we leave behind us the sin that parted us.

You remember how Peter signalised himself on the lake, on the occasion of the second miraculous draught of fishes, when he floundered through the water and clasped Christ's feet. He did not say then, "Depart from me, for I am a sinful man, O Lord!" He had said that before on a similar occasion, when he felt his sin less, but now he knew that the best place for the denier was with his head on Christ's bosom.

So, if we have parted from our Friend, there should be no time lost ere we go back. May it be true of us that we walk with God, so that at last the great promise may be fulfilled about us, " that we shall walk with Him in white," being by His love accounted " worthy," and so " follow," and keep company with, " the Lamb whithersoever He goeth!"

A SOLDIER'S SHOES.

"Your feet shod with the preparation of the gospel of peace."—
EPHESIANS vi. 15.

PAUL drew the first draft of this picture of the Christian armour in his first letter. It is a finished picture here. One can fancy that the Roman soldier to whom he was chained in his captivity, whilst this letter was being written, unconsciously sat for his likeness, and that each piece of his accoutrements was seized in succession by the Apostle's imagination and turned to a Christian use. It is worth noticing that there is only one offensive weapon mentioned—"the sword of the Spirit." All the rest are defensive: helmet, breastplate, shield, girdle, and shoes. That is to say—the main part of our warfare consists in defence, in resistance, and in keeping what we have, in spite of everybody, men and devils, who attempt to take it from us. "Hold fast that thou hast; let no man take thy crown."

Now, it seems to me that the ordinary reader does not quite grasp the meaning of our text, and that it would be more intelligible if, instead of "preparation," which means the process of getting a thing ready, we read "preparedness," which means the state of mind of the man who is ready. Then we have to notice that the little word "of" does duty to express two different relations, in the two instances of its use here. In the first case—"the preparedness of the Gospel"—it states the origin of the thing in question. That condition of being ready comes from the good news of Christ. In the second case—"the Gospel of peace"—it states the result of the thing in question. The good news of Christ gives peace. So, taking the whole clause, we may paraphrase it by saying that the preparedness of spirit, the alacrity which comes from the possession of a Gospel that sheds a calm over the heart and brings a man into peace with God, is what the Apostle thinks is like the heavy hob-nailed boots that the legionaries wore, by which they could stand firm, whatever came against them.

I. The first thing that I would notice here is that the Gospel brings peace.

I suppose that there was ringing in Paul's head some echoes of the music of Isaiah's words, "How beautiful upon the mountains are the feet of Him that bringeth good tidings, that publisheth peace, that bringeth good tidings of good!" But there is a great deal more than an unconscious quotation of ancient words here. For in Paul's thought, the one power which brings a man into harmony with the universe and peace with himself, is the power which proclaims that God is at peace with him. And Jesus Christ is our peace, because He has swept away the root and bitter fountain of all the disquiet of men's hearts, and all their chafing at providences—the consciousness that there is discord between themselves and God. The Gospel brings peace in the deepest sense of that word, and, primarily, peace with God, from out of which all other kinds of tranquillity and heart-repose do come—and they come from nothing besides.

But what strikes me most here is not so much the allusion to the blessed truth that was believed and experienced by these Ephesian Christians, that the Gospel brought peace, and was the only thing that did, as the singular emergence of that idea that the Gospel was a peace-bringing power, in the midst of this picture of fighting. Yes, it brings both. It brings us peace first, and then it says to us, "Now, having got peace in your heart, because peace with God, go out and fight to keep it." For, if we are warring with the devil we are at peace with God; and if we are at peace with the devil we are warring with God. So the two states of peace and war go together. There is no real peace which has not conflict in it, and the Gospel *is* "the Gospel of peace," precisely because it enlists us in Christ's army and sends us out to fight Christ's battles.

So, then, dear brother, the only way to realise and preserve " the peace of God which passes understanding " is to fling ourselves manfully into the fight to which all Christ's soldiers are pledged and bound. The two conditions, though they seem to be opposite, will unite ; for this is the paradox of the Christian life, that in all regions it makes compatible apparently incompatible and contradictory emotions. " As sorrowful "—and Paul might have said " therefore " instead of " yet "—" as sorrowful yet always rejoicing ; as having nothing yet " —therefore—" possessing all things " ; as in the thick of the fight, and yet kept in perfect peace, because the soul is stayed on God. The peace that comes from friendship with Him, the peace that fills a heart tranquil because satisfied, the peace that soothes a conscience emptied of all poison and robbed of all its sting, the peace that abides because, on all the horizon in front of us nothing can be seen that we need to be afraid of—that peace is the peace which the Gospel brings, and it is realised in warfare and is consistent with it. All the armies of the world may camp round the fortress, and the hurtling noise of battle may be loud in the plains, but up upon the impregnable cliff crowned by its battlements there is a central citadel, with a chapel in the heart of it; and to the worshippers there none of the noise ever penetrates. The Gospel which laps us in peace and puts it in our hearts makes us soldiers.

II. Further, this Gospel of peace will prepare us for the march.

A wise general looks after his soldiers' boots. If they give out, nothing else is of much use. The roads are very rough and very long, and there need to be strong soles and well-sewed uppers, and they will be none the worse for a bit of iron on the heels and the toes, in order that they may not wear out in the midst of the campaign. "Thy shoes shall be iron and brass," and these metals are harder than any of the rock that you will have to clamber over. Which being translated into plain fact is just this—a tranquil heart in amity with God is ready for all the road, is likely to make progress, and is fit for anything that it may be called to do.

A calm heart makes a light foot; and he who is living at peace with God, and with all disturbance within hushed to rest, will, for one thing, be able to see what his duty is. He will see his way as far as is needful for the moment. That is more than a good many of us can do, when our eyes get confused, because our hearts are beating so loudly and fast, and our own wishes come in to hide from us God's will. But if we are weaned from ourselves, as we shall be if we are living in possession of the peace of God which passes understanding, the atmosphere will be transparent, as it is on some of the calm last days of autumn, and we shall see far ahead and know where we ought to go.

The quiet heart will be able to fling its whole strength into its work. And that is what troubled hearts never can do, for half their energy is taken up in steadying or quieting themselves, or is dissipated in going after a hundred other things. But when we are wholly engaged in quiet fellowship with Jesus Christ, we have the whole of our energies at our command, and can fling ourselves wholly into our work for Him. The steam-engine is said to be a very imperfect machine, which wastes more power than it utilises. That is true of a great many Christian people; they have the power, but they are so far away from that deep sense of tranquillity with God, of which my text speaks, that they waste much of the power that they have. And if we are to have for our motto "Always Ready," as an old Scottish family has, the only way to secure that is by having "our feet shod with the preparedness" that comes from the Gospel that brings us peace. Brethren, duty that is done reluctantly, with hesitation, is not done. We must fling ourselves into the work gladly, and be always "ready for all Thy perfect will."

There was an English commander, who died some years ago, who was sent for to the Horse Guards one day and asked, "How long will it take for you to be ready to go to Scinde?" "Half an hour," said he; and in three-quarters he was in the train, on his road to reconquer a kingdom. That is how we ought to be; but we never shall be, unless we live habitually in tranquil communion with God, and in the full faith that we are at peace with Him through the blood of His Son. A quiet heart makes us ready for duty.

III. Again, the Gospel of peace prepares us for combat.

In ancient warfare, battles were lost or won very largely according to the weight of the masses of men that were hurled against each other; and the heavier men, with the firmer footing, were likely to be the victors. Our modern scientific way of fighting is different from that. But in the old time, the one thing needful was that a man should stand firm and resist the shock of the enemy, as they rushed upon him. Unless our footing is good we shall be tumbled over by the onset of some unexpected antagonist. And for good footing there are two things necessary. One is a good, solid piece of ground to stand on, that is not slippery nor muddy, and the other is a good strong pair of soldier's boots, that will take hold on the ground and help the wearer to steady himself. Christ has set our feet on the rock, and so the first requisite is secured. If we, for our part, will keep near to that Gospel which brings peace into our hearts, the peace that it brings will make us able to stand, and bear unmoved any force that may be hurled against us. If we are to be "steadfast, unmovable," we can only be so when our feet are shod with the preparedness of the Gospel of peace.

The most of your temptations, most of the things that would pluck you away from Jesus Christ, and upset you in your standing, will come down upon you unexpectedly. Nothing happens in this world except the unexpected; and it is the sudden assaults, that we were not looking for, that work most disastrously against us. A man may be aware of some special weakness in his character, and have given himself carefully and patiently to try to fortify himself against it, and, lo! all at once a temptation springs up from the opposite side; the enemy was lying in hiding there, and whilst his face was turned to fight with one foe, a foe that he knew nothing about came storming behind him. There is only one way to stand, and that is not merely by cultivating careful watchfulness against our own weaknesses, but by keeping fast hold of Jesus Christ manifested to us in His Gospel. Then the peace that comes from that communion will itself guard us. You remember what Paul says in one of his other letters, where he has the same beautiful blending together of the two ideas of peace and warfare: "The peace of God, which passeth all understanding, shall garrison your hearts and minds in Christ Jesus." It will be, as it were, an armed force within your heart which will repel all antagonism, and will enable you to abide in that Christ, through whom and in whom alone all peace comes. So, because we are thus liable to be overwhelmed by a sudden rush of unexpected temptation, and surprised into a sin before we know where we are, let us keep fast hold by that Gospel which brings peace, which will give us steadfastness, however suddenly the masked battery may begin to play upon us, and the foe may steal out of his ambush and make a rush against our unprotectedness. That is the only way, as I think, by which we can walk scatheless through the world.

Now, dear brethren, remember that this text is part of a commandment. We are to put on the shoes. How is that to be done? By a very simple way: a way which, I am afraid, a great many Christian people do not practise with anything like the constancy that they ought. For it is the Gospel that brings the peace, and if its peace brings the preparedness, then the way to get the preparedness is by soaking our minds and hearts in the Gospel of Jesus Christ.

You hear a good deal nowadays about deepening the spiritual life, and people hold conventions for the purpose. All right; I have not a word to say against that. But, conventions or no conventions, there is only one thing that deepens the spiritual life, and that is keeping near the Christ from whom all the fulness of the spiritual life flows. If we will hold fast by our Gospel, and let its peace lie upon our minds, as the negative of a photograph lies upon the paper that it is to be printed upon, until the image of Jesus Christ Himself is reproduced in us, then we may laugh at temptation. For there will be no temptation when the heart is full of Him, and there will be no sense of surrendering anything that we wish to keep when the superior sweetness of His grace fills our souls. It is empty vessels into which poison can be poured. If the vessel is full there will be no room for it. Get your hearts and minds filled with the wine of the kingdom, and the devil's venom of temptation will have no space to get in. It is well to resist temptation; it is better to be lifted above it, so that it ceases to tempt. And the one way to secure that is to live near Jesus Christ, and let the Gospel of His grace take up more of our thoughts and more of our affections than it has done in the past. Then we shall realise the fulfilment of the promise : " He will not suffer thy foot to be moved."

A LIFE LOST AND FOUND.*

"He that loseth his life for My sake shall find it."—MATT. x. 39.

MY heart impels me to break this morning my usual rule of avoiding personal references in the pulpit. Death has been busy in our own congregation this last week, and yesterday we laid in the grave all that was mortal of a man to whom Manchester owes more than it knows.

Mr. Crossley has been for thirty years my close and dear friend. He was long a member of this church and congregation. I need not speak of his utter unselfishness, of his lifelong consecration, of his lavish generosity, of his unstinted work for God and man; but thinking of him and of it, I have felt as if the words of my text were the secret of his life, and as if he now understood the fulness of the promise they contain: "He that loseth his life for My sake shall find it."

Now, looking at these words in the light of the example so tenderly beloved by some of us, so sharply criticised by many, but now so fully recognised as saintly by all, I ask you to consider

I. The stringent requirement for the Christian life that is here made.

Now we shall very much impoverish the meaning and narrow the sweep of these great and penetrating

* Preached after the funeral of Mr. F.W. Crossley.

words, if we understand by "losing one's life" only the actual surrender of physical existence. It is not only the martyr on whose bleeding brows the crown of life is gently placed; it is not only the temples that have been torn by the crown of thorns, that are soothed by that unfading wreath; but there is a daily dying, which is continually required from all Christian people, and is, perhaps, as hard as, or harder than, the brief and bloody passage of martyrdom, by which some enter into rest. For the true losing of life is the slaying of self, and that has to be done day by day, and not once for all, in some supreme act of surrender at the end, or in some initial act of submission and yielding at the beginning, of the Christian life. We ourselves have to take the knife into our own hands and strike, and that not once, but ever, right on through our whole career. For, by natural disposition, we are all inclined to make our own selves, our own centres, our own aims, the objects of our trust, our own law; and if we do so, we are dead whilst we live, and the death that brings life is when, day by day, we crucify the old man with his affections and lusts. Crucifixion was no sudden death; it was an exquisitely painful one, which made every nerve quiver and the whole frame thrill with anguish; and that slow agony, in all its terribleness and protractedness, is the image that is set before us, as the true ideal of every life that would not be a living death. The world is to be crucified to me, and I to the world.

We have our centre in ourselves, and we need the centre to be shifted, or we live in sin. If I might venture upon so violent an image, the comets that career about the heavens need to be caught and tamed, and bound to peaceful revolution round some central sun, or else they are "wandering stars to whom is reserved the blackness of darkness for ever." So, brethren, the slaying of self by a painful, protracted process, is the requirement of Christ.

But do not let us confine ourselves to generalities. What is meant? This is meant—the absolute submission of the will to commandments and providences, the making of that obstinate part of our nature meek and obedient and plastic as the clay in the potter's hands. The tanner takes a stiff hide, and soaks it in bitter waters, and dresses it with sharp tools, and lubricates it with unguents, and his work is not done till all the stiffness is out of it and it is flexible. And we do not lose our lives, in the lofty, noble sense, until we can say—and verify the speech by our actions—"Not my will but Thine be done." They who thus submit, they who thus welcome into their hearts, and enthrone upon the sovereign seat in their wills, Christ and His will—these are they who have lost their lives. When we can say, "I live, yet not I, but Christ liveth in me," then, and only then, have we in the deepest sense of the words "lost our lives."

The phrase means the suppression, and sometimes the excision, of appetites, passions, desires, inclinations. It means the hallowing of all aims; it means the devotion and the consecration of all activities. It means the surrender and the stewardship of all possessions. And only then, when we have done these things, shall we have come to practical obedience to the initial requirement that Christ makes from us all—to lose our lives for His sake.

I need not diverge here to point to that life from which my thoughts have taken their start this morning. Surely if there was any one characteristic in it more distinct and lovely than another, it was that self was dead and that Christ lived. There may be sometimes a call for the actual—which is the lesser surrender—of the bodily life, in obedience to the call of duty. There have been Christian men who have wrought themselves to death in the Master's service. Perhaps he of whom I have been speaking was one of these. It may be that, if he had done like so many of our wealthy men—had flung himself into business and then collapsed into repose—he would have been here to-day. Perhaps it would have been better if there had been a less entire throwing of one's self into arduous and clamant duties. I am not going to enter on the ethics of that question. I do not think there are many of this generation of Christians who are likely to work themselves to death in Christ's cause; and perhaps, after all, the old saying is a true one, "Better to wear out than to rust out." But only this I will say: we honour the martyrs of Science, of Commerce, of Empire. Why should not we honour the martyrs of Faith? And why should they be branded as imprudent enthusiasts, if they make the same sacrifice which, when an explorer, or a soldier, makes it, his memory is honoured as heroic, and his cold brows are crowned with laurels? Surely it is as wise to die for Christ as for England. But be that as it may, the requirement, the stringent requirement, of my text is not addressed to any spiritual aristocracy, but is laid upon the consciences of all professing Christians.

II. Observe the grounds of this requirement.

Did you ever think—or has the fact become so familiar to you that it ceases to attract notice ?—did you ever think what an extraordinary position it is for the son of a carpenter in Nazareth to plant Himself before the human race and say, " You will be wise if you die for My sake, and you will be doing nothing more than your plain duty " ? What business has He to assume such a position as that ? What warrants that autocratic and all-demanding tone from His lips ? " Who art Thou "—we may fancy people saying—" that Thou shouldst put out a masterful hand and claim to take as Thine the life of my heart ? " Ah ! brethren, there is but one answer, " Who loved me, and gave Himself for me." The foolish, loving, impulsive Apostle that blurted out, before his time had come, " I will lay down my life for Thy sake " was only premature ; he was not mistaken. There needed that His Lord should lay down His life for Peter's sake ; and then He had a right to turn to the Apostle and say, " Thou shalt follow Me afterwards," and lay down thy life for My sake. The ground of Christ's unique claim is Christ's solitary sacrifice. He who has died for men, and He only, has the right to require the unconditional, the absolute surrender of themselves, not only in the sacrifice of a life that is submitted, but, if circumstances demand, in the sacrifice of a death. The ground of the requirement is laid, first in the fact of our Lord's Divine nature, and second, in the fact that He who asks my life has first of all given His.

But that same phrase, " for My sake," suggests

III. The all-sufficient motive which makes such a loss of life possible.

I suppose that there is nothing else that will wholly

dethrone self but the enthroning of Jesus Christ. That dominion is too deeply rooted to be abolished by any enthusiasms, however noble they may be, except the one that kindles its undying torch at the flame of Christ's own love. God forbid that I should deny that wonderful and lovely instances of self-oblivion may be found in hearts untouched by the supreme love of Christ! But whilst I recognise all the beauty of such, I, for my part, humbly venture to believe and assert that, for the entire deliverance of a man from self-regard, the one sufficient motive power is the reception into his opening heart of the love of Jesus Christ.

Ah, brethren, you and I know how hard it is to escape from the tyrannous dominion of self, and how the evil spirits that have taken possession of us mock at all lesser charms than the name which "devils fear and fly": "the name that is above every name." We have tried other motives. We have sought to reprove our selfishness by other considerations. Human love— which itself is sometimes only the love of self-seeking satisfaction from another—human love does conquer it, but yet conquers it partially. The demons turn round upon all these would-be exorcists, and say, "Jesus we know... but who are ye?" It is only when the Ark is carried into the Temple that Dagon falls prone before it. If you would drive self out of your hearts— and if you do not it will slay you—if you would drive self out, let Christ's love and sacrifice come in. And then what no brooms and brushes, no spades nor wheelbarrows, will ever do—namely, cleanse out the filth that lodges there—the turning of the river in will do and float it all away. The one possibility for complete, conclusive deliverance from the dominion and tyranny of Self is to be found in the words "For My sake."

Ah, brethren, I suppose there are none of us so poor in earthly love, possessed or remembered, but that we know the omnipotence of these words when whispered by beloved lips, "For my sake"; and Jesus Christ is saying them to us all.

IV. Lastly, notice the recompense of the stringent requirement.

"Shall find it." And that finding, like the losing, has a twofold reference and accomplishment: here and now, yonder and then.

Here and now. Brother, no man possesses himself till he has given himself to Jesus Christ. Only then, when we put the reins into His hands, can we coerce and guide the fiery steeds of passion and of impulse. And so Scripture, in more than one place, uses a remarkable expression, when it speaks of those that believe to the "acquiring of their souls." You are not your own masters until you are Christ's servants; and when you fancy yourselves to be most entirely your own masters, you have promised yourselves liberty and have become the slave of corruption. So if you would own yourselves, give yourselves away.

And such an one "shall find" his life, here and now, in that all earthly things will be sweeter and better. The altar sanctifies the gift. When some pebble is plunged into a sunlit stream, the water brings out the veined colourings of the stone that looked all dull and dim when it was lying upon the bank. Put your whole being, your wealth, your activities, and everything, into that stream, and they will flash in splendour else unknown. Did not my friend, of whom I was speaking, enjoy his wealth far more, when he poured it out like water upon good causes than if he had spent it in luxury and self-indulgence? And shall we not find that everything is sweeter, nobler, better, fuller of capacity to delight, if we give it all to our Master? The stringent requirement of Christ is the perfection of prudence.

"Who pleasure follows pleasure slays," and who slays pleasure finds a deeper and a holier delight. The keenest epicureanism could devise no better means for sucking the last drop of sweetness out of the clustering grapes of the gladnesses of earth than to obey the stringent requirement, and so realise the blessed promise, "Whoso loseth his life for My sake shall find it." The selfish man is a roundabout fool. The self-devoted man, the Christ enthroning man, is the wise man.

And there will be the further finding hereafter, about which we cannot speak. Only remember, how in a passage parallel with this of my text, spoken when almost within sight of Calvary, our Lord laid down not only the principle of His own life but the principle for all His servants, when He said, "Except a corn of wheat fall into the ground and die, it abideth alone; but if it die, it bringeth forth much fruit." The solitary grain dropped into the furrow brings forth a waving harvest a hundredfold. We may not, we need not, particularise, but the life that is found at last is as the fruit an hundredfold of the life that men called "lost" and God called sown.

"Blessed are the dead which die in the Lord; they rest from their labours, and their works do follow them."

CHRIST'S MISSION THE REVELATION OF GOD'S LOVE.

"Herein is love, not that we loved God, but that He loved us, and sent His Son to be the propitiation for our sins."—1 JOHN iv. 10.

THIS is the second of a pair of twin verses which deal with substantially the same subject under two slightly different aspects. The thought common to both is that Christ's mission is the great revelation of God's love. But in the preceding verse the point on which stress is laid is the manifestation of that love, and in our text the point mainly brought out is its essential nature. In the former we read, "In this was *manifested* the love of God," and in the present verse we read, "Herein *is* love." In the former verse John fixes on three things as setting forth the greatness of that manifestation—viz., that the Christ is the Only Begotten Son, that the manifestation is for the world, and that its end is the bestowment of everlasting love. In my text the points which are fixed on are that that Love in its nature is self-kindled—"not that we loved God, but that He loved us"—and that it lays hold of, and casts out of the way, that which, unremoved, would be a barrier between God and us—viz., our sin : "He hath sent His Son to be the propitiation for our sins."

Now, it is interesting to notice that these twin verses, like a double star which reflects the light of a central sun, draw their brightness from the great word of the Master, "God so loved the world, that He gave His only begotten Son, that whosoever believeth in Him should not perish, but have everlasting life." Do you not hear the echo of His voice in the three expressions in the verse before the text—"only begotten," "world," "live"? Here is one more of the innumerable links which bind together in indissoluble union the Gospel and the Epistle. So, then, the great thought suggested by the words before us is just this, that in the Incarnation and Sacrifice of Jesus Christ we have the great revelation of the love of God.

I. Now, there are three questions that suggest themselves to me, and the first is this, What, then, does Christ's mission say about God's love?

I do not need to dwell on the previous question whether, apart from that mission, there is any solid revelation of the fact that there is love in Heaven, or whether we are left, apart from it, to gropings and probabilities. I need not refer you to the ambiguous oracles of nature or to the equally ambiguous oracles of life. I need not, I suppose, do more than just remind you that even the men whose faith grasps the thought of the love of God most intensely, know what it is to be brought to a stand before some of the dreadful problems which the facts of humanity and the facts of nature press upon us, nor need I remind you how, as we see around us to-day, in the drift of our English literature and that of other nations, when men turn their backs upon the Cross, they look upon a landscape all swathed in mists, and on which darkness is steadily settling. The reason why the men of this generation, some of them very superficially, and for the sake of being "in the swim," and some of them despairingly and with bleeding hearts, are turning themselves to a reasoned pessimism, is because they will not see what shines out from the Cross, that God is love.

Nor need I do more than remind you, in a word, of the fact that, go where we will through this world, and consult all the conceptions that men have made to themselves of gods many and lords many, whilst we find the deification of power, and of vice, and of fragmentary goodnesses, of hopes and fears, of longings, of regrets, we find nowhere a god of whom the characteristic is love. And amidst that Pantheon of deities, some of them savage, some of them lustful, some of them embodiments of all vices, some of them indifferent and neutral, some of them radiant and fair, none reveals this secret, that the centre of the universe is a heart. So we have to turn away from hopes, from probability dashed with many a doubt, and find something that has more solid substance in it, if it is to be enough to bear up the man that grasps it and to yield before no tempests. For all that Bishop Butler says, probabilities are *not* the guide of life, in its deepest and noblest aspects. They may be the guide of practice, but for the anchorage of the soul we want no shifting sandbank, but that to which we may make fast and be sure that, whatever shifts, it remains immovable. You can no more clothe the soul in "perhapses" than a man can make garments out of a spider's web. Religion consists of the things of which we are sure, and not of the things which are probable. " Peradventure " is not the word on which a man can rest the weight of a crushed, or an agonising, or a sinking soul; he must have " Verily! verily!" and then he is at rest.

How do we know what a man is? By seeing what a man does. How do we know what God is? By knowing what God does. So John does not argue with logic, either frosty or fiery, but he simply opens his mouth, and in calm, pellucid utterances sets forth the truths and leaves them to work. He says to us, " I do not relegate you to your intuitions; I do not argue with you; I simply say, Look at Him; look, and see that God is love."

What, then, does the mission of Christ say to us about the love of God? It says, first, that it is a love independent of, and earlier than, ours. We love, as a rule, because we recognise in the object to which our heart goes out something that draws it, something that is loveable. But He whose name is " I am that I am " has all the reasons of His actions within Himself, and just as He

"Sits on no precarious throne,
Nor borrows leave to be,"

nor is dependent on any creature for existence, so He is His own motive, He is His own reason. Within that sacred circle of the Infinite Nature, lie all the energies which bring that Infinite Nature into action; and like some clear fountain, more sparkling than crystal, there wells up for ever, from the depths of the Divine Nature, the love which is Himself. He loves, not because we love Him, but because He is God. The very sun itself, as some astronomers believe, owes its radiant brightness and ever-communicated warmth to the impact on, and reception into, it of myriads of meteors and of matter drawn from the surrounding system. So, when the fuel fails, that fire will go out, and the sun will shrivel into a black ball. But this central Sun of the Universe has all His light within Himself, and the rays that pour out from Him owe their being and their motion to nothing but the force of that central fire, from which they rush with healing on their wings.

If, then, God's love is not evoked by anything in His creatures, then it is universal, and we do not need anxiously to question ourselves whether we deserve that it shall fall upon us, and no conscious unworthiness need ever make us falter in the least in the firmness with which we grasp that great central thought. The sun, inferior emblem as it is of that Light of all that is, pours down its beams indiscriminately on dunghill and on jewel, though it be true that in the one its rays breed corruption and in the other draw out beauty. That great love wraps us all, is older than our sins, and is not deflected by them. So that is the first thing that Christ's mission tells us about God's love.

The second is—it speaks to us of a love which gives its best. John says "God *sent* His Son," and that word reposes, like the rest of the passage, on many words of Christ's—such as, for instance, when He speaks of Himself as "sanctified and sent into the world," and many another saying. But remember how, in the foundation passage to which I have already referred, and of which we have some reflection in the words before us, there is a tenderer expression—not merely "sent," but "gave." Paul strengthens the word when he says, "gave *up* for us all." It is not for us to speculate about these deep things, but I would remind you of what I daresay I have had occasion often to point out, that Paul seems to intend to suggest to us a mysterious parallel, when he further says, "He that *spared* not His own Son, but freely gave Him up to death for us all." For that emphatic word "spared" is a distinct allusion to, and quotation of, the story of Abraham's sacrifice of Isaac: "Seeing thou hast not *withheld* from Me thine only son." And so, mysterious as it is, we may venture to say that He not only sent, but He gave, and not only gave, but gave up. His love, like ours, delights to lavish its most precious gifts on its objects.

Now, there arises from this consideration a thought which I only mention, and it is this. Christian teaching about Christ's work has often, both by its friends and its foes, been so presented as to lead to the conception that it was the work of Christ which made God love men. The enemies of Evangelical truth are never tired of talking in that sense; and some of its unwise friends have given reason for the caricature. But the true Christian teaching is, "God so loved . . . that He gave." The love is the cause of the mission, and not the mission that which evokes the love. So let us be sure that, not because Christ died does God love us sinful creatures, but that, because God loves us, Christ died for us.

The third thing which the mission of Christ teaches us about the love of God is that it is a love which takes note of and overcomes man's sin. I have said, as plainly as I can, that I reject the travesty of Christianity which implies that it was Christ's mission which originated God's love to men. But a love that does not in the slightest degree care whether its object is good or bad—what sort of a love do you call that? What do you name it when a father shows it to his children? Moral indifference; culpable and weak and fatal. And is it anything nobler, if you transfer it to God, and say that it is all the same to Him whether a man is living the life of a hog, and forgetting all that is high and noble, or whether he is pressing with all his strength towards light and truth and goodness? Surely, surely they who, in the name of their reverence for the supreme love of God, cover over the fact of His righteousness, are mutilating and killing the very attribute that they are trying to exalt. A love that cares nothing for the moral character of its object is not love, but hate; it is not kindness, but cruelty. Take away the background because it is so black, and you lower the brilliancy of whiteness of that which stands in front of it. There is such a property in God as is fittingly described by that tremendous word "wrath." God cannot, being what He is, treat sin as if it were no sin; and therefore we read, "He sent His son to be the *propitiation* for our sins." The black dam, which we build up between ourselves and the river of the water of life, is to be swept away; and it is the death of Jesus Christ which makes it possible for the highest gift of God's love to pour over the ruined and partially removed barrier and to flood a man's soul. Brethren, no God that is worthy the name can give Himself to a sinful soul. No sinful soul that has not the habit, the guilt, the penalty of its sins swept away, is capable of receiving the life, which is the highest gift of the love. So our twin texts divide what I may call the process of redemption between them ; and whilst the one says, " He sent His Son that we should have life through Him," the other tells us of how the sins which bar the entrance of that life into our hearts, as our own consciences tell us they do, can be removed. There must first be the propitiation for our sins, and then that mighty love reaches its purpose and attains its end, and can give us the life of God to be the life of our souls. So much for my first and principal question.

II. Now, I have to ask, secondly, how comes it that Christ's mission says anything about God's love ?

That question is a very plain one, and I should like to press the answer to it very emphatically. Take any other of the great names of the world's history of poet, thinker, philosopher, moralist, practical benefactor ; is it possible to apply such a thought as this to them—except with a hundred explanations and limitations—that they, however radiant, however wise, however beneficent, however fruitful their influence, make men sure that God loves them ? The thing is ridiculous, unless you are using language in a very fantastic and artificial fashion.

Christ's mission reveals God's love, because Christ is the Son of God. If it is true, as Jesus said, that " He that hath seen Me hath seen the Father," then I can say, " In Thy tenderness, in Thy patience, in Thy attracting of the publican and the harlot, in Thy sympathy with all the erring and the sorrowful, and, most of all, in Thy agony and passion, in Thy cross and death, I see the glory of God which is the love of God." Brother, if you break that link, which binds the man Christ Jesus with the ever-living and the ever-loving God, I know not how you can draw from the record of His life and death a confidence, which nothing can shake, in the love of the Father.

Then there is another point. Christ's mission speaks to us about God's love, if—and I was going to say *only* if—we regard it as His mission to be the propitiation for our sins. Strike out the death as the sacrifice for the world's sin, and what you have left is a maimed something, which may be, and I thankfully recognise often is, very strengthening, very helpful, very calming, very ennobling, even to men who do not sympathise with the view of that work which I am now setting forth, but which is all that to them, very largely, because of the unconscious influence of the truths which they have cast away. It seems to me that those who, in the name of the highest paternal love of God, reject the thought of Christ's sacrificial death, are kicking away the ladder by which they have climbed, and are better than their creeds, and happily illogical. It is the Cross that reveals the love, and it is the Cross as the means of propitiation that pours the light of that blessed conviction into men's hearts.

III. My last question is this: what does Christ's mission say about God's love to me?

We know what it ought to say. It ought to carry, as on the crest of a great wave, the conviction of that Divine love into our hearts, to be fruitful there. It ought to sweep out, as on the crest of a great wave, our sins and evils. It ought to do this; does it? On some of us I fear it produces no effect at all. Some of you, dear friends, look at that light with lack-lustre eyes, or, rather, with blind eyes, that are dark as midnight, in the blaze of noonday. The voice comes from the Cross, sweet as that of harpers harping with their harps, and mighty as the voice of many waters, and you hear nothing. Some of us it slightly moves now and then, and there an end.

Brethren, you have to turn the world-wide generality into a personal possession. You have to say, " He loved *me*, and gave Himself for *me*." It is of no use to believe in a universal Saviour ; do you trust in your particular Saviour ? It is of no use to have the most orthodox and clear conceptions of the relation between the Cross of Christ and the revelation to men of the love of God. Have you made that revelation the means of bringing into your own personal life the conviction that Jesus Christ is *your* Saviour, the propitiation for *your* sins, the Giver to *you* of life eternal ? It is faith that does that. Note that, in the great foundation passage to which I have made frequent reference, there are two conditions put in between the beginning and the end. Some of us are disposed to say, " God so loved the world that every man might have eternal life." That is not what Christ said, " God so loved the world that "—and here follows the first condition—" He *gave His Son* that "—and here follows the second—" he that *believeth on Him* should not perish, but have everlasting life." God has done what it is needful for Him to do. His part of the conditions has been fulfilled. Fulfil yours—" He that believeth on Him." And if you can say, not He is the propitiation for our sin, but for *my* sin, then you will live and move and have your being in a heaven of love, and will love Him back again with an echo and reflection of His own, and nothing shall be able to separate you from the love of God which is in Christ Jesus our Lord.

www.ingramcontent.com/pod-product-compliance
Lightning Source LLC
Chambersburg PA
CBHW030756230426
43667CB00007B/985